DATE DUE		

BUSINESS DEMOGRAPHY

Recent Titles from Quorum Books

Business Demography

A GUIDE AND REFERENCE FOR BUSINESS PLANNERS AND MARKETERS

Louis G. Pol

Q QUORUM BOOKS

NEW YORK
WESTPORT, CONNECTICUT
LONDON

Library of Congress Cataloging-in-Publication Data

Pol, Louis G.
   Business demography.

   Bibliography: p.
   Includes index.
   1. Demography.   2. United States—Population.
   3. Marketing research.   I. Title.
   HB849.41.P63   1987   304.6   87-2494
   ISBN 0-89930-218-1 (lib. bdg. : alk. paper)

British Library Cataloguing in Publication Data is available.

Library of Congress Catalog Card Number: 87-2494
ISBN: 0-89930-218-1

First published in 1987 by Quorum Books

Greenwood Press, Inc.
88 Post Road West, Westport, Connecticut 06881

Printed in the United States of America

∞

The paper used in this bok complies with the
Permanent Paper Standard issued by the National
Information Standards Organization (Z39.48-1984).

10 9 8 7 6 5 4 3 2 1

Copyright Acknowledgments

We gratefully acknowledge the following sources for granting permission to reprint material:

Sections of Chapter 2 are extracted from Louis G. Pol, 1987. *Federal and State Government Data Sources for the Marketing Executive: Information and Uses*. Copyright 1987 by Audits and Surveys, Inc. Reprinted by permission.

Extracts from Martha Farnsworth Riche, 1985. "Directory of Demographic Products and Services," *American Demographics* (July): 34–41. Copyright 1985 by American Demographics, Inc. Reprinted by permission.

Extracts from Mary Mederios Kent and Carl Haub, 1984. *World Population Data Sheet*. Copyright 1984 by Population Reference Bureau. Reprinted by permission.

Appendix 2.1 is reprinted from Martha Farnsworth Riche, 1984. "The State of States' State Data Centers," *American Demographics* (October): 28–37. Copyright 1984 by American Demographics, Inc. Reprinted by Permission.

Figure 5.1 is reprinted from Charles P. Kaplan and Thomas L. Van Valey, 1982. *Census '80: Continuing the Factfinder Tradition*. Reprinted by permission of the U.S. Government Printing Office; U.S. Bureau of the Census.

To My Family

Tables

in business demography. Finally, but certainly not last, Alvin Dorse and Leobardo Estrada deserve a special thank you. It is now more than fifteen years since they first introduced me to demography, and the interest generated by their first lectures and discussions continues.

BUSINESS DEMOGRAPHY

1

What Is Demography?

INTRODUCTION

Historical Perspective

Demography, the study of human population, is a field whose major impact on the understanding of everyday societal events has yet to be fully realized. While demography and demographers have existed for literally thousands of years, until most recently the direct impact of demographic study on the surrounding world has not been realized very far beyond those subareas of inquiry which when combined are labeled *population studies*.[1] Other than Thomas Malthus' famous treatise on population, early demographic work is scarcely known. Until quite recently, contemporary demographic studies have gone almost unnoticed. Many of the field's major journals originated only in the post-World War II era, and almost all are directed toward the small number of professional demographers who understand the technical presentations which are frequently made. Demography's major American professional organization, the Population Association of America, is just a little more than fifty years old. And even today the Association has fewer than 4,000 members.

This little-known subject is gaining stature, however. The importance of a demographic component in understanding world events is beginning to be evidenced in day-to-day communication and virtually all forms of the media. One can hardly pick up a newspaper or magazine or turn on a radio or television without reading or hearing about some aspect of demographic change and how this change is affecting our lives. Whether it is food shortages in Ethiopia, federal legislation affecting the number of legal immigrants entering the United States, or an upturn or downturn in housing starts in the United States, there seems to be a demographic component to the issue of interest.

Magazines such as *Business Week, Time, Forbes, Newsweek,* and *U.S. News and World Report* frequently publish articles on demographic topics.[2] For example, baby boomers, the large number of persons born between 1946 and 1964 who presently make up about one-third of the U.S. population, are continuously discussed in terms of their political beliefs, buying behavior, and the impact that they have on society as they get older. The *Wall Street Journal* often publishes articles connecting demographic and business trends. A proliferation of new demographic journals and magazines have appeared in the last few years, several of which are written with the nonprofessional in mind.

Furthermore, planners from both the public and private sectors are including demographic analyses in their assessment of current business and economic conditions as well as in developing strategic plans for the future. Examples of such planning range from incorporating a demographic dimension in projecting capital expenditures to accounting for demographic factors influencing the soft drink market. Staff demographers are now employed by Time Inc., General Motors, Atlantic Bell, and the Dayton-Hudson Corporation, among other major companies. Academic courses in demography—and applied/business demography—are now taught in a variety of programs.[3]

Concerning academic programs, demography as a course of subject area has been traditionally taught in departments of sociology and economics by persons trained in those fields. Most survey demographic books (those designed to be used in a first course in demography or as reference works) have been written by those same people and, not surprisingly, from the sociologist's, economist's, or simply social scientist's perspective. However, with the increased interest in demography as a more general area of study, there is a need for demographic works written from a different perspective. Businesspersons who want to know more about demography and who wish to learn from examples similar to the problems and opportunities that they encounter should find this book informative and useful.

Though the book is written from a business perspective, many of the introductory topics covered are the same as those addressed in traditional demographic presentations. These topics are introduced early on and provide the basic background material required for a better understanding of the discussions that follow. Nevertheless, the introductory chapters are written for businesspersons and most frequently utilize materials and examples from business fields. Beyond the background chapters, the presentations that follow are written almost entirely from a business point of view. The major goal of integrating demography with business considerations is to bring what is called a *demographic perspective* to problems and opportunities normally not thought of in demographic terms. More specifically, and more importantly, this book adds a demographic dimension to the opportunities and problems of interest to each of the book's readers.

Demographic Perspective

The demographic perspective is simply a manner in which the surrounding world can be viewed. It is "a way of relating basic information to theories about how the world operates."[4] For persons interested in business issues, it means understanding how the population processes discussed in the first section of the book affect the business environment and thus help determine opportunities and problems. By processes it is meant, for example, the increasing or decreasing of birth rates, the aging or "younging" of a population, the increase or decrease in population size, and the geographic redistribution of people. Opportunities and problems are any and all that one has an interest in, and they range from concerns over a decrease in retail sales to identifying market opportunities one to five years in advance. The key is the link between the processes and the opportunity or problem of interest. When coupled with the knowledge and skills of other disciplines, the demographic perspective becomes a powerful tool for understanding how society functions and how changes in society occur.

The demographic perspective, demography, and demographics are terms used interchangeably, though they do not really mean the same thing. Most often, demographics is translated as static characteristics of a population such as average age or median family income. These data are used to describe markets or settings and have intuitive appeal because it is known that buying patterns, for example, vary from one demographically defined group to another. The demographic perspective, however, emphasizes a more in-depth understanding of the connection between demographic characteristics (particularly processes) and behavior. That is, the demographic perspective connects ongoing demographic changes such as an increase in population size with continued alterations in the business environment. This perspective relies on an understanding of historical trends and incorporates forecasts of demographic conditions. Demography, or the science of population study, provides the understanding of the population processes, for example, why birth rates fluctuate or why people move. While this distinction may appear confusing and unnecessary at this time, by the time the book has been read the need for distinguishing what some people call demographics from demography and the demographic perspective should be clear.

Organization of the Book

The remainder of this chapter is devoted to a brief discussion of the major demographic events of the past forty years in the United States with a special emphasis on the business opportunities and problems that are at least partly a product of these events.[5] This discussion provides a general context from which to view the next four chapters: data sources, fertility, mortality, and migration. Together these chapters contain basic demographic data, concepts, measures, and knowledge used in the remaining chapters—the background material required to develop a demographic perspective.

The second section of the book contains four chapters: population composition, geographic concepts, population distribution, and population estimates and projections. This section familiarizes the reader with the descriptive nature of demography along with providing useful information on how geography plays a role in demographic analysis. The discussion on estimates and projections gives background information on the derivation and uses of synthetically produced data.

The last section of the book contains five chapters: population policy, two chapters on data and methods in an applied setting, international business issues, and an overview. This is the applied section of the book, and the majority of demography/business environment relationships are discussed here. Population policy concerns not only how governmental policy (or the lack of it) affects population growth, the distribution of people, and how those people behave, but also the way in which that policy is a major force in helping form the business environment. Policies can range from those at the national level, which function, for example, to limit immigration or fund prenatal care, to those at the local level, which limit population growth. The two chapters on data and methods in an applied setting are designed to show how organizations use a demographic perspective in exploiting opportunities and confronting problems. The chapters demonstrate how the integration of demographic processes, data, and terminology with organization-specific attributes can improve planning. Examples of organizations that have successfully used a demographic dimension in their planning are discussed. The international business chapter takes the concepts and analyses discussed earlier in the book and presents applications from the perspective of developed and developing nations. The overview chapter brings together in a succinct fashion the information covered and reiterates the importance of incorporating the demographic perspective into an organizational and individual context.

Finally, this book is written from a completely American perspective. That is, other than the chapter on international demography (Chapter 13), very little mention is made of the applied/business demographic considerations of other nations. The intention is not to overlook the importance of international business concerns, but to emphasize domestic issues at this time.

DEMOGRAPHIC CHANGE IN THE UNITED STATES: 1945–1985

Demographic change in the United States over the past forty years has been swift and sure. Starting with a 1945 population estimate of 139.8 million, the population increased to 237.5 million by 1985—an increase of nearly 70 percent.[6] This growth has been the product of the interaction of fertility—adding people to the population via births; mortality—subtracting people via deaths; and migration—adding people via the net exchange of persons moving into and out of the United States during a certain time interval. For example, during the 1945–1982 time interval, these components contributed to population growth in the following way:

$$
\begin{aligned}
\text{1982 Population (231,059,000)} = \ &\text{1945 Population (139,767,000)} \\
&+ \text{Births (1945–1981) (137,268,000)} \\
&- \text{Deaths (1945–1981) (63,643,000)} \\
&+ \text{Net Immigrants (1945–1981) (17,667,000)}
\end{aligned}
$$

As can be seen, the relative contribution of each of the components to growth is quite varied and reflects the impact of the post-World War II baby boom and the decline in mortality over the forty-year period, as well as a substantial contribution from immigration. The difference between fertility and mortality accounted for 81 percent of the roughly 91 million-person increase, while net immigration accounted for the remaining 19 percent of the growth.

Fertility

Births and birth or fertility rates have shown a tremendous amount of variation over the forty-year span. Beginning with a low of 2.9 million births in 1945, the annual number increased to 4.3 million by 1961. For each year in the interval 1953 through 1964 there were at least 4 million births—a total of nearly fifty million births over the 12 year period.[7] The time span from 1946 to 1964 is known as the era of the *post-World War II baby boom*. Following this increase in births, a decline in the number of births occurred, bottoming out at about 3.2 million from 1973 through 1976. Since that time the number of births has risen somewhat and currently fluctuates between 3.6 and 3.7 million per year.[8]

The large and sustained increase in the number of births at the end of World War II had, and continues to have, a profound impact on American society. Initially, the effect of the increase was realized in maternity wards and sales of infant-specific goods and services. Only a short time afterward, shortages in classrooms and teachers occurred, and the response was a tremendous increase in school construction and teacher training. And as each successive group (*age cohort*) of the first wave of baby boomers grew one year older, an increased demand for certain products and services was realized. As the baby boom cohorts aged even further, they provided a flood of "new clients" for colleges and universities. After completing their educations, they presented the economy with a marked increase in labor force supply. From 1963, when the age cohort born in 1945 turned age 18, until

1985, the labor force increased from 71.8 to 116.5 million—an addition of 44.7 million persons, or an increase of almost 62 percent.[9] To this day the aging of the baby boom cohorts brings about an increased demand for products and services particular to their ages and lifestyles.[10]

The increases outlined above have had a negative side as well. Baby boomers, especially those born near the end of the boom era, have encountered a labor market glutted with experienced people. The economy has been simply unable to absorb all of those persons who wish to enter the labor force at the skill level they possess and at the salary they expect. Many of the prospective labor force participants have experienced trouble getting any job at all. And a host of those with jobs have found their path to advancement blocked by the sheer number of persons in positions directly above them. The persons whom they wish to replace are no more than a few years older than they are. Unless they quit their jobs and go to work for other companies, which many of them do, they must wait a relatively long time before they move up in the company for which they are presently working. This phenomenon, known as *career plateauing*, presents serious problems for businesses and industries concerned with continued motivation and the resulting reduction in productivity caused by the realization that job advancement is not forthcoming. Of course, the individuals involved become economic and psychological victims of the promotion squeeze.

On the downside of the baby boom where the number of births was significantly smaller—the *baby bust*—once again opportunities and problems are evident. Persons in these smaller birth cohorts are experiencing less competition for school space and are likely to fare better in the job market if for no other reason than there will be fewer of them to compete against each other. However, from an organizational standpoint the decline in numbers has brought about school closings, educational cutbacks, and a reduction in the demand for certain age-specific goods and services. The organizational response, at least at some levels, has been retrenchment, and the number of victims of these cutbacks is substantial. While some organizations have adjusted very well to smaller cohorts by offering new products and services at the same time they retract old ones, others have not fared well at all. Interestingly enough, younger age cohorts have again started to increase in size (remember the number of births per year has increased since 1975) and teacher shortages are reappearing in some sections of the country. There has also been a concomitant increase in interest in goods and services sold to and for persons at these younger ages.

While total births and birth rates are likely to be much more stable over the next twenty years, the impact of what can be called a roller coaster effect of previous birth fluctuations will be felt for many decades in the future. Over the short run, there will once again be large absolute increases in some of the younger age groups (particularly teenagers between now and the middle of the next decade). Over the long run, the effect of the aging of the baby boom cohorts will be evident almost until the time that all of them have died. They will increase the size of every age category they reach from now until the middle of the next century. One the downside, because the age cohorts younger than the baby boomers are smaller, decreases in the absolute number of persons by age cohort will follow as the baby boom cohorts age. Nevertheless, as the baby bust cohorts age, increases in the absolute number of persons will again follow due to the more recent increase in births.

Mortality

The second variable affecting the forty-year change in population is mortality. Though there has been a pattern of only gradual decline in mortality rates, the effect of the decline must not be minimized. In 1945, *life expectancy* at birth, the average number of years a person can expect to live from birth, was 65.5 years. By 1984 it had increased to 74.7 years, or a 14 percent increase over the interval.[11] The overall increase in life expectancy has not been the result of an increase in life chances at all ages. The major contributor has been the more than two-thirds reduction in the *infant mortality rate* (deaths during the first year of life) over the forty-year period from thirty-eight deaths per 1,000 births in 1945 to less than twelve deaths per 1,000 births in 1982.[12] The contribution to overall life expectancy from the older ages has been far less. In 1945 life expectancy at age 65 was 13 years and by 1980 it had increased to nearly 17 years, a 29 percent rise.[13]

The infant mortality decrease and the accompanying increase in life expectancy has presented businesses with a number of opportunities as well as problems. In a sense, the health care opportunities created by higher infant mortality rates and lower levels of life expectancy brought about at least part of the change. The health care industry, and its funding counterparts, responded to high levels of infant mortality by improving health care and medical technology, and now that infant mortality is lower and life expectancy higher, more health care/medical technology is being developed to bring about additional improvement. Overall, we are a physically healthier society than we were forty years ago, and this has resulted in generating demand for new products and services. For example, the age group 85 years old and over is the second fastest growing age segment in the United States today.[14] Those persons 85 and over need and want products and services that are very different from those of younger age groups.

On the negative side, increases in life expectancy can contribute to societal problems. A fast-growing older population with its accompanying health care needs can create increasing demand on a health care system designed to service a younger population. The increase in the number of years between retirement and death, contributed to in part by a declining age at retirement, burdens income maintenance programs that were designed to service a different population.

Migration

The third change factor in U.S. population is migration. The migration component is as volatile as that of fertility in part because it contains two considerations: *immigration*—the exchange of people between the United States and other countries; and *internal migration*—the redistribution of persons already residing in the United States.

With regard to immigration, the pattern of exchange has been one of wide year-to-year fluctuations. Furthermore, three major legislative acts (in 1952, 1965, and 1986) and several other more minor changes in immigration law have occurred over the forty-year interval, altering both the number of persons who can legally enter the country and the composition of those persons. Looking just at the years from the mid–1970's to early 1980's, the number of immigrants and refugees combined entering the United States ranged from 399,000 in 1977 to 808,000 in 1980.[15] During the 1950's immigrants averaged only 252,000 per year.[16] The contribution that immigration makes to overall population growth is increasing. The decades of the 1940's and 1950's saw net immigration account for only 11 percent of all U.S. population growth. During the 1970's, it accounted for 22 percent, and in the early 1980's it made up nearly 25 percent of total growth. One result of net immigration flows, as well as differential growth rates for subsegments of the native U.S. population, is that the overall proportion of the population classified as racial/ethnic minority is increasing. By the turn of the century, the U.S. population could be roughly one-third Black, Hispanic, and Asian.[17] Of course, these figures may change with the passage of other legislation.

The internal migration consideration does not address the issue of growth for the nation as a whole, but it does in part determine both the locations within the country where growth is occurring and locations where future growth is likely to occur. In the forty years since the end of World War II, several new migration streams—movements of large numbers of persons from one part of the country to another—have developed. One stream stopped and was reversed, and another major stream has continued. Americans are relatively mobile. About 17 percent of the population moves from one place to another each year. During the 1970's, one demographer calculated that the average person could expect roughly thirteen permanent changes of address from birth until death, though 1980's estimates exceed twenty moves.[18] While most moves are for a relatively short distance, the longer distance moves over the forty-year period have resulted in a significant redistribution of the population. The major streams of movement include a continuation of the east-to-west stream as well as a relatively new one from what is called the snowbelt to a group of states loosely labeled the sunbelt. Furthermore, the continued decentralization of the population—city to outlying areas—has gone on.

The net result of this movement has been a significant geographic shift of the population, as well as the potential for further growth, to states in the South and Southwest. Conversely, states in the Northeast and Midwest are at a virtual standstill with regard to growth. Three—Ohio, Michigan, and Iowa—are in fact losing population.[19] At the same time, employment opportunities are being lost in the midwestern and northeastern states at an alarming rate. For example, between 1978 and 1982 manufacturing employment in the East North Central states dropped from 5.1 million to 4.1 million—a 20 percent decline.[20] While in the ten-year period from 1972 to 1982 total employees in the United States increased nearly 22 percent, employment in the Northeast and North Central States grew only 9 percent.[21] The redistribution of employment opportunities is likely to give further momentum to the disparity in population growth rates. Projections for the year 2000 show that 60 percent of the population will be located in the South and West, while only 48 percent lived in those regions in 1970.[22] On the other hand, these same projections show 40 percent of the population will live in midwestern and northeastern states compared with the 52 percent that lived there in 1970.[23]

Immigration and internal migration trends and the accompanying redistribution of the population have presented complex situations for businesses to contend with. Areas that are gaining population have had those opportunities that accompany population and industry growth. These areas—like Florida and Arizona, and cities like Orlando and Phoenix—are singled out for their tremendous growth and opportunity. For example, in the 1970's the Orlando Standard Metropolitan Area (SMA) grew 55 percent and gained 161,000 jobs, an increase in employment opportunities of 103 percent from 1970!

An increase in consumers, both individual and industrial, is welcomed by most businesses. However, for other organizations, rapid growth has presented severe problems for servicing the additional members, as well as those already living in growth areas. While industrial and population growth may on the surface seem to be a good thing, rapid—almost uncontrolled—growth can leave states, and in particular municipalities, unable to offer basic services (for example, waste disposal, fire protection) to the rapidly expanding population. Because of its concern for the quality of water and sewage services, Orlando at times has restricted growth by limiting building permits. The result of rapid population growth has been that in some areas municipal and other services can be described as less than adequate. Moreover, some locations have attempted to limit population and industrial growth in part arguing that present service systems cannot adequately supply additional individual and industrial members.

Concerning those regions experiencing population and industrial loss, the picture has been quite different. The loss of jobs has meant higher unemployment rates as well as substantial reductions in tax revenues. Business and industry remaining in these areas, particularly those tied to the local economy, have been negatively affected by the reduction in buying power occurring in those areas.

While there is some evidence that movement out of the Midwest and Northeast is slowing, the present flow, with regard to both population and industry, dictates that differential regional growth (North Central and Northeast the slowest) are likely to continue. This pattern will continue to offer growth opportunities and the problems such growth creates.

The Short and Long Views

Overall, the population of the United States has changed dramatically in the past forty years, though at present a period of relative stability is in place. This relative stability, however, has very interesting short-term and longterm implications. Over the short run—from now until the end of the century—the major impact on the population is likely to come from the continued aging of the baby boom birth cohorts and the increasing impact of net immigration on population growth. The population will gradually age—the average age will increase—and it is quite possible that the level of internal geographic mobility will decline. Business and industry in highgrowth areas will continue to do well in general, though it must be noted that business failures may also increase due to the great amount of competition existing in those places. The problems existing in low-growth areas may be exacerbated by the rapid aging that can occur when a large proportion of the younger population moves to other locations.

The view in the long run is considerably different. Given current and projected fertility, mortality, and migration levels, the population of the United States will not cease growing immediately—barring unforeseen change—until midway through the next century. Shortly afterward it could very well begin to decline. That is, the number of deaths will then outnumber the number of births and net immigrants. One demographer has projected that the population of the United States would stabilize (a point where no growth or decline is occurring) at 108 million in the twenty-second century if current and projected fertility, mortality, and migration levels are maintained. This figure is about 134 million fewer persons than currently reside in the United States! A population this size would be much older and structured much differently from that of today.

SUMMARY

The brief history of the last few pages describes recent population events—and presents some projections—with the goal of providing a background scenario for the chapters that follow. More detail for each component is provided as that topic is addressed.

The following chapter focuses on data sets that demographers use to measure both demographic and economic change. Knowing which data are available and where to obtain the information is imperative if a demographic perspective is to be useful.

NOTES

1. For the most part, these subareas have been sociology, economics, and political science, though significant interaction with statistics, mathematics, biology, and education has also occurred.

2. See, for example, Susanna McBee. 1984. "Here Come the Baby Boomers." *U.S. News and World Report* (November 5): 68–73; Businessweek staff. 1984. "Baby Boomers Push for Power." *Businessweek* (July 2): 52–62; Barbara Kantrowitz. 1986. "Three's a Crowd." *Newsweek* (September 1): 68–76.

3. Cheryl Russell. 1984. *The Business of Demographics.* Population Bulletin Vol. 39, No. 3 (June). Washington, D.C.: Population Reference Bureau.

4. John R. Weeks. 1986. *Population: An Introduction to Concepts and Issues.* Belmont, California: Wadsworth, p. 26.

5. For a more thorough treatment of demographic trends, see Landon Y. Jones. 1980. *Great Expectations.* New York: Ballantine Books; and Bryant Robey. 1985. *The American People.* New York: Truman Talley Books.

6. U.S. Bureau of the Census. 1986. *Statistical Abstract of the United States, 1986.* Washington, D.C.: U.S. Government Printing Office, table 5.

7. U.S. Department of Health and Human Services. National Center for Health Statistics. Annual. *Vital Statistics of the United States.* Washington, D.C.: U.S. Government Printing Office.

8. An excellent discussion of the post-World War II baby boom can be found in Leon Bouvier. 1980. *America's Baby Boom Generation: The Fateful Bulge.* Population Bulletin Vol. 35, No. 1. Washington, D.C.: Population Reference Bureau.

9. U.S. Bureau of the Census. 1986. *Statistical Abstract of the United States, 1986,* table 658.

10. See, for example, Edward L. Kain. 1984. "Surprising Singles." *American Demographics* (August): 16–39; and Eileen Prescott. 1983. "New Men." *American Demographics* (August): 16–45.

11. U.S. Department of Health and Human Services. National Center for Health Statistics. 1984. *Vital Statistics of the United States.* Vol. 2, Section 6. Washington, D.C.: U.S. Government Printing Office, table 6–5; and U.S. Bureau of the Census. 1986. *Statistical Abstract of the United States, 1986,* table 106.

12. U.S. Bureau of the Census. 1986. *Statistical Abstract of the United States, 1986,* table 112; U.S. Bureau of the Census. 1975. *Historical Statistics of the United States, Colonial Times to 1970.* Washington, D.C.: U.S. Government Printing Office, series B123–147.

13. U.S. Bureau of the Census. 1986. *Statistical Abstract of the United States, 1986,* table 108; U.S. Bureau of the Census. 1975. *Historical Statistics of the United States, Colonial Times to 1970.* Series B99–106.

14. U.S. Bureau of the Census. 1984. *Projections of the Population of the United States by Age, Sex and Race: 1983–2080.* Current Population Reports, Series P–25, No. 952. Washington, D.C.: U.S. Government Printing Office, table 6.

15. Population Reference Bureau Staff. 1982. *U.S. Population: Where We Are; Where We're Going*. Population Bulletin Vol. 37, No. 2. Washington, D.C.: Population Reference Bureau, figure 10.

16. U.S. Bureau of the Census. 1986. *Statistical Abstracts of the United States, 1986*, table 127.

17. Estimate arrived at by combining projections from U.S. Bureau of the Census. 1984. *Projections of the Population of the United States by Age, Sex and Race: 1983–2080*, table 6; and Leon Bouvier, Cary Davis, and Robert Haupt. 1983. *Projections of the Hispanic Population in the United States 1990–2000*. Washington, D.C.: Population Reference Bureau, table A–1.

18. Larry Long. 1973. "New Estimates of Migration Expectancy." *Journal of the American Statistical Association* 68:37–45; Mohamed Bailey and David F. Sly. 1985. "Metropolitan-Nonmetropolitan Migration Expectancy in the United States, 1965–1980." Paper presented at the annual meeting of the Southern Regional Demographic Group, Austin, Texas.

19. U.S. Bureau of the Census. 1986. *Statistical Abstract of the United States, 1986*, table 13.

20. U.S. Bureau of the Census. 1984. *Statistical Abstract of the United States, 1984*. Washington, D.C.: U.S. Government Printing Office, table 706; and U.S. Bureau of the Census. 1979. *Statistical Abstract of the United States, 1979*. Washington, D.C.: U.S. Government Printing Office, table 680.

21. U.S. Bureau of the Census. 1984. *Statistical Abstract of the United States, 1984*, table 706.

22. U.S. Bureau of the Census. 1985. *Statistical Abstract of the United States, 1985*. Washington, D.C.: U.S. Government Printing Office, tables 12 and 14.

23. U.S. Bureau of the Census. 1985. *Statistical Abstract of the United States, 1985*, tables 12 and 14.

2

Demographic Data: The Numbers and Their Sources

INTRODUCTION

There are many uses of demographic data for the business executive. In fact, it might be argued that the only restriction to finding uses is a person's own limited vision about which data are available and how they can be used—a problem that this book is designed to at least partially remedy. Many executives view population variables as indicators of conditions and changes in the business environment: the expansion and contraction of existing markets as well as the creation of new ones. Demographic data on the size and age structure of a population, for example, assist in telling the executive which segments of a market are growing, and if population projections are utilized, which segments are likely to grow the fastest in the future. Population data are also of value in the formulation of business strategies such as deciding which segments to target, estimating and projecting demand for products and services, and determining labor force needs and supplies. Finally, demographic data are regarded by many executives as basic information crucial to the day-to-day operations performed by a business enterprise.

Demographic data sets come from a variety of federal and state agencies, though some of the specific sources of population information, such as expenditure and health surveys, are not strictly demographic. They contain demographic components, but their major focus is nondemographic. The

Sections of this chapter were extracted from Louis Pol. 1987. *Federal and State Government Data Sources for the Marketing Executive: Information and Uses.* New York: Audits and Surveys, Inc.

reader can be the judge concerning the importance of the demographic/
nondemographic distinction.

Because there are a relatively large number of data sources being generated
by a host of federal and state agencies, a highly detailed discussion of each
source is not possible in the space of a single chapter. What is presented is a
brief summary of a variety of sources: the agency that collects the data; what
information is collected; in what form the data are available (printed reports,
microfiche, computer tape, and/or diskette); for which geographic areas the
data are tabulated; and how frequently the data are gathered. For those
readers who wish to obtain more detail about one or more of these data sets,
the bibliographic citations at the end of the chapter should prove useful.
Furthermore, much more detail on the uses of these data is provided in the
chapters on demographic data and expertise in the large and small enterprise
context. Last, some judgment has been exercised in the presentation of these
sources, and, with a few exceptions, only those data sets perceived to be most
useful to business executives are presented. Those exceptions are the information vital to providing demographers and nondemographers with information related to population growth (fertility, mortality, and migration).
Following the discussion of data sources, five brief examples of how these
data can be used to solve business problems or take advantage of business
opportunities are offered.

From a business research perspective, these data should be seen as a
supplement to an organization's internal records and part of an overall plan
for the analysis of secondary data (data already in existence). The data may
be linked, with appropriate caution and caveats, to other internal and external data sets to create synthetic information systems, incidence and prevalence rates, and measures of business success and/or failure not usually
available to the business executive. Furthermore, the data sets described can
easily be integrated into a research agenda that calls for the collection and
analysis of primary data (for example, surveys and focus groups). The key to
any analysis is to locate and utilize the information most appropriate to the
problems or opportunities at hand, even if this involves the merging of
several different sources of data.

Another important topic of interest concerns the areal units—that is,
geographic areas—for which these data are tabulated. While some data sets
are available for very small areal units such as city blocks and census tracts
for Standard Metropolitan Areas (SMAs), others are aggregated only at the
county level and above. Due to relatively small sample sizes for several
nationwide surveys, some data are available only for regions (groups of
states) and the United States as a whole. Of extreme importance is a knowledge of the advantages and limitations of the extent to which any of these
data are geographically subdivided, and whether or not the data available on
computer tape or diskette allow for aggregations different from those seen in
published reports. While some discussion of geographic units of availability

is included for each of the data sets presented, the references at the end of the chapter include the detailed explanations needed by consumers of the information.[1] Furthermore, Chapter 6 contains definitions of geographic units as well as information on how these units can be of use to the business executive.

Also worthy of note is the cost of obtaining these data. Published reports can be purchased very inexpensively (generally, less than $5 per volume) and are available for examination—no cost—at many public and university libraries. Data on microfiche are also available at many public and university libraries, though they are sometimes more expensive to purchase. Data accessible on computer tape vary in cost, though many national-level surveys can be obtained in their entirety for less than $150. Special unpublished tabulations are available from various federal and state agencies for the cost of computer time and postage. State data centers (there is one in each state) sometimes serve as an intermediary between the consumer and state/federal agencies by providing archived data at little or no cost to individuals requesting them. A list of those centers, including address and telephone number, is provided as an appendix to this chapter. Data available on diskette also vary in cost, though the general trend has been that the data in this form are becoming less expensive. Finally, state and national statistical abstracts contain summary data from a host of sources and can prove to be quite useful in a variety of contexts.

For presentation purposes, the data sets have been organized into four general categories. The first contains censuses or complete count data, though it should be noted that under the general rubric census data, a great deal of sampling does take place. For example, while the 1980 Census of Population and Housing was a complete count of persons for the first seven population and first twelve housing items on the questionnaire (short form), data for the remaining questions were gathered from only about one-sixth of the households in the total population (long form). The second data set category contains information, such as births and deaths, extracted from vital records. These registration systems are an excellent source of information and have been in existence for varying lengths of time, though some do not cover all areas of the United States. The third data category includes sample surveys such as the U.S. Census Bureau's Current Population Survey and the Bureau of Labor Statistics' Consumer Expenditure Survey. Most of these surveys are conducted on a periodic basis, and many are carried out annually. The last group presented contains derived data such as population estimates and projections. These data sets take statistics from other information sources, such as censuses and surveys; they synthesize those data and make assumptions about past and/or future behavior in order to create data not normally collected, and/or make projections for some time in the future. Figure 2.1 graphically presents the four categories and examples of data sets falling within each rubric.

Figure 2.1
Data Source Categories

Category	Sources
Census	Population and Housing Economic County Business Patterns Foreign Trade Statistics
Vital Registration	Births and Deaths Marriages and Divorces Abortions
Surveys	Current Population Consumer Expenditure Annual Housing Income and Program Participation Public Health
Derived	Population Estimates and Projections Labor Force Projections Income Projections

Over the past five years, a variety of vendors of census and survey data as well as surveyed information have appeared in the marketplace. The last section of the chapter includes a general discussion of these vendors along with some comments with regard to issues that should be considered in making a choice among vendors. A list of data vendors can be found in the sources cited in the notes.

DATA SOURCES

Censuses

Census of Population and Housing. Simply stated, a census is a simultaneous complete count of people characterized by individual enumeration and periodicity. That is, all individuals are counted and the taking of a census is done at regular intervals. Article 1, Section 2 of the U.S. Constitution calls for the completion of a decennial census for the purposes of determining congressional representation and for taxation apportionment to be carried out within three years after the first meeting of the U.S. Congress. Fulfilling those constitutional requirements, there has been a census of population in the United States every ten years since 1790 (periodicity), though the appearance of the census forms and information gathered from those enumerations have varied greatly. The census of 1790 collected information about only six factors including the name of family head and the number of free white males 16 years old and over; free white males under age 16; free white females; all other free persons; and slaves, in each household. However, the 1980 census of population and housing (housing became part of the population data-gathering activities in 1940), conducted by the U.S. Bureau of the Census, contained thirty-three population and thirty-two housing inquiries, not including many question subparts. The information collected in the 1980 census of population and housing among other factors included the following: respondent and household member characteristics such as age, sex, language spoken inside home, and occupation, along with housing unit data—rent paid, whether or not the housing unit had an air conditioner, and dollar value of a one-family owner-occupied house.

The census of population and housing has undergone many changes in the evolution to its present form. Among the major milestones are the initiation of the collection of data on agriculture, commerce, and manufacturing in 1820 (now part of the economic censuses discussed later in this chapter); the introduction of tabulating machines in 1870; the establishment of a permanent census bureau in 1902; the introduction of sampling to census data collection activities in 1940; computerized data management initiated in 1950–1951; the transition from an individual enumerator to a mail-out mail-back data collection format in 1960; and the near completion of the format transition by 1980. A much more extensive census history and a discussion of the evolution of census forms can be found in Kaplan and Van Valey (1980), the U.S. Bureau of the Census (1979), and Shryock and Siegel (1973).[2]

The geographic areas for which the data are available are the most extensive of any data set reviewed in this chapter. While some of these geographic units are not defined until Chapter 6, they include the United States as a whole, regions and divisions of the United States (state groupings); states; urban and rural areas, counties, metropolitan statistical areas (MSAs—formerly SMSAs), urbanized areas, cities, urban places, census tracts, blocks, block groups, neighborhoods, enumeration districts, and zip codes. However, not all of this geographic precision has been in existence since 1790. For example, MSAs, in their present form, were not designated until 1950 (small area metropolitan statistics for areas such as tracts and blocks are therefore also not available before 1950), and zip code data do not exist for years before 1970.

Census of population data are available in printed reports, including a U.S. summary; individual state, and special reports; five summary computer tape files (each with different levels of geographic and data detail); and on microfiche. In addition, a microdata public use sample tape (identifying data for individuals have been removed) is also available for conducting custom analyses, and individual records include geographic codes that allow for data aggregation at several levels. These microdata files are available for 1950 through 1980.

Economic Censuses—Overview. While most thinking with regard to census data concerns the census of population and housing, economic census data have been gathered since 1810 when information on manufacturers was first collected. Specific economic censuses, however, are of much more recent vintage. In 1840, data collection for agriculture and mineral industries was initiated, followed by governments (1840—limited data—and 1850); transportation (1880); construction (1889); retail, wholesale, and service trade (circa 1930); and foreign trade (1940). Enterprise statistics, which cover the "modern" economic census program initiated in 1954, include retail and wholesale trade; service, mineral, and construction industries; manufacturers; and transporation.[3]

Economic censuses are now conducted by the U.S. Bureau of the Census every five years in years that end in 2 and 7, though data collection has not always followed that pattern. For example, the census of agriculture was conducted every five years for years ending in 4 and 9 until 1974. Recent data are available on microfiche, on computer tape, and in printed form. For some of the economic censuses, geographic availability covers the United States; regions, or groups of states; each state including the District of Columbia, Puerto Rico, Guam, the Virgin Islands, and Northern Marianas; Standard Metropolitan Areas (SMAs); counties; and incorporated places of 2,500 or more inhabitants. However, for many the geographic units are much more limited. Participation on the part of enterprises is mandatory (Title 13, U.S. code), though the same law provides for confidentiality, and therefore the data are available only in aggregated form.

Census of Manufacturers. In general, manufacturing involves the mechanical or chemical transformation of materials or substances into new products. Data on establishments that engage in manufacturing are collected in the portion of the economic census that gathers data on manufacturers. These data cover activity classified by Standard Industrial Classification (SIC) codes ranging from the manufacturing of food and kindred products to instruments and related products.[4] The principal data collected on all economic censuses cover employment, payrolls, inventories, capital expenditures, cost of materials, and products shipped. These data, cross-classified by SIC code and geographic unit (United States, region, state, SMA, county, and selected places), are tabulated and made available on microfiche, on computer tape, and in printed form. Historical data for comparison purposes are sometimes provided in printed reports.

The annual survey of manufacturers (ASM) provides census-type information for intercensal periods. Based on a sample of about 55,000 manufacturers from the census of manufacturers, detailed data are gathered on production, shipment, and/or inventories for sample establishments. Because of the small sample size for the ASM, data for geographic units smaller than SMAs are not available, and the data for states and SMAs are not all-inclusive.

Census of Wholesale Trade, Retail Trade, and Service Industries. The census of wholesale trade includes the sale of merchandise to retailers and repair shops; industrial, commercial institutional, or professional business users; farmers for farm use; governments; or other wholesalers. It also covers agents or brokers who buy merchandise for, or sell merchandise to, such clients or customers.[5] The principal types of establishments enumerated are merchant wholesalers, manufacturers' sales branches and manufacturers' sales offices, and merchandise agents and brokers. The major SIC groups included are 50 and 51. The geographic areas covered are the same as those discussed in the census of manufacturers. The census gathers information on businesses that vary from those producing durable goods such as motor vehicles to those generating nondurable goods such as paper and paper products. Once again, these data are tabulated and cross-classified by geographic area and other economic and financial characteristics (for example, payroll and employment). The information is made available in printed form, on microfiche, and on computer tape.

The census of retail trade enumerates all establishments engaged primarily in selling merchandise for personal or household consumption and rendering services incidental to the sale of those goods.[6] These cover SIC codes 52 through 59. Data for direct sellers with no paid employees and post exchanges are not included. The basic data also do not include information for establishments that are auxiliary (for example, the primary function is providing a service, such as a warehouse). The establishment records do include data on type of business, sales, payroll, number of employees, and legal form of organization. Tabulations and cross-classifications, much like those discussed in the census of manufacturers, are produced. Geographic areas of availability are the same as well. The U.S. Census Bureau also tabulates and publishes monthly retail sales reports for the largest metropolitan markets.

The census of service industries includes data for those businesses that provide lodging, amusement, education, repairs, and other types of services.[7] The types of establishments covered range from hotels and boardinghouses to social service providers. The SIC codes covered are 70 through 79. The data collected from service providers includes federal income tax status (taxable or tax exempt), receipts and revenues, payroll, employment, size of establishment, legal form of organization, and other specialized data such as sources of receipts and number of hotel rooms. These data are tabulated and categorized by SIC code and are obtainable from published sources, on microfiche, and on computer tape. Geographic coverage includes the United States, regions, states, SMAs, and places of 2,500 or more persons.

Census of Agriculture. The census of agriculture provides periodic information on farming, ranching, and related activities in the United States.[8] A farm is defined (1982 definition) as any place from which the sale of agricultural products amounted, or normally would amount, to $1,000 in the census year. Much like the census of population and housing, all farms are canvassed concerning basic items, and a sample of farms (20 percent in 1982) is queried with regard to more detailed factors. Examples of data collected include acreage, crops, land use, livestock and poultry, use of fertilizer, and market value of land and buildings. The data are available at the county, state, and national levels on computer tape, on microfiche, and in printed form. In many of the printed documents, historical data for comparison purposes are available. Tabulations produced generally include the number of farms and farm-related activities classified by geographic unit, for example, counties.

Census of Governments. Census data for governments cover federal, state, and local governmental bodies, including how they are organized and what their functions are.[9] With regard to local governments, municipalities, townships, school districts, and special districts are included for enumeration and tabulation, though only data for the United States and states (an inside and outside SMA distinction is made) are available. More detailed data gathered concern taxable property values; government employment, including numbers of employees, payroll, labor-management policies, and worker benefits; and government finances—revenues, expenditures, and indebtedness. Again, these data are available for years ending in 2 and 7. The U.S. Bureau of the Census also conducts periodic surveys on government employment and finances, though the geographic areas for which these data are available are more limited than those included in the census data.

Census of Transportation. The 1982 census of transportation consisted of three surveys—truck inventory and use; commodity transportation; and nonregulated carriers and public warehousing—though the number of surveys conducted in a given census year has fluctuated over time.[10] The data are available on microfiche, on computer tape, and in printed form. The geographic units of availability include the entire United States and states. Transportation statistics are covered in SIC code 42. The truck inventory and use survey gathers information on the characteristics and operational use of nongovernmental truck resources including body type, load size, principal products carried, and average miles per truck. The commodity transportation survey collects data on intercity commodity shipments originating in the fifty states and the District of Columbia. Nonregulated carriers and public warehousing data contain information on the number of carriers, employment and payrolls for warehouses, and legal form of organization for establishments.

Census of Construction. Covering SIC codes 15 through 17 and 6552, the 1982 census of construction industries collected data from establishments through the use of eight questionnaires. A construction establishment is defined as a relatively permanent office or other place of business that has been established for the management of more than one project or job and is expected to be maintained on a continuing basis.[11] The information gathered covers corporations, individual proprietorships, and partnerships, and is available for the United States, regions, individual states, and the District of Columbia. The basic data collected include, among other information, the number of proprietorships, number of employees, payrolls, payments for materials and utilities, capital expenditures, and business receipts. The data are then categorized by geographic unit. Ongoing surveys gather construction data on a more frequent basis (as often as monthly) and for relatively small geographic units (that is, cities and counties).

County Business Patterns. Even though the county business pattern data-gathering activities are ongoing and the data are derived from administrative records and current survey data, they do constitute a complete count of businesses and are therefore discussed here. Information is collected by the U.S. Bureau of the Census. The data included cover those for establishments and are cross-classified by SIC code.[12] The information is extracted from administrative records (see U.S. Code 8501–8508), and aggregation includes payroll (first quarter and total annual) and mid-March employment. The resulting tabulations contain data on the number of employees and payroll cross-classified by detailed SIC codes. This also allows for tabulations that contain the number of establishments by employee size category for each SIC code. The data are extracted from the Census Standard Establishment List. Industry classifications are assigned on the basis of the nature of the business supplied in applications for employee identification numbers (Treasury Form SS–4).

The data are available for counties, states, and the entire United States for every year since 1964 and for selected years from 1946 to 1964. However, before 1974, nonmanufacturing industry data were not gathered on an establishment basis, and therefore longitudinal analyses that contain time periods before and after 1974 should contain the appropriate caveats. Another factor worthy of note concerns the comparison of economic census and county business pattern data in years when the economic censuses are conducted. The data are not directly comparable because while the county business pattern source relies on administrative records, the economic censuses report data are individual establishments. The differences that appear in the two sources are sometimes large, and simultaneous users of the data sets should proceed with caution. The data are available on microfiche, on computer tape, and in printed form through the U.S. Bureau of the Census.

Foreign Trade Statistics. Though not a strictly census-derived data source (these are really registration data), given their close relationship to other economic census data and their complete count nature, foreign trade statistics are discussed here. The data are produced via the transmission of import and export documents from U.S. Customs officials to the U.S. Bureau of the Census and are available for individual months and years. The source of data for imports is the formal entry form that must be filed when merchandise enters a customer's warehouse or is released from customs service custody.[13] Export information includes records of the physical moving of merchandise from the United States to a foreign country. The information available for detailed commodity categories includes country of origin and destination, quantity of import/export, value of import/export, customs district of entry, and method of transportation. The data are available in printed form, and private computer tape processing centers can make tapes available.

Vital Statistics

The official registration of vital events in the United States—the responsibility of the National Center for Health Statistics (NCHS)—has a relatively long and complex history. Vital events for the most part include live births, deaths, fetal deaths (stillbirths), marriages, divorces, induced abortions, adoptions, annulments, and legal separations, though for the purpose of this presentation the focus is on the first six. While the registration of vital events was initiated long before 1776 in some colonies, it was not until 1900 that an official vital event registration area comprising states was designated (the death registration area). A vital event registration area comprises states that theoretically have a 90 percent coverage of the vital event in question and make use of standard questions on the form (document) where the event is recorded. In 1915 a birth registration area was designated, followed by marriage, 1957; divorce, 1958; and induced abortions, 1977. However, not all registration areas include all of the states in the United States. Birth and death registration areas were complete (all states included) in 1933. In 1984 there were forty-three states in the marriage registration area; thirty-one states in the divorce registration area; and twelve states in the induced abortion registration area. Nevertheless, some statistics published on marriages and divorces include data from all states and the District of Columbia. Data gathering and compiling is the joint responsibility of the NCHS and cooperating states.

Data with regard to vital events include the date of the event; the age, sex, and race of the person(s) to whom the event occurred; where the event occurred; and the residence of the person to whom the event occurred. Examples of items specific to each event are the following:

1. Births—age of father, and mother's and father's education
2. Deaths—cause of death and contributing causes
3. Marriages—number of previous marriages for bride and groom
4. Divorces—children under age 18 affected by the divorce
5. Induced abortion—period of gestation, and number of previous live births.

Vital events data are available frequently (monthly updates and yearly summaries) through the *Monthly Vital Statistics Report* published by the NCHS. Provisional data in these reports are available as soon as two months after the month in question has occurred, though the final data (not provisional) take much longer to be published. Yearly summaries with detailed tabulations are available in NCHS's volumes, *Vital Statistics of the United States*, but the time lag between the end of the year and data publication is quite long (four years for the 1982 data).[14]

Surveys

As stated earlier, the distinction between censuses and surveys has blurred in recent years because many data collection activities formally labeled censuses are in fact surveys. This occurrence is not surprising given the tremendous increase in data collection costs and improvements in the development and implementation of sampling procedures. However, sampling activities do have a cost, the most obvious one is that data for small areas (for example, cities and counties, and in some instances states as well) are simply not reliable or made available in published form due to small sample sizes. Nevertheless, surveys do provide good quality data for regions and the United States as a whole; and the data are available for fairly frequent intervals. That is, the consumer does not have to wait five or ten years between censuses to have current information.

Current Population Survey. The current population survey (CPS) is an ongoing data collection activity engaged in by the U.S. Bureau of the Census. The survey provides data on the social and economic characteristics of the entire U.S. population for frequent intervals during the intercensal time period.[15] The information collected is much like that gathered in the census of population and housing. (For example, the characteristic age, occupation, marital status, education, and race/ethnicity are ascertained for individuals.)

Geographic units for which data are available in published form include the United States, regions of the United States, state groupings, metropolitan-nonmetropolitan residence, central city-outside central city for metropolitan-nonmetropolitan residence, urban-rural, and farm-nonfarm. Data for smaller geographic units are less reliable because of the relatively small sample size for these areal units though the analysis of the data on computer tape makes it possible to extract data for some specific cities. The CPS sample size has ranged from 45,000 to 63,000 households over the last fifteen years; in 1976, however, about 155,000 households were queried with a special focus on income and education matters. Written reports are published many times each year, with specific months being devoted to special topics. For example, the March CPS is devoted to presenting data on geographic mobility. Residence changes over the past year are cross-tabulated by other social and economic characteristics such as age, race/ethnicity, education, income, marital status, and occupation.

Data are available for households, families and individuals within households, and families. In addition to the published reports, CPS microdata are available on computer tape and, like many of the other data sets described in this chapter, can be ordered directly from the Census Bureau.

Consumer Expenditure Survey. Expenditure surveys have a long history in the United States.[16] Initially (1888 to 1891) data were collected as a result of tariff negotiations between the United States and European nations. Later (1901 and 1917–1919), information was needed concerning rapid increases in the cost of living. Surveys during the depression (1934–1936) were seen as requisites for economic planning. The first in a series of very detailed data-gathering efforts was conducted in 1960–1961, and sampled respondents were asked to recall the previous year's general expenditures. However, with regard to detailed food expenditures, the period of recall was seven days. The 1972–1973 Consumer Expenditure Survey expanded that data-gathering period to quarters and divided the collection of data into an interview panel survey (quarterly) and a diary, with separate samples for each questionnaire. The most recent data are collected by an interviewer every three months over a twelve-month period and via a consumer diary, which gathers complete information for two consecutive one-week periods. Presently, the survey is continuous with data being collected every quarter. Prior to 1982, expenditures were obtained from a sample of all spending units. In October 1981, due to budget constraints, rural areas were eliminated from the sample. In 1984 data collection for the rural population resumed.

Data collection activities are currently conducted by the U.S. Bureau of the Census under contract with the Bureau of Labor Statistics (BLS). The interview survey covered approximately 43,000 consumer units in 1980–1981 while the diary survey gathered data from about 20,000 consumer units in the same time interval. Data are available in printed form through bulletins published by the BLS and on computer tape for the United States as a whole and regions (state groupings). Beginning in 1980–1981, data for SMAs are available.

The Consumer Expenditure Survey contains a wealth of information ranging from a host of social and economic characteristics to very detailed information on expenditures. The social and economic data include factors such as age, income by source, marital status, education, and race/ethnicity, while the broad expenditure categories range from money spent on food (both in home and out of home) to money spent on vehicle insurance. Once again, the expenditure data are quite detailed. For example, money spent on categories of expenditures such as living room tables and chairs and men's nightwear are gathered. Data appearing in the published bulletins generally cross-tabulate social and economic characteristics by expenditure categories, though virtually any type of cross-tabulation can be done using the micro-data available on computer tape.

American Housing Survey. The American Housing Survey (AHS), often called the Annual Housing Survey, has gathered information on a variety of housing-related topics from a sample of households annually since 1973.[17] Data collection is conducted jointly by the U.S. Department of Housing and Urban Development and the U.S. Bureau of the Census. Each two years there is a national sample of about 56,000 households surveyed as well as a concentrated data collection effort in selected SMAs. There are 61 SMAs in all in the AHS sample, and a survey is conducted in each SMA approximately every four years. Besides having SMA and U.S. data, information for regions (groups of states) is also available.

Data gathered in the survey include these characteristics: home ownership status, monthly housing costs for owners and renters, size of housing unit, type of heating equipment, the presence or absence of air conditioning, and whether or not a telephone is available. Information is available in printed form as well as on computer tape and microfiche through the U.S. Bureau of the Census.

National Family Growth Survey. The National Family Growth Survey, conducted by Westat, Inc., under contract with the National Center for Health Statistics, is the latest in a long line of U.S. national fertility surveys. Cycle III, the 1982–1983 survey, consisted of interviews with 7,969 women, regardless of marital status, with the focus of the inquiry including preg-nancy history, contraceptive use, childbearing expectations, marital history, and labor force participation. Demographic characteristics of those inter-viewed such as age, income, occupation, and race were also collected. The data gathered, in conjunction with information from previous surveys, allow demographers to study trends in subjects such as contraceptive use where no other data (vital registration and other survey) are available.

Because of the relatively small sample size, only national (U.S.) data are available. Data are available in published reports and on computer tape though there are restrictions on the access to the data on tape for a time after the tape is created.[18]

Survey of Income and Program Participation. The Survey of Income and Program Participation (SIPP) was initiated in 1983 to gather information on income distribution and poverty in the United States. While the data are intended to be used to study federal and state aid programs (for example, food stamps, supplementary security income, and aid to families with de-pendent children) for the purpose of estimating future program costs and to assess the impact of altering eligibility rules or benefit levels, these data can provide information useful to other interested parties.[19] The survey contains three distinct elements: one regarding demographic characteristics, the sec-ond concerning labor force activity and income sources, and the third focusing on specialized modules such as work histories and health character-istics. The sample includes interviews with persons in about 21,000 house-holds nationwide, who are interviewed at four-month intervals over two and one-half years. New panels are selected to replace those who have completed the cycle. The tabulations produced include, among others, income sources cross-classified by demographic data, labor force status cross-classified by income and program participation, and sources and amounts of program income cross-classified by demographic characteristics. The data are avail-able in published reports and on computer tape.

Public Health Surveys. Of particular interest to those marketing executives engaged in health care planning and marketing are several data sets that contain data on illnesses and injuries gathered from individuals, doctors, and hospitals. In the following paragraphs, three data sets that represent the range of the types of health care data collected are presented. All three data sets are available in published reports or on computer tape. They have been selected from a much longer list of health care–related surveys conducted mainly by the National Center for Health Statistics.

The *National Health Interview Survey* has been conducted annually since 1957 by the U.S. Bureau of the Census on behalf of the NCHS.[20] The sample size is approximately 40,000 households nationwide, yielding good quality U.S. and regional estimates of health-related activities. Data gathered in the survey include acute and chronic health conditions; injuries and accidents; visits to physicians, dentists, and hospitals; days spent in bed; and financial costs associated with getting medical care. In addition, demographic infor-mation is collected, and the cross-tabulation of the health and demographic factors provide useful information. Given the relatively long history of this data set, trends and changes in health conditions and visits to medical professionals may be established with year-to-year comparisons.

The *National Hospital Discharge Survey* has been conducted by the NCHS annually since 1965.[21] The data collected are from hundreds of hospitals and for thousands of patient records. In 1980, for example, 420 participating hospitals yielded about 224,000 medical records. The data provide national and regional estimates on the use of nonfederal short-stay hospitals. The data set includes the demographic characteristics of dis-charged patients such as age and sex as well as conditions diagnosed, length of stay in the hospital, and expected source of payment. These data are cross-tabulated, and discharges per 1,000 population and average length of stay are calculated and compared across demographic groups. Again, trends and movements away from past patterns are possible to ascertain because of the frequency of data collection.

The *National Ambulatory Medical Care Survey* collects descriptive data about medical care provided in doctors' offices.[22] The survey was initiated in 1973 and comprises information provided by a representative sample of U.S. doctors of medicine and osteopathy whose primary jobs are office-based, patient-care practice. Excluded are visits to hospital-based physicians, certain specialists, and physicians who are principally engaged in teaching, research, or administration. The sampled physicians complete records for a systematic random sample of their office visits over a weekly reporting period. Data on office visits, reasons for visits, diagnostic services ordered, medication therapy ordered or provided, and principal diagnosis rendered are tabulated and cross-classified by demographic factors such as age, sex, and race/ethnicity.

Derived Data

As stated previously, producing derived or synthetic data involves a merging of existing information, along with patterns in that information, with assumptions about unmeasured or future phenomena in order to construct estimates and/or projections. With regard to demographic data, the types of estimates and projections generated include those for populations (along with components for births, deaths, and migrants), labor force, and income. In general, an estimate is a figure such as population size for a date that has already passed though no specific census or survey was conducted in order to enumerate that population. For example, a population figure for July 1, 1985, for the state of Florida is an estimate because no enumeration of that population took place, and information on measurable events (births and deaths) between the April 1, 1980, census of population and July 1, 1985, and assumptions about another event (migration) were required to produce the later figure. Projections take events that already have occurred (such as a population count) and combine those events with educated guesses about events that might change the population count (births, deaths, in- and out-migrants) to arrive at a population figure for some time in the future. More discussion concerning the distinction between estimates and projections is provided in the presentation of the various data sets. However, if more detail with regard to various estimating methods is desired, the references for this section should be consulted.[23] Chapter 8 presents a detailed presentation of the methodologies used to generate derived data.

Consumers of estimates and projections should always keep in mind that these are derived figures and are therefore subject to error, particularly in places that are changing rapidly (if change is not sufficiently reflected in the assumptions). Baseline data and assumptions should be studied carefully to ensure their accuracy and reasonableness, and periodic checks of population projections with actual counts and population estimates should be performed to measure how accurate the projections are.

Population Estimates—U.S., State, and County. Population estimates provide the data consumer with relatively up-to-date detailed information about the size and structure of a given population. The data can be used to ascertain the size and composition of a population at one point in time or to

jected. The state figures on personal income and earnings by industry are a product of disaggregating the U.S. totals.

USES OF DEMOGRAPHIC DATA

While the topic of how demographic data can be used by the business executive world could easily be the subject of a lengthy manuscript, the present section provides a general overview and some examples concerning the saliency of the data. More extensive discussions of data uses can be found in Chapters 11 and 12. For presentation purposes, examples have been divided into three categories—individual consumer and industrial markets (including segmentation and targeting), locational analysis, and measuring demand or future sales. However, other uses of these data (for example, to assist in producing financial estimates and in planning for labor force supply) have been demonstrated. The reader should keep in mind that the discussion below is applicable in both the small- and large-business context.

With regard to individual consumer and industrial markets, a host of data are available for a range of functions including profiling of consumers, segmenting markets, identifying the geographic location of industrial markets, and determining if these markets are changing (for example, increasing or decreasing). Market profiles include a demographic dimension, and customer profiles can be measured in terms of their age, race, sex, and income components. If it is known that the age structure of a population is changing (for example, becoming older as in the case of the United States) and a product or service is sold mostly to younger persons, then a change in business strategy must occur if sales are to be maintained. Levi Strauss has learned to link its sales strategies to fluctuations in age structure (blue jeans sales are concentrated in the younger ages): A more diverse product line and blue jeans with a "skosh" more room were developed in the 1970's to counteract the effects of an aging market.[30] Data of particular value are census of population information for population counts and compositional information; population estimates and projections for counts and compositional change since the last census; and economic census and county business pattern information for the characteristics and location of industrial customers and competitors, as well as to ascertain the general strength of specific markets. Furthermore, data such as those from the Consumer Expenditure Survey for two or three time intervals can assist both in profiling present spending patterns and ascertaining how those patterns have changed over time.

Segmenting markets also has a demographic component, given that product and service consumption is sometimes concentrated in some relatively distinct demographic segments. By merging demographic and psychographic data, business executives can learn a great deal about who their customers are and can gain useful information about segments that can be targeted at a later time. Data that can be used for this purpose include nationwide census of population figures or data for specific geographic areas. These data in turn can be linked to internal company records (information about present customers) and any special survey data that provide more extensive information about present and future customers. Included in the survey data may be information on lifestyles, attitudes, and opinions. Gathering and analyzing longitudinal data (including estimates and projections) allow the planner/researcher to measure change and potential change in the market.

Determining the location and characteristics as well as change in industrial markets can also be accomplished through analyses of demographic data. *County Business Patterns*, for example, provides SIC code-specific data each year for each county in the United States. Concentrations of certain types of customers and potential customers can be determined, and by measuring change in these markets the researcher/strategist can determine which markets are growing, declining, or remaining generally unchanged. Several businesses that the author has worked with have used *County Business Patterns* data to assist in the location of concentrations of potential customers and competitors over a variety of county aggregations. Of course, any analysis of this type requires detailed knowledge of present customers as well as targeted future customers.

With regard to locational analysis, demographic data can again be quite useful. Functions can include determining the best location for a new business or a relocation site for an existing business. The most obvious examples are taken from the statements made above, where the demographic characteristics of potential individual customers and the location of industrial consumers have been ascertained. In many instances businesses want to locate near customers, and demographic data (both population- and industry-specific) can provide the needed information on the geographic locations of the highest concentrations of potential customers. Population estimates and projections give valuable data with regard to where the highest concentrations of potential customers are likely to be in the future. Data on income projections show the future aggregate buying power of these customers. For example, when large and small businesses desire to locate or relocate, they wish to gather as much information as possible about the business environment in the areas of potential location. These data include demographic characteristics. One major hotel chain looks at a number of key factors including population, the number of major competitors, the number of firms with 100 or more employees, and the number of daily commercial airline flights, in order to select sites for new hotel construction. Their formula for decision making is based on the success of hotels that they are presently operating (vacancy rates and revenue are two of their success measures), and success is linked to the above factors through a mathematical formula. Recently a list of 150 potential new markets was reduced to 33 through the use of this formula.

Measuring and projecting future demand for products and services is another key area where demographic data have become instrumental to market planners. Demand and projected demand of sales are to some extent population driven (number and types of customers), and if incidence or prevalence rates for the products or services of interest can be assembled, then demand figures can be derived. An incidence or prevalence rate is no more than the number of new or existing occurrences (for example, the new purchases or ongoing ownership of a particular type of automobile) divided by the population at risk to buying such a car.

Baylor Hospital in Dallas, Texas, uses incidence and prevalence rates to project local health care needs and thus the demand for its own services.[31] The rates are calculated using the hospital's own internal or area data on disease or procedures, as well as information from some of the national health care surveys discussed earlier. Year-to-year fluctuations are ascertained and rates are adjusted for local conditions. The next step is to link the rates to population projections in order to forecast the number of persons who will require various types of services. Time, Incorporated uses a similar procedure to forecast magazine-specific readership.[32] Readership rates are calculated through the use of historical data on the demographic characteristics of past and present readers. These rates are then multiplied by national population projections of persons in these demographic categories to arrive at a readership (sales, including subscriptions) forecast. For example, sales for *Sports Illustrated* are forecast to plateau because the greatest concentration of readers are young adults, and the number of young adults in the United States is actually declining right now.

DATA VENDORS

Presently there are at least forty U.S. vendors of demographic and related data including psychographics, health care utilization, purchasing power indices, and information on specific markets.[33] All of these firms make those data available for the geographic areas desired (zip codes and census tracts to states and the entire United States). Many vendors provide estimates of demographic characteristics (for example, population counts and characteristics of those populations such as median education level) for non-census/nonsurvey years. The estimates are available annually for very small geographic areas such as zip codes. The estimation procedures utilized by the companies vary, and the potential consumer of these data should look carefully into the methodological procedures before purchasing and utilizing the data. Projections for a limited number of variables are also available, and again the reader is advised to proceed with caution. The data are available in printed form, on computer tape, and on diskette, and the data on diskette can be easily analyzed using software packages such as Lotus 1-2-3 and dBase III. Some vendors allow the consumer access through personal computers (PCs) to data sets and software available on a mainframe computer. Furthermore, the software required to do mapping of characteristics is also available from some companies. This software also has the capability of locating areas with certain prespecified characteristics.

Costs of the data vary considerably by company and by data needs. Also, reduced-priced data sets are often available and the general trend has been for the data to become less expensive. Potential buyers of these data should first identify their data needs and then shop around for the company that (1) provides the most reliable data, (2) makes those data available in the form most useful to the consumer (for example, IBM PC-compatible diskette), and (3) sells those data relatively inexpensively. Some companies also allow (in some cases require) the consumer to subscribe to an updating service at a reduced price for later years. In addition, the prospective consumer should also consider the company's reputation for assistance/consulting when first setting up a data system. The assistance/consulting can range from help in setting up a data base to choosing a microcomputer system and software.

Finally, seminars are now being conducted in various cities on the uses, availability, and calculation of demographic data. *American Demographics* magazine, for example, has conducted seminars on the uses and "how-to's" of building a demographic information system. These seminars include presentations on the advantages of these information systems and specific examples on how the systems may be used. Donnelly Marketing Information Services has conducted seminars on changing consumer lifestyles, which contain a demographic component. It is suggested that the reader explore the range of services offered and pricing structure of the various seminars before deciding to attend one.

NOTES

1. For an extensive discussion about Census Bureau geography see Charles P. Kaplan and Thomas L. Van Valey. 1980. "Geography for a Changing Society." Pp. 129–158 in Kaplan and Van Valey (eds.), *Census '80: Continuing the Factfinder Tradition*. Washington, D.C.: U.S. Government Printing Office.

2. Charles P. Kaplan and Thomas L. Van Valey. 1980. "Twenty Censuses." Pp. 9–36 in Kaplan and Van Valey (eds.), *Census 80: Continuing the Factfinder Tradition*. Washington, D.C.: U.S. Government Printing Office; Henry S. Shryock and Jacob S. Siegel. 1973. *The Methods and Materials of Demography*. Vol. 1. Washington, D.C.: U.S. Government Printing Office, pp. 15–24; and U.S. Bureau of the Census. 1979. *Twenty Censuses*. Washington, D.C.: U.S. Government Printing Office.

3. U.S. Bureau of the Census. 1983. Factfinder for the Nation. *Enterprise Statistics*. CFF No. 19 (Rev.). Washington, D.C.: U.S. Government Printing Office.

4. U.S. Bureau of the Census. 1986. *1982 Census of Manufacturers: General Summary*. Washington, D.C.: U.S. Government Printing Office; and U.S. Bureau of

the Census. 1983. Factfinder for the Nation. *Statistics on Manufacturers*. CFF No. 15 (Rev.). Washington, D.C.: Government Printing Office.

5. U.S. Bureau of the Census. 1984. *1982 Census of Wholesale Trade: Geographic Area Series—United States*. Washington, D.C.: U.S. Government Printing Office; and U.S. Bureau of the Census. 1983. Factfinder for the Nation. *Wholesale Trade Statistics*. CFF No. 11 (Rev.). Washington, D.C.: U.S. Government Printing Office.

6. U.S. Bureau of the Census. 1983. *1982 Census of Retail Trade: Geographic Area Series—United States*. Washington, D.C.: U.S. Government Printing Office; and U.S. Bureau of the Census. 1983. Factfinder for the Nation. *Retail Trade Statistics*. CFF No. 10 (Rev.). Washington, D.C.: U.S. Government Printing Office.

7. U.S. Bureau of the Census. 1984. *1982 Census of Service Industries: Geographic Area Series—United States*. Washington, D.C.: U.S. Government Printing Office; and U.S. Bureau of the Census. 1983. Factfinder for the Nation. *Statistics on Service Industries*. CFF No. 12 (Rev.). Washington, D.C.: U.S. Government Printing Office.

8. U.S. Bureau of the Census. 1985. *1982 Census of Agriculture: Geographic Summary*. Washington, D.C.: U.S. Government Printing Office; and U.S. Bureau of the Census. 1983. Factfinder for the Nation. *Agricultural Statistics*. CFF No. 3 (Rev.). Washington, D.C.: U.S. Government Printing Office.

9. U.S. Bureau of the Census. 1984. *1982 Census of Governments: Government Employment, Employment of Major Local Governments*. Washington, D.C.: U.S. Government Printing Office; and U.S. Bureau of the Census. 1983. Factfinder for the Nation. *Statistics on Governments*. CFF No. 17 (Rev.). Washington, D.C.: U.S. Government Printing Office.

10. U.S. Bureau of the Census. 1985. *1982 Census of Transportation: United States*. Washington, D.C.: U.S. Government Printing Office; and U.S. Bureau of the Census. 1983. Factfinder for the Nation. *Transportation Statistics*. CFF No. 13 (Rev.). Washington, D.C.: U.S. Government Printing Office.

11. U.S. Bureau of the Census. 1985. *1982 Census of the Construction Industries: Geographic Area Series—U.S. Summary*. Washington, D.C.: U.S. Government Printing Office; and U.S. Bureau of the Census. 1983. Factfinder for the Nation. *Construction Statistics*. CFF No. 9 (Rev.). Washington, D.C.: U.S. Government Printing Office.

12. U.S. Bureau of the Census. 1986. *County Business Patterns, 1984: United States*. Washington, D.C.: U.S. Government Printing Office.

13. U.S. Bureau of the Census. 1981. *U.S. Exports—Schedule E: Commodity by Country, February 1981*. Washington, D.C.: U.S. Government Printing Office; and U.S. Bureau of the Census. 1981. *U.S. General Imports—Schedule A: Commodity by Country, February 1981*. Washington, D.C.: U.S. Government Printing Office.

14. For example, see U.S. Department of Health and Human Services. National Center for Health Statistics. 1985. *Vital Statistics of the United States, 1981*. Vol. 1—Natality. Washington, D.C.: U.S. Government Printing Office; and U.S. Department of Health and Human Services. National Center for Health Statistics. 1985. Monthly Vital Statistics Report. *Advance Report of Final Marriage Statistics, 1982*. Vol. 34, No. 3, Supplement. Hyattsville, Maryland: U.S. Public Health Service.

15. See, for example, U.S. Bureau of the Census. 1985. *Household and Family*

Characteristics: March 1984. Current Population Reports, Series P–20, No. 398. Washington, D.C.: U.S. Government Printing Office.

16. U.S. Bureau of Labor Statistics. 1985. *Consumer Expenditure Survey: Interview Survey, 1980–81*. Bulletin 2225. Washington, D.C.: U.S. Government Printing Office; and U.S. Bureau of Labor Statistics. 1986. *Consumer Expenditure Survey: Diary Survey, 1982–1983*. Bulletin 2245. Washington, D.C.: U.S. Government Printing Office.

17. U.S. Bureau of the Census. 1985. *Annual Housing Survey: 1983*. Current Housing Reports, Series H–150–83. Washington, D.C.: U.S. Government Printing Office.

18. Christine Bachrach and William Moser. 1984. *Use of Contraception in the United States, 1982*. Advancedata from Vital and Health Statistics, No. 102. Hyattsville, Maryland: U.S. Public Health Service.

19. U.S. Bureau of the Census. 1985. *Economic Characteristics of Households in the United States: First Quarter 1984*. Current Population Reports, Series P–70, No. 3. Washington, D.C.: U.S. Government Printing Office.

20. B. Bloom. 1982. *Current Estimates from the National Health Interview Survey, United States*. Vital and Health Statistics. National Center for Health Statistics. Series 10, No. 41. Washington, D.C.: U.S. Government Printing Office.

21. E. Graves. 1982. *Expected Principal Source of Payment for the Hospital Discharges: United States, 1979*. Vital and Health Statistics. National Center for Health Statistics. Advancedata, Series 2, No. 75. Washington, D.C.: U.S. Government Printing Office.

22. D. A. Knapp and H. Koch. 1984. *The Management of New Pain in Office-Based Ambulatory Care: National Ambulatory Medical Care Survey, 1980 and 1981*. Vital and Health Statistics. National Center for Health Statistics. Advancedata, Series 2, No. 97. Washington, D.C.: U.S. Government Printing Office.

23. For a detailed discussion on population estimates and projections, see Norfleet W. Rives, Jr., and William J. Serow. 1984. *Introduction to Applied Demography-Data Sources and Estimation Techniques*. Beverly Hills, California: Sage Publications.

24. U.S. Bureau of the Census. 1985. *Estimates of the Population of the United States by Age, Sex, and Race, 1980–1984*. Current Population Reports, Series P–25, No. 965. Washington, D.C.: U.S. Government Printing Office.

25. U.S. Bureau of the Census. 1985. *State Population Estimates, by Age and Components of Change: 1980 to 1984*. Current Population Reports, Series P–25, No. 970. Washington, D.C.: U.S. Government Printing Office.

26. U.S. Bureau of the Census. 1985. *County Intercensal Estimates by Age, Sex, and Race, 1970–1980*. Current Population Reports, Series P–23, No. 139. Washington, D.C.: U.S. Government Printing Office; and U.S. Bureau of the Census. 1985. *Patterns of Metropolitan Areas and County Population Growth: 1980–1984*. Current Population Reports, Series P–25, No. 976. Washington, D.C.: U.S. Government Printing Office.

27. U.S. Bureau of the Census. 1979. *Illustrative Projections of State Populations by Age, Race, and Sex: 1975–2000*. Current Population Reports, Series P–25, No. 796. Washington, D.C.: U.S. Government Printing Office.

28. U.S. Bureau of Labor Statistics. 1985. *Monthly Labor Review* 108 (November). Washington, D.C.: U.S. Department of Labor; and U.S. Bureau of

Labor Statistics. 1984. *Employment Projections for 1995*. Bulletin 2197. Washington, D.C.: U.S. Government Printing Office.

29. U.S. Bureau of Economic Analysis. 1985. *Survey of Current Business 65*, No. 5. Washington, D.C.: U.S. Government Printing Office.

30. John Wyek. 1984. "The Levi Strauss Strategy." Transcript of talk given at Strategic Demographics for U.S. Markets Conference (March). San Francisco, California.

31. John McWhorter. 1985. "Local Area Demographic Estimates: Small Is Beautiful." Paper presented at the annual meeting of the Southern Regional Demographic Group. Austin, Texas.

32. Scott McDonald. 1984. "Use and Limitations of Demographic Analysis in a Communications Business." Paper presented at the annual meeting of the Population Association of America (May). Minneapolis, Minnesota.

33. Martha Farnsworth Riche. 1985. "The Business Guide to the Galaxy of Demographic Products and Services." *American Demographics* (June): 23–33; and Martha Farnsworth Riche. 1985. "Directory of Demographic Products and Services." *American Demographics* (July): 34–41.

APPENDIX 2.1: STATE DATA CENTERS

Alabama
Center for Business and Economic
    Research
University of Alabama
P. O. Box AK
University, AL 35486
Edward Rutledge
(205) 348-6191

Alaska
Alaska Department of Labor
P. O. Box 1149
Juneau, AK 99802
Katherine Lizik
(907) 465-4513

Arizona
The Arizona Department of
    Economic Security
1300 West Washington, 1st Flr.
P. O. Box 6123-045Z
Phoenix, AZ 85005
Linda Strock
(602) 255-5984

Arkansas
IREC-College of Business Adm.
University of Arkansas
33rd and University Avenue
Little Rock, AR 72204
Forrest Pollard
(501) 371-1971

California
Department of Finance
1025 P Street
Sacramento, CA 95814
Linda Sage
(916) 322-4651

Colorado
Division of Local Government
Colorado Dept. of Local Affairs
1313 Sherman Street, Rm. 520
Denver, CO 80203
Reid Reynolds
(303) 866-2351

Connecticut
Comprehensive Planning Division
Office of Policy and Management
State of Connecticut
80 Washington Street
Hartford, CT 06106
Theron A. Schnure
(203) 566-3905

Delaware
Delaware Development Office
99 Kings Highway
P.O. Box 1401
Dover, DE 19903
Gary Smith
(302) 736-4271

District of Columbia
Data Services Division
Mayor's Office of Planning and
    Development
Room 458, Lansburgh Bldg.
420 7th Street, N.W.
Washington, D.C. 20004
Albert Mindlin
(202) 727-6533

Florida
Executive Office of the Governor
Office of Planning and Budget
The Capitol
Tallahassee, FL 32301
Leslie Hazlett
(904) 488-4512

Georgia
Georgia Office of Planning and Budget
270 Washington St., S.W. Rm. 608
Atlanta, GA 30334
Tom Wagner
(404) 656-2191

Hawaii
State Department of Planning and
    Economic Development
P.O. Box 2359
Honolulu, HI 96804
Robert Schmitt
(808) 548-3082

Idaho
Division of Economic and
    Community Affairs
700 W. State Street
State Capitol Bldg., Rm. 108
Boise, ID 83720
Alan Porter
(208) 334-3416

Illinois
Division of Planning and
    Financial Analysis
Illinois Bureau of the Budget
William Stratton Bldg. Rm. 605
Springfield,IL 62706
Kathy Roberts
(217) 782-5414

Indiana
Indiana State Library
140 North Senate Avenue
Indianapolis, IN 46204
Sandi Thompson
(317) 232-3733

Iowa
Office of the State Demographer
Iowa Office for Planning and
    Programming
523 East 12th St.
Des Moines, IA 50319
Mary Tavegia
(515) 281-3738

Kansas
State Library
State Capitol Building, Rm. 343
Topeka, KS 66612
Marc Galbraith
(913) 296-3296

Kentucky
Urban Studies Center, Dept. SDC
University of Louisville
Gardencourt Campus
Alta Vista Road
Louisville, KY 40292
Vernon Smith
(502) 588-6626

Louisiana
Louisiana State Planning Office
P. O. Box 44426
Baton Rouge, LA 70804
Karen Paterson
(504) 342-7410

Maine
Division of Economic Analysis and
    Research
Maine Department of Labor
20 Union Street
Augusta, ME 04330
Raynold Fongemie
(207) 289-2271

Maryland
Maryland Dept. of State Planning
301 West Preston Street
Baltimore, MD 21201
Arthur Benjamin
(301) 383-5664

Massachusetts
Center for Massachusetts Data
Executive Office of Communities and
    Development
100 Cambridge Street, Rm. 904
Boston, MA 02202
Charles McSweeney
(617) 727-3253

Michigan
Michigan Information Center
Department of Management and Budget
Office of the Budget/LLPD
P.O. Box 30026
Lansing, MI 48909
Laurence Rosen
(517) 373-2840

Minnesota
State Demographic Unit
Minnesota State Planning Agency
101 Capitol Square Bldg.
550 Cedar Street
St. Paul, MN 55101
Eileen Barr
(612) 296-4886

Mississippi
Center for Population Studies
The University of Mississippi
Bondurant Building, Rm. 3W
University, MS 38677
Michelle Ratcliff
(601) 232-7288

Missouri
Missouri State Library
308 High Street, P.O. Box 387
Jefferson City, MO 65102
Jon Harrison
(314)751-4552

Montana
Montana Census and Economic
    Information Center
Montana Dept. of Commerce
1429 9th Street
Capitol Station
Helena, MT 59620-0401
Patricia Roberts
(406) 444-2896

Nebraska
Bureau of Business Research
200 CBA, University of
    Nebraska, Lincoln
Lincoln, NE 68588
Jerry Deichert
(402) 472-2334

Nevada
Nevada State Library
Capitol Complex
401 North Carson
Carson City, NV 89710
John Kerschner
(702) 885-5160

New Hampshire
Office of State Planning
State of New Hampshire
2½ Beacon Street
Concord, NH 03301
Jim McLaughlin
(603) 271-2155

New Jersey
New Jersey Dept. of Labor
Division of Planning and Research
CN 388 - John Fitch Plaza
Trenton, NJ 08625-0388
Connie O. Hughes
(609) 984-2593

New Mexico
Economic Development and
    Tourism Dept.
Bataan Memorial Building
Santa Fe, NM 87503
Ann Glover
(505) 827-6200

New York
Division of Economic Research
    and Statistics
New York Department of Commerce
Twin Towers, Room 1005
99 Washington Avenue
Albany, NY 12245
Mike Batuitis
(518) 474-5944

North Carolina
North Carolina Office of State
    Budget and Management
116 West Jones Street
Raleigh, NC 27611
Francine Ewing
(919) 733-7061

North Dakota
Dept. of Agricultural Economics
North Dakota State University
Agricultural Experiment Station
Morrill Hall, Rm. 207
P. O. Box 5636
Fargo, ND 58105
Richard Rathge
(701) 237-8621

Ohio
Ohio Data Users Center
Ohio Department of Economic and
    Community Development
P. O. Box 1001
Columbus, OH 43216
Keith Ewald
(614) 466-7772

Oklahoma
Department of Economic and
    Community Affairs
Lincoln Plaza Bldg. Suite 285
4545 North Lincoln Blvd.
Oklahoma City, OK 73105
Karen Selland
(405) 528-8200

Oregon
Intergovernmental Relations Division
Executive Building
155 Cortage St., N.E.
Salem, OR 97310
Jon Roberts
(503) 373-1996

Pennsylvania
Institute of State and
    Regional Affairs
Pennsylvania State University
Capitol Campus
Middletown, PA 17057
Bob Surridge
(717) 948-6336

Puerto Rico
Puerto Rico Data Center
Puerto Rico Planning Board
Minillas Government Center
North Bldg., Avenida De Diego
P. O. Box 41119
San Juan, PR 00940
Nolan Lopez
(809) 726-7210

Rhode Island
Rhode Island Statewide Planning
    Program
265 Melrose Street, Rm. 203
Providence, RI 02907
Joyce Karger
(401) 277-2656

South Carolina
Division of Research and
    Statistical Services
Budget and Control Board
State of South Carolina
Rembert C. Dennis Bldg. B341
1000 Assembly Street
Columbia, SC 29201
Mike MacFarlane
(803) 758-3986

decreased in the United States, the reference may be to a change in the average number of children women are having or merely to a trend toward more or fewer births. While the average number of births per woman and total births are certainly related, knowing the value of one does not guarantee knowledge about the size of the other. For example, while the average number of births per woman remained fairly stable during the late 1970's, total births rose because more women entered their childbearing years. The increase in the number of women in their childbearing years can easily offset a decline in average births per woman.

Fecundity, on the other hand, refers to the physiological ability to reproduce without regard to any societal context whatsoever. A *fecund* woman, in general, has few if any problems conceiving and carrying a child to term. Women who are infecund have also been labeled *sterile* or physically unable to have children, while *subfecund* women have difficulty conceiving and/or carrying a child to term. Another term frequently seen in the demographic literature is *infertile* and is operationally defined as the inability to conceive after one year of intercourse without contraception. Estimates for 1965, 1976, and 1982 show a generally consistent proportion of American women classified infertile—13.3, 14.3, and 13.9 percent, respectively.[1] Fecundity is also affected by age at *menarche*—the onset of menstruation—and *menopause*—the end of menstruation. There is a strong relationship between age and infertility, and in 1982 the percentage of women classified infertile increased from 2.1 at ages 15–19 to 27.2 at ages 40–44.[2] Furthermore, between 1900 and 1980 average age at menarche declined approximately three years from 15 to 12.

As a result of the interaction of social norms, economic and political conditions, biological limitations sometimes related to nutrition, and health care standards, very few populations reproduce at or near their theoretical biological maximum. If, for example, a woman entered a sexual union at age 18, had a child at age 19, and then bore a child every two years until she was 45, 14 births would occur. Today in the United States, women are averaging somewhat less than two births over a lifetime, and given the relatively low percentage of infertile women discussed above, some types of social constraints certainly must be in place.

These constraints, or partial determinants of the number of births a woman will eventually have, are mediated by what have been labeled factors intermediate to fertility outcomes. These factors specifically refer to (1) exposure to intercourse, (2) exposure to conception, and (3) the likelihood of having a live birth once a conception has taken place.[3] Figure 3.1 shows in graph form the fertility process from social factors to fertility outcome. Without intercourse, conception, and a fetus that remains viable until the end of the pregnancy term, there can be no fertility outcome. However, the model views these three factors as intermediate in the sense that social and economic conditions (for example, social norms and income conditions) in

Figure 3.1
The Effect of Intermediate Variables on Fertility

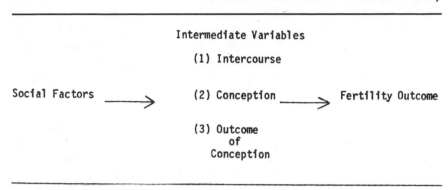

Intermediate Variables

(1) Intercourse

Social Factors ————→   (2) Conception ————→ Fertility Outcome

(3) Outcome
of
Conception

turn affect factors such as marriage rates and the desire to have children (intermediate variables). Interaction between these two sets of conditions ultimately determines fertility levels. Finally, the intermediate variables should be seen as interdependent in producing fertility outcomes. That is, intercourse and conception variables, for example, interact to produce fertility outcomes.

Among the factors affecting exposure to intercourse are age at marriage, extent of nonmarriage, time spent between or outside marriage, and frequency of intercourse.[4] Even though there has been a relatively recent and substantial increase in births outside marriage, over 80 percent of all births still occur to married women.[5] The remaining 20 percent is discussed later in the chapter.

Concerning age at marriage, age at first marriage has shown a gradual increase since 1950. From 1950 to 1980, average age at first marriage increased from 22.8 to 23.6 years for males and 20.3 to 21.8 years for females. By 1982, these figures had risen to 24.1 and 22.3 respectively.[6] While this increase may appear on the surface to be a small one, it, in conjunction with several other factors such as increased female labor force participation, explains a great deal about the U.S. fertility decline discussed in Chapter 1 and presented in more detail later in this chapter. More dramatic, however, has been the increase in the percentage of adults who have never been married. Looking at the ages 30–34, the percentage of persons who have never been married increased from 11.9 to 20.9 for males and 6.9 to 13.3 for females from 1960 to 1984. That is, more than 15 percent of the population 30–34 years of age has never been married.[7]

Recent data show a marked increase in the proportion of marriages terminating in divorce. While in the 1940–1945 time period 14.2 percent of all marriages ended in divorce, by 1975–1980 the proportion had risen to 45.4 percent. Comparing the interval 1940–1945 with 1975–1980, 2.1 and 11.3 percent respectively of a white woman's life was spent either widowed or divorced—an increase of 9.2 percent. For blacks, the increase was from 5.9 to 20.9 percent. And if the years spent before the first marriage are eliminated from consideration, whites and blacks spent 17.1 and 39.3 percent, respectively, of their adult lifetimes single, separated, or divorced, using the 1975–1980 time period as the reference.[8] Overall, separation and divorce reduce fertility, though for some groups of women the effect of remarriage and the desire to "cement" new marriages leads to increased fertility in subsequent marriages.[9]

Much less information has been reported about frequency of intercourse. The mean coital frequency reported in the 1970 National Fertility Survey was 8.2 times during the four weeks preceding the survey. Among those women using contraceptives, coital frequency increases as the age of the woman increases.[10] The comparable mean frequency for unmarried female teenagers in 1976 was 2.6.[11] However, in the years since the formulation of the Davis-Blake framework (1956) the increase in contraceptive availability and use has left this factor a less important determinant of fertility.

Factors affecting conception include infecundity (involuntary and voluntary—that is, sterilization), contraceptive use, and breast feeding. Breast feeding is included because it lengthens the period of natural infertility following a birth. Involuntary infecundity has already been discussed and affects approximately 13 percent of all women 15–44 years of age. Concerning sterilization, there has been a large increase over the last two decades in the proportion of males and females who have been sterilized. From 1965 to 1982 the increase in the percentage of all men aged 15–44 who had been sterilized was over 10 percent, from 5.2 to 15.4. The concomitant percentage for females was 7.2 and 25.6.[12] Above age 30, sterilization is the most prevalent method of contraception, and overall it ranks second in popularity to the pill.[13]

Contraceptive use varies along two important dimensions: age of woman and type of contraceptive used. In 1982, at the ages 15–19, a little less than 25 percent of all women used contraceptives, with nearly two-thirds of these women using the pill. By the ages 25–29, nearly two-thirds of the women used some type of contraceptive, though only slightly more than one-third used the pill.[14] Not only was there an increase in sterilization, but IUD and diaphragm use rose sharply.

Finally, the incidence of breast feeding has increased markedly over the past decade. While less than one-fourth of all women breast-fed in the early 1970s, more than half do now. Furthermore, nearly one-third breast-feed for three or more months. Among the highest educated women, those with more than a bachelor's degree, nearly three-fourths breast-feed; about one-half of these women breast-feed for more than three months.[15]

Factors affecting the likelihood of having a live birth, once a conception has taken place, are *spontaneous* and *induced abortions*. Concerning spontaneous abortions, it has been estimated that over 50 percent of all fertilized ova are naturally lost before a live birth can take place.[16] One estimate suggests that 35 percent of all fertilized ova are lost before the first menstrual period and another 14 percent are lost between the first missed period and delivery.[17]

When a pregnancy is aborted voluntarily, it is called an induced abortion. Reported induced abortion has increased markedly since the 1973 Supreme Court decision that in general ruled state laws banning induced abortions unconstitutional.[18] From 1973 to 1982 there was an increase of induced abortions from 745,000 to over 1.5 million. This translates as an increase from 239 induced abortions per 1,000 live births in 1973 to 426 per 1,000 live births in 1982, though the ratio has been relatively stable since 1980.[19] Caution, however, must be exercised in viewing these figures because part of the increase is probably due to the higher incidence of nonreported induced abortions during the early 1970's.

Fertility measurement is discussed over the next several pages. While the discussion is at times somewhat tedious, measurement is one of the nuts-and-bolts functions of the demographer. Of greatest importance to the reader, however, is the understanding that each of these measures provides different information about fertility and thus gives a variety of useful data with regard to the business environment.

FERTILITY MEASURES

Now that factors affecting fertility have been discussed, it is necessary to address how fertility outcomes are measured. At the individual or micro level this is relatively easy—the woman in question either did or did not have a live birth. And births over a lifetime can be counted. This task is performed by the birth registration system in the United States. However, fertility is generally measured at the aggregate or macro level (for example, country or regional level), and therefore a series of measures has been developed at the macro level for expressing fertility outcomes as rates.

The reason for expressing fertility outcomes as rates has to do with the need for some type of standardization. That is, one region of a country may have more births than another simply because it contains more people (women) and not because women are averaging more births. So the number of births can be standardized by dividing the number of births by some population figure, thereby creating a rate. There are several types of fertility rates receiving frequent use, and together they form a logical progression from less to more specific, depending on what denominator is used for calculating the rate.

Furthermore, fertility rates are in general expressed in *cross-sectional* terms; that is, at one point in time. They are *period* specific and tied to the data at hand in the sense that they are generally calculated from figures tabulated over a relatively short period of time (one to three years). These period rates can be misleading, however, in that they do not tell us how a *cohort* of women will behave throughout a lifetime of childbearing. A cohort of women are women with a common set of characteristics—in this case age. If the reader wants to know about the fertility behavior of the cohort of women born between 1955 and 1960, he or she must wait until those women complete their childbearing before knowing precisely how many children on average the women will have. The period rates discussed below actually capture fertility of all cohorts at one time, but only at the time specific to the measurement. They do, however, allow demographers to hypothesize about future fertility as well as make comparisons and chart trends because many data collection systems are continuous or at least periodic.

Finally, it should be noted that the data required for the calculation of fertility rates often come from these three sources discussed in Chapter 2: (1) census of population figures for the denominators of rates and the number of children ever born to women in census years, (2) population estimates for the denominators of rates in intercensal years, and (3) the number of births from vital registration data for the numerators of the rates. Survey data do provide information for producing estimates of some rates.

Crude Birth Rate

The *crude birth rate* (CBR) is the number of births per 1,000 persons for some given year. It can be expressed as

$$\text{CBR} = \frac{\text{Number of births in year X}}{\text{Midyear population in year X}} \times 1,000.$$

Multiplication by 1,000 has the effect of reducing the number of digits after the decimal point. For 1982 the CBR for the United States was

$$\text{CBR} = \frac{3,713,000 \text{ (births 1982)}}{232,062,00 \text{ (midyear population in 1982)}} \times 1,000 = 16.0$$

or 16 births per 1,000 persons. This compares with a CBR of 15.0 in 1978, 14.6 in 1975, and 24.9 in 1955. While the CBR is adequate for making very general comparisons and has the advantage of requiring only two pieces of information, it has two major shortcomings. First, the denominator includes people not *at risk* to having a birth. The concept at risk refers to a person or group of persons being in a sense eligible for occurrence of some phenomenon. Everyone is at risk to dying, though the risk for some is greater than for others. A more limited population is at risk to having children, though the CBR in a sense assumes everyone is at risk. All males and younger and older females are not at risk to having births. Second, the CBR hides or masks differences in age structures of populations. That is, fertility rates are greatly affected by age structure—specifically, the proportion of all women who are in the "childbearing" years. So, for example, two populations with the same population size could have dissimilar CBRs simply because one population had 20 percent of its females in the childbearing ages, while the other had 35 percent. Therefore, more refined measures of fertility have been developed.

General Fertility Rate

The *general fertility rate* (GFR) is a refinement of the CBR in that the denominator of the rate is females aged 15–44—the approximate population at risk to having a child. The GFR is expressed as

$$GFR = \frac{\text{Total number of births in year X}}{\text{Midyear populatin of women aged 15–44 in year X}} \times 1000.$$

For 1982 the GFR is calculated in the following fashion:

$$GFR = \frac{3,713,000}{54,621,000} \times 1,000 = 68.0.$$

By comparison, the GFR was about the same (67.8) in 1977 and higher (88.0) in 1967. In 1955 it was much larger (118.5). While the GFR is clearly an improvement over the CBR, it does require an additional piece of information—the number of females 15–44 years of age—and therefore means that the demographer needs to know not only the size but the age-sex structure of the population in question in order to arrive at the appropriate rate denominator.

Age-Specific Fertility Rates

The *age-specific fertility rate* (ASFR) is a more precise measure of fertility. Instead of having one rate, as is the case with the CBR and GFR, multiple rates—one for each five-year age interval for women 15–44—are generally calculated. In other words, there are individual fertility rates produced for women 15–19, 20–24, and beyond, up to the age interval 40–44. Furthermore, rates for other ages, under 15 and over 44, can be generated to capture either very early or very late fertility. Five-year intervals are used out of convenience, not necessity. When early fertility is being measured, shorter age intervals, for example, 13–14, are frequently used.

One additional data requirement must be met for calculating ASFRs. Birth data (births) must be classified by the age of the mother when she gave birth. In general, an ASFR is computed

$$\text{ASFR} = \frac{\text{Births in a year to women aged X to X}+5}{\text{Midyear population of women aged X to X}+5 \text{ in year Y}} \times 1{,}000.$$

6.0For 1982 the ASFR for women 20–24 was

$$\text{ASFR}_{20-24} = \frac{1{,}206{,}000}{10{,}836{,}000} \times 1{,}000 = 111.3.$$

ASFRs for women aged 20–24 were 121 per 1,000 women in 1973 and twice that, 242, in 1955.

Six ASFRs are calculated for women 15–44 years of age when five-year intervals are utilized: 15–19, 20–24, 25–29, 30–34, 35–39, and 40–44. Sometimes handling all six rates is unwieldy because year-to-year comparisons really require looking at six individual relationships. Therefore, demographers have developed three summary measures that incorporate all six ASFRs.

Total Fertility Rate

The *total fertility rate* (TFR) is a hypothetical measure of fertility. It is a period measure—for one point in time—for which cohort types of generalizations are sometimes made. Specifically, it measures the number of children a *just* 15-year-old-woman would have *if* age-specific fertility rates remained the same until she was 44. Now, of course, all ASFRs will not remain constant for this thirty-year time interval. But to the extent that actual ASFRs over the thirty-year period taken together approximate the TFR calculated, the TFR can be a good approximation of completed fertility. Once again, the only way to measure completed fertility is to wait until the childbearing years are over. Frequently, fertility information is required long before this rather lengthy interval is over, and the TFR can provide it. Finally, it should be noted that the cohort fertility rates, completed fertility, for women just ending their childbearing years often mask birth rate fluctuations occurring at earlier ages.

The TFR is calculated

$$\text{TFR} = (\text{ASFR} \times 5.)$$

In 1982, the TFR was

Age	ASFR	ASFR × 5
15–19	52.9	264.5
20–24	111.3	556.5
25–29	111.0	555.0
30–34	64.2	321.0
35–39	21.1	105.5
40–44	3.9	19.5
Total	364.4	1822.0

The 1,822.0 figure refers to 1,822 births per 1,000 women aged 15–44, and therefore women are averaging 1.8 births over a lifetime. Comparable data for past years show a great deal of year-to-year variation. Given the discussion from Chapter 1, one would expect high TFRs during the post-World War II baby boom and low TFRs during the baby bust, and this turns out to be true. During the 1955–1959 time interval, the TFR averaged 3,690. By 1976, the TFR had dropped to 1,738.

Two refinements of the TFR have been developed in order to more adequately reflect what might be called reproductive capability. While it is true that only through sexual intercourse, and in some cases artificial insemination, does a pregnancy occur, females are the only members of the species who are capable of becoming pregnant and carrying a child to term at the present time. Therefore, an additional measure of fertility, one that reflects the births of females, is required. Furthermore, not all of these female births will in fact survive to the end of their own reproductive years, so an additional fertility measure has been developed to account for the affects of what might be called premature mortality.

Gross Reproduction Rate

The *gross reproduction rate* (GRR), takes the TFR and "corrects" it to account only for female births. In other words, it is a TFR for female births. The GRR was created to measure fertility *replacement*. Given that females are the only members of the species who can bear children, the GRR tells us how well females are reproducing themselves. A value of 1,000 means that women are exactly replacing themselves, while values greater and less than 1,000 reflect fertility over and under replacement. Much like the TFR, the GRR is the average number of female births a cohort of women entering their childbearing years would have over a lifetime *if* age-specific fertility rates (the sex distribution of births is accounted for as well) remained constant. The

GRR is calculated by multiplying each ASFR by the proportion of total births in that age interval who are females, and then summing all ASFRs the same way to produce a TFR. In equation terms

$$GRR = (ASFR^F \times 5);$$

$ASFR^F$ is the age-specific fertility rate for female births only. In 1982, the GRR was approximately 890. By comparison, the GRR was 1,212 in 1945, rose to 1,783 in 1960, and declined to 876 in 1975. However, without accounting for deaths to women before they complete childbearing, the concept of replacement-level fertility is somewhat unclear. Therefore, a measure that "corrects" the GRR for mortality is discussed.

Net Reproduction Rate

The *net reproduction rate* (NRR) "corrects" the GRR by accounting for the mortality likely to occur during the time interval in question. For each $ASFR^F$, a mortality correction factor is introduced because not all of the female children born will live through all of their reproductive years. Those who do die before or during their childbearing years will obviously not be at risk to having children throughout the interval (ages 15–44), and some adjustment for their reduced childbearing must be made. Again a value of 1,000 reflects just replacement-level fertility. In simple terms:

$$NRR = (ASFR^F \times \text{mortality correction}).$$

The NRR measures the number of female births per 1,000 females of childbearing age a cohort of women entering their childbearing years would have if age-specific fertility *and* age-specific mortality rates remained constant. Age-specific mortality rates are discussed in Chapter 4. In 1982, the NRR was approximately 870, compared with 1,132 in 1945, 1,715 in 1960, and 853 in 1975.

Cohort Measures of Fertility

As discussed earlier, *cohort* measures of fertility measure the childbearing experiences of women of a given age—generally the five-year intervals used in calculating period measures of fertility. Generally speaking, women are asked in censuses and surveys how many children (live births) they have had in their lifetime. Subsequently, these data are categorized by the age of the woman respondent. Looking at the oldest women, those above age 44, demographers obtain what might be considered a cohort version of a TFR, except that the assumption about ASFRs remaining constant no longer need be made. This cohort measure, *children-ever-born*, is a measure of completed fertility for women at those ages. For women 45–49 years of age, the number of children-ever-born per 1,000 women was 2,492 in 1950, 2,402 in 1960, 2,854 in 1970, and 3,096 in 1983, reflecting the completed fertility from the end of the Great Depression through to the post-World War II baby boom. It is also possible to examine cohort rates—children-ever-born—for women who have not completed their fertility. This allows the data user to assess trends in both the overall number of births and the timing (at what ages women have their children) of fertility. Looking at the 15–19 cohort, children-ever-born numbered 604 in 1950, 792 in 1960, 636 in 1970 and 760 in 1983. Since 1970, the fertility of very young women, as reflected in children-ever-born figures, has increased. Furthermore, many fertility surveys also include a question regarding how many children a woman expects to have over her lifetime.

TRENDS IN U.S. FERTILITY

Number of Births

While the measures of fertility discussed above provide a good way of illustrating changes in various aspects of fertility over time, year-to-year presentations show in greater detail changes in U.S. fertility patterns since the end of World War II. However, first fluctuations in the number of births since 1945 are explored. Looking at Table 3.1, the reader can see the effect of the post-World War II baby boom discussed in Chapter 1 as reflected in the number of births. Starting at a low of 2.9 million births in 1945, this number rose to 4.0 million by 1953 and peaked at 4.3 million for each year 1957 to 1961. The baby bust is shown by the decline in the number of births from 4.3 million in 1961 to 3.1 million by 1975. In terms of the crude birth rate (CBR) in 1945 it stood at 20.4, increased to 25.3 in 1957, and declined to 14.6 by 1975. Since 1975, the number of births has increased (this is sometimes called the boomlet) by about one-half million births per year to around 3.7 million. The CBR has increased slightly to around 16.

Total Fertility Rate

Table 3.2 shows the trend in the total fertility rate (TFR) over the same time period. Starting at 2,491 in 1945, the TFR increased by nearly 50 percent to 3,654 by 1960—in only a ten-year period! More dramatically, however, over the next twenty years it declined to a little less than 50 percent of its peak value, to 1,774. Recalling that the net reproduction rate is a measure of fertility replacement for those same years, it stood at 1,132 in 1945, 1,715 in 1960, and 853 in 1975. An NRR of 853 shows fertility considerably below replacement—the average number of female births required for adult females to replace themselves. In other words, females were only averaging .85 female births over a lifetime in 1975. While the TFR stood a little higher, 1,829 in 1982, than it had in 1975, it was still considerably

Table 3.1
Annual Births to U.S. Women: 1945–1984

Year	Births (in millions)	Year	Births (in millions)
1945	2.9	1965	3.8
1946	3.4	1966	3.6
1947	3.8	1967	3.5
1948	3.6	1968	3.5
1949	3.6	1969	3.6
1950	3.6	1970	3.7
1951	3.8	1971	3.6
1952	3.9	1972	3.3
1953	4.0	1973	3.1
1954	4.1	1974	3.2
1955	4.1	1975	3.1
1956	4.2	1976	3.2
1957	4.3	1977	3.3
1958	4.3	1978	3.3
1959	4.2	1979	3.5
1960	4.3	1980	3.6
1961	4.3	1981	3.6
1962	4.2	1982	3.7
1963	4.1	1983	3.6
1964	4.0	1984	3.7

Sources: U.S. Bureau of the Census. 1975. Historical Statistics of the U.S.,
           Colonial Times to 1970, Part 1, Series B1-4. Washington D.C.:   U.S.
           Government Printing Office; U.S. Bureau of the Census, Statistical
           Abstract of the United States 1986, Washington, D.C.: U.S.
           Government Printing Office, table 81.

below replacement-level fertility. The fact that U.S. fertility is presently below replacement level has important implications for long-term U.S. population growth and will be discussed in more detail at the end of this chapter and again in Chapter 10, which focuses on population policy.

Children-Ever-Born

Children-ever-born (CEB) data for the same time period are provided in Table 3.3. Remembering that the CEB measure is a true cohort measure, examination of CEB data for women aged 45–49 can provide accurate information on completed fertility. Looking at Table 3.3, it can be seen that completed fertility in general has increased since 1950. Starting with a CEB of 2,492 in 1950, the rate increased to 2,854 by 1970 and peaked at 3,185 in 1980—a rise of 28 percent from 1950. That is, women who were at the end of their childbearing years in 1980 had averaged slightly more than three births during the period beginning roughly in 1931 and ending in 1980. However, as previously discussed, looking at the CEB for women at the end of their childbearing years can be somewhat misleading because these data

Table 3.2
Total Fertility Rate for U.S. Women: 1945–1982

Year	Total Fertility Rate (births per 1,000 women aged 15 to 49)
1945	2,491
1950	3,091
1955	3,580
1960	3,654
1965	2,913
1970	2,480
1975	1,774
1980	1,840
1982	1,829

Sources: U.S. Bureau of the Census. 1986. Statistical Abstract of the United States, 1986, table 82; U.S. Bureau of the Census. 1975. Historical Statistics of the U.S., Colonial Times to 1970, Part 1, Series B11-19. Washington, D.C.: U.S. Government Printing Office.

Table 3.3
Children Ever Born for U.S. Women Aged 45 to 49: 1950–1983

Year	Children Ever Born[a]
1950	2,492
1954	2,436
1960	2,402
1965	2,603
1970	2,854
1975	3,152
1980	3,185
1983	3,096

[a]Data are for ever-married women.

Source: U.S. Bureau of the Census. 1986. Statistical Abstract of the United States, 1986, table 92.

tell us nothing about recent trends in fertility. For example, focusing on women 25–29 years of age, women who have not completed their fertility, it can be seen that CEB, while standing at 1,930 in 1954, decreased to 1,389 by 1983—a decline of 28 percent. A more marked decline at the ages 20–24 is evident. Peaking at 1,441 in 1960, the CEB fell to 930 in 1983—a reduction of 35 percent!

Furthermore, in examining data on *fertility expectations*—the number of children women tell researchers they expect to have over a lifetime—changing fertility norms are even more evident. In 1967, 7.4 percent of the women who were married at the time of the survey expected to have either one or no children at all. Fifty-five percent said they expected to have three or more children. By 1982, expectations had changed considerably. Nineteen percent gave a zero or one expectation and only 25 percent expected three or more children.[20] While all women 30–34 years of age had an actual fertility rate of 1,674 births per 1,000 women, they expected to have 2,029 births over a lifetime.[21]

The careful reader of the last several pages has noticed the discrepancy between the most widely used measures of fertility—TFR, CEB, and birth expectations. Once again the TFR is a period rate which is an aggregate of age-specific fertility behavior at one point in time. Changes in fertility behavior, either through the changes in fertility norms or the *timing of fertility* (at what age women bear their children), effect the rate either upward or downward, and the TFR cannot reflect these changes. While the completed CEB reveals actual fertility, it can do so only for women who are at the end of their childbearing years. And though CEB data at early ages provide information about changing fertility norms (lower fertility), they also can reflect timing changes (children being born later in life) and therefore are not a true measure of changing overall fertility. Expectations, on the other hand, are educated guesses—though they do include already completed fertility—and are therefore subject to change as social norms and economic conditions change. All three measures have their distinct advantages and disadvantages, and each falls short of the crystal ball fertility measure that demographers would all like to have.

Childlessness

While the impact of women expecting zero or one and less than four children has had a profound effect on overall fertility, the impact of *childlessness*—not having any children at all—on overall fertility rates is worthy of note. Childlessness may be divided into two components—*involuntary*, or those women who through no conscious act of their own cannot conceive and/or carry a child to term—and *voluntary*—those women who through their own volition choose not to bear any children. So when data on childlessness are discussed, they contain the contribution of both components. However, the extent of involuntary childlessness is not precisely known, and therefore it is difficult to guage exactly what proportion of women are choosing not to have any children. The proportion of women at the end of their childbearing years who are involuntarily childless may be less than 8 percent—the percentage of all women aged 40–44 who were childless in 1984.[22]

Table 3.4 shows the percentage of all women who were childless, catego-

Table 3.4
Percent of All United States Women Aged 20 to 24 and 30 to 34 Who Are
Childless: 1950–1984

Year	Aged 20-24	Aged 30-34
1950	33.3	17.3
1954	24.3	13.4
1960	24.2	10.4
1965	28.0	7.2
1970	35.7	8.3
1975	42.3	8.8
1980	40.4	13.7
1984	40.7	15.8

Source: U.S. Bureau of the Census. 1986.   Statistical Abstract of the United
States, 1986, table 92.

rized by two age groups (20–24 and 30–34) for the years 1950–1984. The two age groups were selected because they represent what are currently early and late childbearing age intervals in the United States, though it must be pointed out that fertility at ages younger than 20 and older than 34 is not inconsequential. Looking at the table, it can be observed that a relatively large increase in childlessness occurs at both ages, though it does appear that the figures for ages 30–34 are returning to pre–1960 levels. Of particular interest are differences between the percentages exhibited during the post-World War II baby boom and the most recent years. From 1960 to 1984, the percentage of women in their early twenties who were childless increased nearly 19 percent, and between 1965 and 1984 the percentage of women 30–34 years of age who were childless increased over 8 percent. Recent analysis of survey data has shown that a substantial proportion of women who are childless but say they intend to have children change their minds to a childless preference over a fairly short period of time.[23] Therefore, it is quite possible that the relatively high percentages seen for the 20–24-year-olds will translate into even higher proportions as these women become older.

Teenage Fertility

While teenage fertility—births to women under 20 years of age—accounted for only 15.6 percent of all births in the United States in 1980, the age-specific fertility rate (ASFR) for women under 20 is one of the highest in the world—twice as high as the rates for France, Denmark, and Ireland and more than ten times the rate of Japan![24] Beyond the relatively high ASFR, there are several related issues that make teenage fertility a topic of concern in the United States. These issues can be categorized as those affecting the welfare of the teenagers bearing the children and those related to the health of the children themselves.

Concerning the welfare of the teenage mothers, there are both health and social considerations. The maternal death risk is 60 percent higher than that of older mothers, and teenage mothers are 1.3 times more likely to suffer from nonfatal anemia or toxemia than mothers age 20 and above.[25] While the direction of causality is not clear, teenage mothers are poorly educated—eight out of ten mothers aged 17 and under never complete high school—and therefore lack the skills to compete in today's job market. They suffer high rates of unemployment and welfare dependency.[26] Furthermore, their marriages (48 percent of the births are to unmarried women) tend to be unstable. Early childbearing also results in a significantly larger number of births over a lifetime.[27]

With regard to the health of their children, teenagers' babies are two to three times more likely to die soon after birth than babies born to older mothers. The incidence of low birth weight (less than 2,500 grams, or 5.5 pounds) is twice as high for teenage mothers, and one recent study has shown that births to mothers 15 years old and younger are 2.4 times more likely to suffer from neurological defects than infants born to mothers in their twenties.[28]

Induced Abortion

Pre–1973 data concerning induced abortion in the United States is sketchy and so it is difficult to get much of a historical perspective regarding the effect of induced abortion on the overall fertility rate. Looking only at the 1982 data on induced abortion—1.5 million—there were 426 abortions for every 1,000 live births.[29] Even if it is assumed that one-third of these pregnancies would not have resulted in live births as a result of spontaneous abortion and other complicating factors, without induced abortion over 1 million more births would have occurred. In other words, hypothetically there would have been 4,653,000 births, not the 3,612,000 reported—or an increase of 29 percent!

Births to Unmarried Women

The last issue to be considered in this section concerns the proportion of births occurring to women outside marriage. Recalling the intermediate variable scheme discussed earlier, it was based in part on the assumption that all or at least the vast majority of fertility occurred to women who were married. In 1955, there were only 183,000 births to unmarried women, and these births made up less than 5 percent of all births. In 1982, the 715,200 births outside marriage made up over 19 percent of all fertility. Among black

Americans, in 1982 over 55 percent of all births were born to unmarried women. Without question, the models of how fertility is affected (that is, intermediate variables) must be changed in order to accommodate behavior norms of the 1980's.

EXPLANATIONS FOR CHANGES IN BIRTH RATES

Social Norms

Perhaps the easiest way to explain the post-World War II baby boom and the following baby bust is to say that fertility norms changed. That is, women and men simply changed their minds with regard to the number of children they wished to have. Furthermore, it can be argued that better contraceptives and the availability of induced abortions aided them in adhering to their own wishes. This explanation is probably accurate but is too simple because it does not explain why fertility norms changed. It does not identify the specific aspects about the relationship between structural changes in society and lowered fertility desires. The explanation also assumes that people have the number of children they desire.

In order to understand fertility norm changes, identification and understanding of previous fertility norms must take place. Examining first fertility levels in the early part of this century, it can be observed (data not shown) that completed fertility (CEB) averaged close to four births per woman. And fertility at this time was lower than it had been in the nineteenth century. The question to be answered is, Why did women at that time (the early twentieth century) bear that many children, though it must be emphasized that the CEB figure for women 45–49 in the early 1980's was only one child fewer. The answer in part lies in the way children were viewed. Today children offer love, affection, a fulfillment of expectations, and a certain type of status, but for the most part, until they are much older, they are consumers of goods and services. Therefore, the utility, or joy, in having children results from the psychic pleasure derived by their existence. Children in general are not seen as producers, or providers of labor, nor are they responsible for their parents' well-being when they are no longer able to work.

However, earlier in U.S. history (pre-twentieth century) children performed different functions than they do today. They provided the same joy as children do today, but they were also economic producers. They began working at younger ages and provided a form of old age security. They were an integral part of the family economic system that was so crucial in the survival of rural America. Overall, it can be argued that as the United States became more urbanized and industrialized, functions performed by children—and family structure as a whole—changed to the extent that high fertility norms began to be replaced by lower ones. Changing fertility norms in the latter part of the twentieth century are a product of already lower fertility expectations, coupled with other changes, which include a continued transition from extended to nuclear and other types of families, increased female labor force participation, more liberal societal attitudes with regard to the nonfamily roles of women, and a change in the degree of importance of having children in a differently structured society. Together these factors brought about a reduction in fertility desires.

Economic Explanations

Not independent of the social norm explanations are several economic models designed to give insight into the decline in fertility in the twentieth century. As it turns out, these models also do a reasonably good job of explaining the post-World War II baby boom and baby bust though these explanations are not without problems. One model, developed by University of Chicago economist Gary Becker, views children as a consumption good requiring both time and money to acquire. Briefly, borrowing from classical microeconomic theory, a utility function can be derived for each individual couple that expresses the trade-offs between the couple's desire for children and all other goods and services that compete with children for time and money.[30] Also of concern is the quality of children. Not only does the element time modify the expected increase in children that accompanies increases in income, but the desire to improve the quality of the children already born (for example, providing them a better education) has the effect of negating the increased income effects by absorbing money that could be spent acquiring additional children. However, the model is limited in that (1) it assumes that this couple behaves in a rational manner and (2) it assumes that no children are born that are unwanted; that is, there is perfect contraceptive effectiveness.

A second model, developed by Richard Easterlin, is sometimes referred to as the *relative-income hypothesis*.[31] According to Easterlin, fertility is the product of present levels of income along with a desired level of living that is developed during an earlier time in a person's life. That is, men acquire a desire for a certain standard of living during their adolescent years, and this is based to a large extent on the standard of living of their parents. As these men reach their years of marriage and having children—their early twenties—they compare their present standard of living with their desired standard, and to the extent that the actual meets or exceeds the desired, early marriage and childbearing occur. However, if the actual standard is less than the desired, marriage and childbearing are put off. This model fits the baby boom and bust well in that during the boom the point of reference (time during which desires were being formed) was the Depression, so from the late 1940's through the 1950's actual standards of living exceeded the desired. The result was earlier marriage and an increase in fertility. As the point of reference changed to better economic times during the 1960's and 1970's, young men found themselves living in harder economic times, relatively

Table 3.5
Labor Force Participation Rates for Single and Married Women with Children:
1950–1985

Year	Single	Married With Children Aged 6-17 Only	Married With Children Less Than 6 Years of Age
1950	50.5	28.3	11.9
1955	46.4	34.7	16.2
1960	44.1	39.0	18.6
1965	40.5	42.7	23.3
1970	53.0	49.2	30.3
1975	57.0	52.4	36.6
1980	61.5	61.7	45.1
1985	65.2	67.8	53.4

Sources: U.S. Bureau of the Census. 1986. Statistical Abstract of the United States, 1986, tables 674 and 675; U.S. Bureau of the Census. 1975. Statistical Abstract of the United States, 1975, table 565.

speaking, and therefore delayed marriage and reduced childbearing was seen. The model also can explain reasonably well secular trends in U.S. fertility during the nineteenth century.

The relative-income hypothesis nevertheless leaves some important questions unanswered.[32] First, Easterlin provides no evidence that family background accounts for all or even the major proportion of the aspirations of young adults. Peer groups certainly account for some and perhaps a great deal of the desired lifestyle. Second, the changing status of females, particularly with regard to female labor force participation, is not incorporated into the model. Wives' and single women's aspirations and income levels significantly affect childbearing and marriage decisions that are made today. And labor force participation and child rearing are more and more likely to be occurring at the same time childbearing decisions are being made. While labor force participation rates of all women have risen consistently over the past thirty years—more than 52 percent of all adult women are currently in the labor force—increases in labor force participation rates of single and married women with children show very interesting patterns.

Table 3.5 presents labor force participation rates for single and married women with children of varying ages for 1950 to 1985. The proportion for single women, which provides a point of comparison for the married women

Table 3.7
Fertility Differences (Lifetime Births Expected) by Race and Ethnicity for Currently
Married Women 30 to 34 Years of Age: 1973, 1978, 1985

Year	Race/Ethnicity				
	White	Black	Percent of White	Spanish Origin	Percent of White
1973	2,762	3,332	120.6	3,784	137.0
1978	2,395	2,789	116.4	2,980	124.4
1985	2,139	2,521	117.9	2,712	126.8

Source: U.S. Bureau of the Census. 1986. Fertility of American Women: June 1985, table 5.

1985, expectations for blacks were nearly .3 children higher than whites, while Spanish-origin expectations exceeded that of Anglos by nearly .6 births.

Level of Education

Table 3.8 provides information on educational differences in fertility. Once again, the differences are substantial—more than 1.7 children between the lowest and highest educated women. Even the difference between a high school and a college graduate is more than one-half child. As educational

Table 3.8
Fertility Differences by Educational Attainment for Ever-Married Women 35 to 44
Years of Age: 1985

Educational Attainment of Wife	Children Ever Born
All Education Levels	2,321
Not a High School Graduate	3,059
High School, 4 years	2,339
College: 1 or more years	2,010

Source: U.S. Bureau of the Census. 1986. Fertility of American Women: June 1985, table 2.

levels increase from (1) not high school to high school and (2) high school to college, the reduction in fertility is 32 and 21 percent, respectively.

Major Occupational Group

Occupational differences in fertility (lifetime births expected) are much smaller than those seen in previous tables. Table 3.9 presents the differences, and the largest—that between managerial-professional and operators—is a little more than .9 births. Managerial, technical, and service workers' wives all expect about the same number of births (2.1–2.3) over a lifetime.

Family Income

Data with regard to income category differences in fertility are shown in Table 3.10. There is a clear pattern of fertility decline in moving from the lowest to the highest income group, though the range is about one-half birth—a decline of 20 percent. These differences are not as great as the differences seen for age at first marriage and educational groupings.

Summary

In sum, these data illustrate the wide fertility differentials in the United States today and suggest that broad fertility variations are likely to exist in the future. Overall, if age at first marriage remains relatively high and educational attainment increases, aggregate fertility can be expected to remain low, all other factors remaining the same. However, to the extent that

Table 3.9
Fertility Differences by Major Occupational Group of Husband for Currently Married Women 35 to 44 Years of Age: 1985

Major Occupation Group of Employed Civilian Husband	Children Ever Born
Total Employed	2,322
Managerial-Professional	2,111
Technical, Sales, and Administrative Support	2,160
Service	2,385
Precision Production	2,589
Operators	2,939

Source: U.S. Bureau of the Census. 1986. Fertility of American Women: June 1985, table 3.

Table 3.10
Fertility Differences by Family Income for Currently Married Women (Wife
Working) 35 to 44 Years of Age: 1985

Income Level	Children Ever Born
All Income Levels	2,202
Under $10,000	2,538
$10,000 to $14,999	2,557
$15,000 to $19,999	2,382
$20,000 to $24,999	2,366
$25,000 to $29,999	2,312
$30,000 to $34,999	2,220
$35,000 and over	2,031

Source: U.S. Bureau of the Census. 1986. Fertility of American Women: June
1985, table 3.

blacks and Spanish-origin persons become a larger proportion of the population, fertility could well increase. Fertility norms do become altered and fertility-social-economic variable relationships are likely to change over time. These are complex relationships that must be continuously monitored and studied.

LOW FERTILITY IMPLICATIONS—THE BUSINESS ENVIRONMENT

The low fertility rates seen in the United States today in some ways can be considered a continuation of declining fertility rates that were evident in late-nineteenth-century America. The post-World War II baby boom was merely an aberration in a historical trend toward lowered fertility, though the significance of the baby boom should not be overlooked. Fertility rates (expressed as TFRs and CEBs) seem to have plateaued recently, and in certain years the TFR has actually risen slightly. These year-to-year fluctuations, however, are for the most part a response to changing age structure. Most demographers look for the NRR to remain below replacement, though some demographic analysis has predicted a small but detectable rise in fertility. No one has forecast any large and sustained increase in fertility rates. It must be emphasized, however, that TFRs could decrease much more. In several Western European nations, the TFR is at or below 1.5.[34]

By now the reader is probably asking, "What does low fertility mean for the national, regional, or local business environment?" First, the implications for population growth must be considered. Leaving aside a detailed discussion of the effect of mortality and immigration on population growth—these are topics for chapters 4 and 5—without enough immigration to offset less than replacement level fertility, population growth will eventually cease—in about another 50–100 years if some U.S. Census Bureau population projections are correct.[35] While that may seem like a long time in the future, slowed growth is presently affecting the business environment as the population ages and, therefore, the structure of consumption changes. The effect of slowing population growth is being felt today in ways ranging from the decreased sales of baby-related goods and services to the increased demand for elderly health care. Furthermore, beyond this 50–100-year period lies potential population decline, which is certain to elicit fear on the part of policymakers and the public in general.

As was stated above, one of the effects of low fertility rates is that the population of the United States is becoming an older one. In 1984, over 28 million persons (11.8 percent) were 65 years old or older, an increase of about 8 million since 1970, when persons 65 and above made up 9.2 percent of the population.[36] Recent population projections show these figures to increase to between 58 and 65 million, or over 22 percent of the total population, by the year 2030.[37] At that point in time, the median age of the population will have increased from 30 years in 1980 to between 41 and 44 years.[38] These data illustrate the rapid growth in what is now labeled the "mature market."

What these figures do not reflect are the marked changes in figures for other ages that are occurring at the same time. The overall change in *age structure*—the way in which the total population is distributed with regard to age—means that the age structure of individual consumers along with that of the labor force which provides goods and services to those consumers is changing as well. Those changes must be met with altered strategies on the part of business and government in order to see that desired products and services are available in sufficient quantities. But these goods and services cannot be provided without adjusting for the changing age structure of those producing and providing these goods and services.

At the individual level, declining growth is bringing about a social restructuring of the United States. Recalling that data on the increase in childlessness and labor force participation of mothers, along with the decrease in persons in their early thirties who are married, it can be seen that the traditional husband-wife (stay at home) -children family home has been altered. While a large number of these traditional families still exist, other acceptable alternative lifestyles are being lived. Once again, consumption patterns are being altered as the need for convenience goods rises (working mothers) and discretionary income increases as a result of fewer births. The decrease in traditional families (recall the increases in childlessness and not getting married) brings about smaller household sizes. Household size is related to consumption; for example, smaller households spend more dollars per capita on food away from home and less per capita on furniture. Also at the individual level are the still existing job squeeze problems facing the baby boom cohorts discussed in Chapter 1.

While this discussion has certainly not exhausted all the implications of lower fertility rates and fewer overall births, the reader should have a general idea concerning the segments of the business environment affected by the charges. A more extensive discussion of the impact of fertility, mortality, and migration trends on the business environment is withheld until Chapters 11, 12 and 13, which focus on specific business issues.

NOTES

1. W. Pratt, W. Mosher, C. Bachrach, and M. Horn. 1984. *Understanding U.S. Fertility*. Population Bulletin Vol. 39, No. 5. Washington, D.C.: Population Reference Bureau, table 11.

2. W. Pratt et al. 1984. *Understanding U.S. Fertility*, table 11.

3. Kingsley Davis and Judith Blake. 1956. "Social Structure and Fertility: An Analytic Framework." *Economic Development and Cultural Change* 4: 211–235.

4. Voluntary and involuntary abstinence have been excluded from this discussion. New categories such as fertility outside of marriage and the extent of nonmarital teenage sexual activity should be added to the list of intercourse variables.

5. In 1950 the proportion of all births to unmarried women was 3.9 percent. By 1982, 19.4 percent of all births were to unmarried women. Source: U.S. Bureau of the Census. 1986. *Statistical Abstract of the United States, 1986*. Washington, D.C.: U.S. Government Printing Office, tables 81 and 94.

6. U.S. Bureau of the Census. 1986. *Statistical Abstract of the United States, 1986*, table 124.

7. U.S. Bureau of the Census. 1986. *Statistical Abstract of the United States, 1986*, table 56.

8. Thomas J. Espenshade. 1984. "Demographic Forces Shaping the Future of the Family." Paper presented at the annual meeting of the Southern Regional Demographic Group. Orlando, Florida.

9. See Arland Thornton. 1978. "Marital Dissolution, Remarriage and Childbearing." *Demography* 15: 361–380; and Janet Kalwat. 1983. *Divorce, Remarriage and Childbearing: A Study of Fertility Differences between Women in First and Second Marriages*. Unpublished Ph.D. dissertation, Princeton University, for a more detailed discussion on the relationship between remarriage and fertility.

10. See pp. 64–68 in Charles F. Westoff and Norman B. Ryder. 1977. *The Contraceptive Revolution*. (Princeton, New Jersey: Princeton University Press.

11. See pp. 85–88 in Melvin Zelnik, John Kantner, and Kathleen Ford. 1981. *Sex and Pregnancy in Adolescence*. Beverly Hills, California: Sage Publications.

12. W. Pratt et al. 1984. *Understanding U.S. Fertility*, table 8.

13. Population Reference Bureau Staff. 1984. "Sterilization, Breastfeeding on the Rise." *Population Today* 12 (December): 20.

14. W. Pratt et al. 1984. *Understanding U.S. Fertility*, table 8.

15. W. Pratt et al. 1984. *Understanding U.S. Fertility*, table 12.

16. Melville G. Kerr. 1971. "Perinatal Mortality and Genetic Wastage in Man." *Journal of Biosocial Science* 2: 223–237.

17. W. H. James. 1970. "The Incidence of Spontaneous Abortion." *Population Studies* 24: 241–245.

18. See Malcolm Potts, Peter Diggory, and John Peel. 1977. *Abortion*. London: Cambridge University Press, pp. 332–376, for an excellent discussion of the state laws rules unconstitutional by the U.S. Supreme Court in 1973.

19. U.S. Bureau of the Census. 1986. *Statistical Abstract of the United States, 1986*, table 103.

20. U.S. Bureau of the Census. 1986. *Statistical Abstract of the United States, 1984*. Washington, D.C.: U.S. Government Printing Office, table 92.

21. U.S. Bureau of the Census. 1986. *Fertility of American Women: June 1985*. Current Population Reports, Series P–20, No. 406. Washington, D.C.: U.S. Government Printing Office, table 5.

22. U.S. Bureau of the Census. 1986. *Statistical Abstract of the United States, 1986*, table 92.

23. Mark Merwin and Louis Pol. 1983. "Childlessness: A Panel Study of Expressed Intention and Reported Fertility." *Social Biology* 30: 318–327.

24. U.S. Bureau of the Census. 1986. *Statistical Abstract of the United States, 1986*, table 83; and Alan Guttmacher Institute. 1976. *11 Million Teenagers*. New York: Planned Parenthood Federation, figure 1.

25. Alan Guttmacher Institute. 1976. *11 Million Teenagers*, p. 23.

26. Alan Guttmacher Institute. 1976. *11 Million Teenagers*, pp. 25–26.

27. Alan Guttmacher Institute. 1976. *11 Million Teenagers*, pp. 28–29.

28. Alan Guttmacher Institute. 1976. *11 Million Teenagers*, p. 22.

29. U.S. Bureau of the Census. 1986. *Statistical Abstract of the United States, 1986*, table 105.

30. Gary Becker. 1960. "An Economic Analysis of Fertility." Pp. 209–231 in *Demographic and Economic Change in Developed Countries*. Universities-National Bureau of Economic Research Conference Series 11. Princeton, New Jersey: Princeton University Press, pp. 209–231.

31. Richard Easterlin. 1973. "Relative Economic Status and the American Fertility Survey." Pp. 170–223 in Eleanor B. Sheldon (ed.), *Family Economic Behavior: Problems and Prospects*. Philadelphia: J. B. Lippincott Company.

32. Deborah Freedman. 1976. "Fertility, Aspirations and Resources: A Symposium on the Easterlin Hypothesis." *Population Development Review* 2 (3–4): 411–415.

33. William Butz and Michael Ward. 1979. "The Emergence of Countercyclical U.S. Fertility." *American Economic Review* 69: 318–328.

34. Population Reference Bureau Staff. 1985. "Take a Number." *Population Today* 13 (February): 10.

35. U.S. Bureau of the Census. 1984. *Projections of the Population of the United States by Age, Sex and Race: 1983–2080*. Current Population Reports, Series P–25, No. 952, table E.

36. U.S. Bureau of the Census. 1984. *Statistical Abstract of the United States, 1984*, table 30.

37. U.S. Bureau of the Census. 1984. *Projections of the Population of the United States by Age, Sex and Race: 1983–2080*, tables E and F.

38. U.S. Bureau of the Census. 1984. *Projections of the Population of the United States by Age, Sex and Race: 1983–2080*, table C.

4

Mortality—The Feared Study

INTRODUCTION

A discussion of mortality is not a very pleasant topic by virtually any standard. Nevertheless, mortality—the study of death including how long people live, at what ages they die, and what they die from—is the second key component of the demographic equation, and therefore population change. In conjunction with births, the number of deaths over a specific time interval determines whether or not the world population is growing, and how rapidly growth is taking place. At the national and subnational levels, mortality and out-migration are pitted against fertility and in-migration to determine population growth or decline. However, the study of mortality is a much more complex and interesting undertaking than merely ascertaining how many deaths occurred over a particular time period or identifying a contribution to overall growth. Before these complexities and the ways in which mortality is measured are discussed, a brief overview of the importance of mortality to the understanding of the business environment is presented.

The connection between mortality and the growth in the overall consumer population is quite clear. If the number of deaths is large enough, then there can be no increase, and perhaps a decrease, in the absolute number of consumers. A significant increase in deaths for selected social and economic groups can bring about a measurable decline in specific consumer segments. Without consumers, the number of businesses is reduced if all other factors remain the same. A low-growth or no-growth population is also marked by an aging consumer population, though historically that has not always been the case. By *aging* it is meant that there is an increased proportion of the total population at the middle and upper ages.

Moreover, if deaths are classified by the age at which a person dies, it is possible to specifically determine how different probabilities of dying at various ages affect the age structure of the entire consumer population. *Age structure* is defined as the proportion of persons at various age intervals within a population. For example, at the turn of the century when life expectancy was less than 50 years in the United States, a discussion of the opportunities existing in what has been labeled the "mature market," those persons 55 years of age and older, took on a different meaning than it does today. Simply stated, the mature market was virtually nonexistent in 1900. Presently, growth in this population, and in particular the increase in the population 70 years old and over, represents booming markets for the housing, health care, and travel industries, as well as others. In addition, the general improvement in the health of the older population fosters a change in the patterns of goods and services bought by this population, as well as the purchasing habits shared with younger age cohorts. Better health brings a higher proportion of older persons who are capable of independent living (shared consumption patterns), though services such as different housing arrangements, which are designed to prolong independent living, represent a unique set of needs.

The increase in *life expectancy*, the number of years a person can be expected to live from any age, and the concomitant change in age structure affect other components of the business environment. In conjunction with the increase in overall life expectancy has come, until recently, a widening gap in life expectancy between males and females. That is, life expectancy at birth is about seven years longer for women, and the result is a female-dominated group of consumers at the older ages. This sex imbalance becomes more marked as age increases. In 1984, for example, there were approximately 117 females for every 100 males at age 65 and above. At age 80 and above, there were about 166 females for every 100 males. And female consumers have a very different set of product and service demands than their male counterparts.

At the other end of the age continuum, more children are surviving their first year of life, once again changing the composition of consumers. These are the consumers who in many ways are most different from the remainder of the buying population because of their total dependence on others to purchase goods and services for them. They also represent more than 3.6 million new consumers every year. In 1920, approximately 85 out of 1,000 persons born died in their first year of life. In 1984, only about 11 out of 1,000 suffered the same fate.

Specific to the business environment concerns of the health care industry are the changes in the composition of death causes and types of illnesses that have occurred since the beginning of the century. In 1900, infectious and parasitic diseases combined to be the major cause of death in the United States. By comparison, malignant neoplasms—cancer—was not a major cause. In the 1980's, infectious and parasitic diseases are major causes only for the very old and the very young. Cancer is the second leading cause of death. Heart and cardiovascular causes account for 38 percent of all mortality. This reshaping of what can be called the death structure of the United States has affected the demand for most health care-related goods and services including the need for new drugs, specialized diagnostic equipment, different physical facilities, and training for those engaged in the diagnosis and treatment of diseases.

A final concern with regard to the relationship between mortality and the business environment is the interaction among longevity, health care costs, pensions, and public policy related to providing adequate housing and quality health care and overseeing pensions for the aged. To the extent that public policy affects the providers of services either by regulating the amount of money that can be charged for services or by adjusting the amount of money paid to the elderly in the form of old age insurance, the private sector is affected. The initiation of diagnostic-related groups (DRGs), for example, has left many hospitals, doctors, and nursing homes aggressively attempting to attract more private-pay and fewer medicare patients. The resulting competition has resulted in increased marketing efforts and the provision of more upscale services in some hospitals. On the other hand, a great deal of concern is being expressed by politicians and health care professionals with regard to the availability of health care services to public-pay patients, many of whom are older.[1] Any legislation designed to guarantee health insurance to these older members of society is sure to have a strong impact on the industry.

Concerning housing, it is well known that there is a shortage of reasonable-quality rental units in many large cities in the United States. The elderly are particularly vulnerable to these problems, given that a high proportion of them have a limited ability to pay for housing and are in a fixed income situation. One partial solution proposed by housing expert Chester Hartman would see the creation of government capital grants to build 200,000 units of new social housing and 400,000 units of rehabilitated housing annually.[2] Though it has been argued that this is an area of housing that the public sector has to a great extent ignored, the creation of 600,000 units of housing each year through grants by the federal government would to some extent affect the business environment of the housing industry.

With regard to pension regulation, a great deal of congressional concern is being expressed over how the $1 trillion pool of pension capital is being managed. Companies that have terminated plans have also received significant tax windfalls, though the major issue focuses on whether or not pension plans, many of which are underfunded, can provide workers with previously promised income at retirement.[3] New laws passed by Congress to regulate these plans will most likely affect not only those receiving benefits, but how current pension funds can be managed.

The overall decrease in mortality and the resulting change in age structure go beyond concerns of individual consumers to issues regarding personnel and the staffing of key positions within organization, the purchasing of goods and services by industrial buyers, and the creation of new markets. Thus entire industries are coming into existence as a result of the substantial numbers of persons who in earlier periods of history would have long since died. Additional discussion of these and related issues appears in Chapter 6 on population composition and in Chapters 11 and 12, which focus on demography in the large- and small-business context.

The organization of the remainder of the chapter is as follows: Initially, various ways in which mortality is measured are discussed along with an explanation of what the measures do and do not reveal. The second section focuses on trends in mortality in the United States from around 1930 to the present. Trends in mortality include changes in the number of deaths, death rates, life expectancy, and the cause of death structure. The final section of the chapter returns to the implications of present mortality rates as well as how the historical trend and projected changes in mortality are affecting the United States. In the last section of the chapter, the major emphasis is on how the historical data and forecasts are linked to changes in the business environment.

MEASURING MORTALITY—DEATH RATES AND LIFE TABLES

Death is the permanent cessation of life after birth has taken place, though deaths prior to a live birth, fetal deaths, are aggregated as a separate category. While the definition of death may seem simple and straightforward, recent medical and legal developments have added a great deal of complexity to death-related issues because of the advanced technology available to keep persons alive who, without very specialized treatment, would die. However, though the medical, legal, and political communities are continuing to debate the issues related to what constitutes death and when artificial and heroic means of prolonging life can be stopped, mortality statistics are not greatly affected by these concerns at the present time.

As discussed in Chapter 2, data that measure mortality are gathered through vital registration, though information on a closely related issue, *morbidity*—the study of the spread, incidence, and prevalence of illness—is obtained from various health surveys as well as ongoing research work at the National Institutes of Health, The Centers for Disease Control, and a number of research hospitals throughout the United States.

Death Rates

Much in the same way a crude birth rate was calculated in Chapter 3, a *crude death rate* can be derived. The crude death rate (CDR) is expressed as

$$\text{CDR} = \frac{\text{Number of deaths in year X}}{\text{Midyear population in year X}} \times 1{,}000.$$

For 1982, the CDR for the United States was

$$\frac{1{,}975{,}000}{232{,}062{,}000} \times 1{,}000 = 8.5,$$

or 8.5 deaths per 1,000 persons. The data for the numerator come from the death registration data set described in Chapter 2 and the numerator is a population estimate from the U.S. Census Bureau's population estimates and projections. This is the same denominator used for calculating the crude birth rate in Chapter 3. The 1982 CDR compares with a CDR of 8.8 in 1980, 9.5 in 1970, 9.6 in 1950, and 10.8 in 1940.

However, it is important to realize that the probability of dying varies greatly by age. For example, the proportion of persons younger than 1 year of age who die in a year is about 1 percent. The proportion of 10-to-15-year-olds who die in a five-year interval is about one-tenth of 1 percent. At the ages 80–85 the proportion increases to about one-third. Therefore, it is important to consider again the concept *population at risk* that was introduced in Chapter 3. While everyone is at risk to death, wide variation in probabilities by age calls for measures of mortality specific to age. And just as age-specific fertility rates were calculated in Chapter 3, the generation of age-specific mortality rates is also important. In general, *age-specific death rates* (ASDRs) are arrived at through the following formula:

$$\text{ASDR} = \frac{\text{Deaths to persons age X to X}+5 \text{ in year Y}}{\text{Number of persons age X to X}+5 \text{ in year Y}} \times 1{,}000;$$

X to X + 5 is a five-year age interval.

In 1982, the ASDR for 20-to–24-year-olds was

$$\text{ASDR} = \frac{24{,}930}{21{,}754{,}000} \times 1{,}000 = 1.15 \text{ deaths per 1,000 persons aged 20–24.}$$

While the calculation of a five-year-interval age-specific death rate is illustrated above and tends to be the interval width most often used in the calculation of ASDRs, there is nothing inherent in the methodology of data sets that prevents calculating ASDRs for wider or narrower age ranges. In fact, at ages where mortality is high and/or increasing or decreasing it is common to calculate rates for narrower age bands. The *infant mortality rate* (IMR), which measures death in the first year of life, by definition only corresponds to the population under 1 year of age, and therefore, the age interval is one year. It is calculated because the probability of death during the first year of life is relatively high, while probabilities beyond the first year are much lower. The formula for the IMR is

$$\text{IMR} = \frac{\text{Deaths to persons under 1 year of age in year X}}{\text{Births to persons in year X}} \times 1,000.$$

Worthy of note is the fact that the denominator is the number of births in year X and *not* the population younger than 1 year of age. In 1982 the IMR was

$$\text{IMR} = \frac{42,401}{3,713,000} \times 1,000 = 11.4 \text{ deaths per 1,000 live births.}$$

Additional refinements of the IMR are frequently used, though their calculations are not presented here. The IMR is usually divided into the following two components: *neonatal* and *post-neonatal*, with the former measuring mortality in the first twenty-eight days of life and the latter reflecting mortality between twenty-nine days and one year. The reasoning underlying the before and after twenty-eight-day distinction relates to the causes of death during the first year. In general, causes of death at or before twenty-eight days are regarded for the most part as related to congenital abnormalities and problems arising during pregnancy. Deaths beyond twenty-eight days are seen as more related to environmental factors such as nutrition and postnatal care.

Other measures of early mortality include the *fetal death ratio*, which is a surrogate measure of fetal wastage (stillbirths); the *perinatal mortality rate*, which measures late fetal deaths and early infant mortality (the first seven days, or in some instances the first twenty-eight days of life); and the *maternal mortality rate*, which is a measure of mortality for women who die during childbirth.[4]

Other refinements of age-specific and crude death rates are sometimes incorporated. Without presenting an overly complex set of issues, mortality rates have been adjusted for a variety of reasons using several different techniques. Sometimes, age-specific and crude death rates are calculated for a three-year interval in order to add stability to the rates if year-to-year fluctuations in mortality are evident. The arithmetic is simple and instead of having one year's deaths in the numerator, three years' deaths are added in the numerator and the sum is divided by three. This provides an average figure for deaths over the three-year period. The rate denominator is the midpoint population for the three-year interval.

A further mortality adjustment seen in the literature is called *standardization*, though more specifically the terms *direct standardization* and *indirect standardization* are used. Standardization, which can be used for adjusting fertility and other rates, is used in comparing crude death rates for two countries, two regions, or two points in time. The crude death rate is a product of the number of deaths occurring in an area as well as that area's age structure. That is, given the very different probabilities of dying evident for different ages—with the probability of dying being lowest at the younger, but not youngest, ages—a younger population produces fewer deaths than an older one even if the size of both populations is the same. However, the fact that deaths and the crude death rate in the latter population are larger than in the former should not be interpreted as being the result of better health standards, and thus lower mortality, in the area with a younger age structure. For example, Mexico has a smaller crude death rate than the United States. The lower CDR results because Mexico has a much younger age structure and therefore a high concentration of persons in the least-likely-to-die age categories. Standardization allows the researcher to hold constant age structures and then comparisons of death rates can be made. That is, age-specific death rates, which combine to make up the crude death rate, are applied to a common age structure and then crude death rate comparisons made. When standardization is performed, the *age-adjusted crude death* rate is higher for Mexico than the United States.

Cause-specific mortality rates are also calculated and published in a number of the reports discussed in Chapter 2. These rates, nevertheless, usually are not very refined in that the deaths attributable to a certain cause are divided by the total population and expressed as deaths by cause per 100,000 persons. For example, the 1982 crude death rate of 8.5 deaths per 1,000 persons can be decomposed into 3.26 deaths per 1,000 persons attributable to diseases of the heart, 1.87 deaths per 1,000 persons attributable to malignant neoplasms (cancer), and 0.68 deaths per 1,000 persons attributable to cerebrovascular diseases. Moreover, it is possible to determine what percentage of overall mortality each specific cause accounts for, simply by dividing the number of deaths attributable to a given cause by the total number of deaths. In 1982, diseases of the heart made up 38 percent of all deaths with malignant neoplasms and cerebrovascular diseases accounting for 22 and 8 percent, respectively. More specific rates by cause *and* by age are produced when the situation dictates. Death records make it possible, for example, to examine the cause of death structure at certain ages. Examining specific cause-of-death data for infant deaths show that the leading causes of death are sudden infant death syndrome (12.4 percent of all infant deaths), respiratory distress syndrome (9.5 percent), and disorders relating to short gestation and unspecified low birth weight (8.5 percent).[5]

Life Tables

A relatively complex but extremely useful mortality measurement technique is called the *life table*. These are the same life tables generated by actuaries for use by insurance companies for the determination of premiums. Life tables provide a host of information about the patterns of mortality within a population including the probability of dying and life expectancies at any age. *Multiple decrement life tables* allow for the joint or multiple probabilities of events that result in a person's exiting from a population.[6]

Table 4.1 presents an abridged life table for the United States in 1982. Based on age-specific mortality rates, death probabilities can be calculated for each age and other functions of the life table derived. The probability of dying during the age interval can be approximated by the formula:

$$\text{Probability of dying } (n^q x = \frac{n^M x}{1 + \frac{1}{2}\, n^M x} \; ;$$

$n^M x$ is the age-specific death rate for the age interval in question.[7] So, for example, using the age-specific death rate calculated earlier, the probability of dying during the interval 20–25 years of age in 1982 is as follows:

$$\frac{.00572}{1 - \frac{1}{2}(.00572)} = .0057.$$

While the age-specific mortality rate is extremely close to q_x for the age interval, for ages where $n^M x$ is large, the numbers are considerably different and therefore $n^M x$ cannot be used as a substitute for the probability of dying.

All life table functions taken together are derived on the basis of one assumption: Age-specific death probabilities remain constant over the period of the life table. That is, if life expectancy at birth, e_o, is 74.6 years, then age-specific death probabilities at all ages must remain constant. A change in any of the probabilities results in a shorter or longer life expectancy, depending on whether the probabilities increased or decreased over time. Therefore, life expectancies derived from any life table must be interpreted with caution and with a view toward prospective changes in medical and health technology. While the life expectancy at birth today in the United States is 74.6 years, age-specific death probabilities are likely to decrease over time and any child born now will have a life expectancy somewhat greater than 74.6 years.

The x to x + n column merely refers to the age intervals, such as 5–9 years for the population. Single-year intervals could have been chosen along with other age, sex, and race combinations. Other functions are defined as follows:

$n^q x$—the proportion of persons alive at the beginning of the interval who died during the interval. For example, 1.15 percent of the population born died during their first year of life. This is the same as the probability of dying.

Table 4.1

Abridged Life Table for the United States: 1982

Age Interval	Proportion Dying	of 100,000 born alive		Stationary Population		Average Remaining Lifetime
Period of life between two exact ages stated in years	Proportion of persons alive at beginning of age interval dying during interval	Number living at beginning of age interval	Number dying during age interval	In the age interval	In this and all subsequent age intervals	Average number of years of life remaining at beginning of age interval
x to $x+n$	nq_x	l_x	nd_x	nL_x	T_x	e_x
0-1 year	0.0115	100,000	1,155	98,999	7,455,187	74.6
1-5 years	0.0023	98,845	225	394,857	7,356,188	74.4
5-10 years	0.0014	98,620	140	492,724	6,961,331	70.6
10-15 years	0.0014	98,480	140	492,105	6,468,607	65.7
15-20 years	0.0043	98,340	424	490,738	5,976,502	60.8
20-25 years	0.0057	97,916	560	488,198	5,485,764	56.0
25-30 years	0.0059	97,356	577	485,337	4,997,566	51.3
30-35 years	0.0066	96,779	640	482,364	4,512,229	46.6
35-40 years	0.0084	96,139	804	478,814	4,029,865	41.9
40-45 years	0.0127	95,335	1,215	473,837	3,551,051	37.2
45-50 years	0.0208	94,120	1,958	466,011	3,077,214	32.7
50-55 years	0.0334	92,162	3,074	453,603	2,611,203	28.3
55-60 years	0.0508	89,088	4,526	434,735	2,157,600	24.2
60-65 years	0.0763	84,562	6,451	407,426	1,722,865	20.4
65-70 years	0.1131	78,111	8,831	369,338	1,315,439	16.8
70-75 years	0.1619	69,280	11,219	319,241	946,101	13.7
75-80 years	0.2330	58,061	13,529	256,955	626,860	10.8
80-85 years	0.3362	44,532	14,973	184,521	369,905	8.3
85 years and over	1.0000	29,559	29,559	185,284	185,284	6.3

Source: U.S. Department of Health and Human Services. National Center for Health Statistics. 1984. Advance Report of Final Mortality Statistics, 1982. Monthly Vital Statistics Report, Vol. 33, No. 9.

l_x—known as the radix; an arbitrary 100,000 persons are chosen as the starting point. As deaths occur during each interval they are subtracted, and l_x becomes smaller; 100,000 minus 1,155 ($n^d x$ which is the number of deaths in the interval 0–1 year) equals 98,845, the number of persons alive at age 1.

$n^d x$—the number of deaths occurring during the age interval given the number of persons alive at the beginning of the interval, l_x, and the proportion of persons dying during the interval. Deaths in the age interval $n^d x$ are derived by multiplying $n^d x$ by $n^q x$.

$n^t x$—the number of person-years lived during the interval. This involves multiplying the number of persons alive at the end of the interval by the width (number of years) of the interval and adding that product to the assumed number of years that those dying during the interval lived. To calculate $n^t x$ for the ages 1–4 in the life table, the following factors were considered: Persons in the l_x column for the ages 5–10 years have all lived four years. Multiplying 98,620 by 4 years equals 394,480 person-years. In addition, the 225 persons dying lived an average of 1.67 years. This information was derived from the official death records. Multiplying 225 by 1.67 equals 377 person-years. The sum of 394,480 and 377 equals 394,857, the number appearing as L_x in column 4, row 2.

T_x—the reverse sum of $n^t x$ values. For example, T_{80-85} is equal to the sum of T_{85} and over and T_{80-85}, or 185,284 + 184, 621 = 369,905.

e_x—the life expectancy at any age. For example, life expectancy at age 5 is 70.6 years. This column is derived by dividing T_x by l_x. Life expectancy at birth, for example, divides 7,455,187 by 100,000, which yields 74.6 years.

Life tables provide a host of information about mortality conditions, and it is possible to trace trends in mortality by assembling life table data for more than one time period. Comparative life table analysis can yield information on life expectancy differentials by sex and race for any age. Though life expectancy at birth is more than seven years longer for females than it is for males, the difference narrows to six years at age 40, three years at age 60, and two years at age 80. Jointly looking at race and sex differences, larger differentials emerge. Black females outlive black males by nearly nine years from birth. White females outlive black males by fourteen years from birth.

While these data have serious social, economic, and political implications with regard to markets, the differentials indicate that two very different populations exist when race and sex differences are considered. Therefore, when race and sex segmentation and targeting are considered, differential life expectancies must be incorporated in order to develop the best business plans. Again, using the black male versus white female example, out of 100,000 white females born (l_0), over 85,000 are alive at age 65 (l_{65-70}). For black males, the figure (l_{65-70}) is about 57,000, or only about two-thirds of the white female population. Certainly this differential has serious implications for segmenting the mature, or any other, market. Based on the above data, it can be said that the black male population is considerably younger than the remaining three sex/race groupings. Coupled with additional psychographic and behavioral information, specific strategies regarding products, advertising appeals, and perhaps distribution channels could be developed for this very different market segment.

Other information that can be gained from the examination of life tables includes determining at what age(s) life expectancy declines the most, observing the fluctuation patterns in the number of deaths; and if life tables for more than one time period are used, ascertaining at what ages life expectancy increases have been the greatest. The expected number of deaths in any age interval is used to assist in determining premiums for those participating in life insurance plans. Probabilities of failure, foreclosure, or other types of business demise are used to arrive at premiums for other types of insurance.

Survival ratios, a way of determining the proportion of persons surviving from one age interval to the next, can be calculated and used to determine what percentage of persons alive now can be expected to be alive at some point in the future. Survival ratios are derived by dividing one L_x figure by another L_x, depending on how far forward or backward the user wishes to look. For example, the survival ratio of the age interval 75–80 living to the interval 80–84 from Table 4.1 is

$$\text{Survival ratio} = \frac{L_{80\text{-}84}}{L_{75\text{-}80}} = \frac{184{,}621}{256{,}955} = .718, \text{ or } 71.8 \text{ percent.}$$

That is, about 72 percent of the persons who were alive at age 75 will also be alive at age 80. Cause-specific life tables allow the measurement of the effect of the hypothetical removal of certain causes of death on overall life expectancy, though the same basic principles could be used to learn more about the hypothetical effect of changing business conditions on business failures.

The purpose of this chapter is not to make the reader an expert in mortality measurement, but to generate an appreciation for the variety of measures available, what information each measure can provide, and what implications for the business environment those data have. One of the best ways to begin appreciating the effect of mortality on the business climate is to observe trends in mortality. The following section presents several trends and utilizes the measures of mortality already discussed.

TRENDS IN MORTALITY

Table 4.2 presents changes in the annual number of deaths in the United States between 1935 and 1984. The data are gathered as part of the national registration of deaths discussed in Chapter 2. As can be seen, annual deaths have increased by about 600,000 over the forty-seven year period and further increases in total deaths are inevitable as the age structure of the United States becomes older.

If total births (Chapter 3) are combined with these death data, an interest-

Table 4.2
Total Number of Deaths in the United States: 1935–1984

Year	Deaths[a]
1984	2,039
1980	1,990
1975	1,893
1970	1,921
1965	1,828
1960	1,712
1955	1,529
1950	1,452
1945	1,402
1940	1,417
1935	1,393

[a]Deaths in 1,000s.

Sources: U.S. Bureau of the Census. 1975. Historical Statistics of the United States, Colonial Times to 1970. Bicentennial Edition, Part I, Washington, D.C., U.S. Government Printing Office, Series B 1-4; U.S. Bureau of the Census. 1986. Statistical Abstract of the United States, 1986. Washington, D.C., U.S. Government Printing Office, table 109; U.S. Department of Health and Human Services, National Center for Health Statistics. 1986. Advance Report of Final Mortality Statistics, 1984. Monthly Vital Statistics Report, Vol. 35, No. 6., Washington, D.C.: U.S. Government Printing Office, table 1.

ing pattern emerges. In 1940 there were 2.6 million births to go along with the 1.4 million deaths, or a difference of 1.2 million persons. By 1955, the year corresponding to about the middle of the post-World War II baby boom period, there were nearly 4.1 million births versus 1.5 million deaths—a difference of 2.6 million persons. In only fifteen years the number of persons being added to the U.S. population via the difference between births and deaths increased by 1.4 million persons annually. In 1984 there were 3.7 million births versus 2.0 million deaths, or an increase of 1.7 million persons. Thus, 900,000 fewer persons were added through the difference in fertility and mortality in 1984 compared with 1955. As the number of births stabilizes and deaths increase, the increase in population due to the difference in fertility and mortality will decrease. At some point in the future, it could well be the case that annual deaths exceed annual births. Recent population projections show that the number of deaths will equal the number of births (about 3.5 million) around the year 2030.[8] If the balance between immigration and emigration is not large enough, population loss is inevitable. The population loss scenario is discussed in more detail in Chapters 10 and 14—with regard to population policy and in conjunction with a view toward future population.

Table 4.3 presents age-specific mortality rates for eleven age categories for four time periods between 1935 and 1984. Marked rate reductions are evident for several ages—82 percent for age younger than 1, 89 percent for ages 1–4, 80 percent for ages 5–14, and 70 percent for ages 25–34. Even at the older ages, mortality rate decline is evident—43 percent for ages 75–84, and 32 percent for ages 85 and over. Overall, while mortality has decreased

Table 4.3
Death Rates by Age for the United States: 1935–1984

	1935	1950	1970	1984
< 1	60.9[a]	33.0	21.4	10.9
1-4	4.4	1.4	0.8	0.5
5-14	1.5	0.6	0.4	0.3
15-24	2.7	1.3	1.3	1.0
25-34	4.0	1.8	1.6	1.2
35-44	6.2	3.6	3.1	2.0
45-54	11.6	8.5	7.3	5.2
55-64	23.2	19.0	16.6	12.9
65-74	48.7	41.0	35.8	28.5
75-84	113.1	93.3	80.0	64.0
85 +	224.2	202.0	163.4	152.2

[a]Deaths per 1,000 population.

Sources: U.S. Bureau of the Census. 1975. Historical Statistics of the United States, Colonial Times to 1970. Series B 181-192; National Center for Health Statistics. 1984. Advance Report of Final Mortality Statistics, 1984. Monthly Vital Statistics Report, Vol. 35, No. 6, table 2.

Table 4.4

Infant and Maternal Mortality Rates in the United States: 1920–1984

Year	Infant Mortality[a]	Maternal Mortality[b]
1984	10.9	0.8
1980	12.6	0.9
1970	20.0	2.2
1960	26.0	3.7
1950	29.2	8.3
1940	47.0	37.3
1930	64.6	67.3
1920	85.8	79.9

[a]Deaths per 1,000 live births.

[b]Deaths per 10,000 live births.

Sources: U.S. Bureau of the Census. 1975. Historical Statistics of the United States, Colonial Times to 1970. Series B 136-147; U.S. Bureau of the Census. 1986. Statistical Abstract of the United States, 1986, table 112; U.S. Department of Health and Human Services, National Center for Health Statistics. 1986. Advance Report of Final Mortality Statistics, 1984. Monthly Vital Statistics Report, Vol. 35, No., 6, table F.

at all ages, the greatest improvements have come at the younger ages, particularly in the age group that makes up infant mortality.

Table 4.4 presents infant mortality rates from the years 1920–1984 along with maternal mortality rates. While the infant mortality rate in 1984 was only 13 percent of what it had been in 1920, the *maternal mortality rate*, calculated by dividing the number of women dying because of childbirth complications in a given year by the number of births in that same year, was only about 1 percent of its former figure. Finally, the infant mortality data when combined with those from Table 4.3 provide the background information that explains the tremendous increase in longevity experienced over a period of roughly sixty years. The increase in persons at every age has also been accompanied by the betterment of health for persons at each of those ages.

Table 4.5
Life Expectancy at Birth by Sex in the United States: 1900–1984

Year	Males	Females
1984	71.2	78.2
1980	70.0	77.5
1975	68.8	76.6
1970	67.1	74.8
1960	66.6	73.1
1950	65.6	71.1
1940	60.8	65.2
1930	58.1	61.6
1920	53.6	54.6
1910	48.4	51.8
1900	46.3	48.3

Sources: U.S. Bureau of the Census. 1975. Historical Statistics of the United States, Colonial Times to 1970. Series B 107-115; U.S. Bureau of the Census. 1986. Statistical Abstract of the United States, 1986, table 106; U.S. Department of Health and Human Services, National Center for Health Statistics. 1986. Advance Report of Final Mortality Statistics, 1984. Monthly Vital Statistics Report, Vol. 35, No. 6, table 4.

Table 4.5 provides additional evidence of increased longevity. It shows life expectancies at birth for males and females for eleven intervals between the years 1900 and 1984. Over that time period, life expectancy has increased nearly thirty years (62 percent) for females and about twenty-five years (54 percent) for males.

Observe that the sex differential in mortality was only two years (females living longer) in 1900. By recalling the data on maternal mortality from Table 4.4, a partial explanation to the widening gap in life expectancies can be found. As maternal mortality rates declined, life expectancy differentials increased. By 1960 when maternal mortality rates had fallen to extremely low levels, the difference in life expectancy had increased to 6.5 years. However, also observe that the life expectancy difference has narrowed from 7.8 to 7.0 years since 1975. While the explanation for the narrowing of sex

Table 4.6
Life Expectancy at Age 65 and 85 in the United States: 1950–1984

	Age 65	Age 85
1984	16.8	6.1
1980	16.4	5.9
1975	16.0	6.2
1965	14.6	4.7
1955	14.2	5.1
1950	14.1	4.9

Sources: U.S. Department of Health, Education and Welfare. 1954. Vital Statistics of the United States, 1950. Volume 1, Washington, D.C., U.S. Government Printing Office, table 8.06; U.S. Department of Health, Education and Welfare. 1957. Vital Statistics of the United States, 1955. Volume 1, table AZ; U.S. Department of Health, Education and Welfare. 1967. Vital Statistics of the United States, 1965. Volume II - Mortality, Part A, table 5-4; U.S. Bureau of the Census. 1977. Statistical Abstract of the United States, 1977, table 96; U.S. Bureau of the Census. 1984. Statistical Abstract of the United States, 1984, table 103; U.S. Department of Health and Human Services, National Center for Health Statistics. 1986. Advance Report of Final Mortality Statistics, Monthly Vital Statistics Report, Vol. 35, No. 6, table 3.

differences includes many factors, the general reasoning given cites increased female labor participation and subsequent stress-induced mortality and morbidity along with the increased percentage of females who are smoking as evidence that women are adopting lifestyles more conducive to earlier death. Nevertheless, much more research regarding this topic remains to be conducted.

Table 4.6 shows life expectancy data focusing only on two ages, 65 and 85. These ages were selected for presentation because they represent ages known for recent large increases in absolute numbers (age 65 and over) as well as substantial percentage increases (age 85 and over). Overall, life expectancy at the older ages is quite long. As was observed in Table 4.1, because the probabilities of dying are very different as a person gets older, life expectancy at each age varies as well. For example, though life expectancy at birth is 74.6 years for both sexes, it rises to 75.6 years if a person survives to age 5 (70.6 years, which is the life expectancy at age 5 in addition to five years that have already been lived). Therefore, at the older ages, life expectancy far exceeds 74.6 years. In row 1 of column 1, it can be seen that life expectancy at age 65 in 1982 was 81.8 years (16.8 years plus the sixty-five years that had been already lived).

By looking at trends over the last thirty years, a precise measurement of what contribution to overall life expectancy an increase in life expectancy at ages 65 and 85 can be obtained. Between 1950 and 1982, life expectancy increased by 8.1 percent and 10 percent for males and females, respectively (data from Table 4.5). The increase in life expectancy at ages 65 and 85 (both sexes combined—data from Table 4.6) was 19.1 and 28.6 percent, respectively. While life expectancy at birth increased substantially over the thirty-two-year period, increases at the older ages were even more marked.

Closely related to increases in life expectancy are the changes in mortality structure evidenced in Table 4.7. The rates, expressed as deaths attributable to that specific cause per 100,000 persons, were selected from a much longer list of rates. The choice was based jointly on what were the major causes of death in 1900 and 1982. Overall, causes of death have changed radically since the turn of the century. While major cardiovascular disease is the single leading group cause of death for both years, the rate per 100,000 increased by only 26 percent over the eighty-two year period. On the other hand, the rate for malignant neoplasms rose more than 187 percent, from 64 to 184 deaths per 100,000 population. More remarkable, however, was the decline in rates for the three remaining diseases—739 percent for influenza and

Table 4.7
Major Causes of Death in the United States: 1900–1982

	Major Cardiovascular	Influenza & Pneumonia	Tuberculosis	Gastritis, Dueodentis, Enteritis, Colitis	Malignant Neoplasms
1982	417.6[a]	21.1	0.8	≤ 1.0	187.2
1970	496.0	30.9	2.6	0.6	162.8
1940	485.7	70.3	45.9	10.3	120.3
1920	364.7	207.3	113.1	53.7	83.4
1900	345.2	202.2	194.4	142.7	64.0

[a]Deaths per 100,000 population.

Sources: U. S. Bureau of the Census. 1975. Historical Statistics of the United States, Colonial Times to 1970. Series B 167-180; U. S. Bureau of the Census. 1986. Statistical Abstract of the United States, 1986. table 114.

pneumonia; 2,150 percent for tuberculosis; and 14,260 percent for gastritis, duodentis, enteritis, and colitis.

In sum, while there are multiple measures of mortality, the key to using any of the measures in a business context is knowing how the information is to be used. If the businessperson is interested in the growth or decline of the children's market, for example, then national or local births and migration provide the initial data concerning the size and growth of that market. However, mortality, particularly infant mortality, must be accounted for in adjusting market size estimates. On the other hand, the reader with a need for data on the mature market should be most interested in life expectancies and survival ratios at the older ages as well as the relative health condition of the persons surviving to those ages.

As mentioned earlier, life table functions are used to assist in determining premiums for various types of insurance. Without question, actuaries who must make judgments about a host of phenomena such as the ability of ships to survive in convoys during wartime, the probability of plant shutdowns, or the likelihood of a fire take on great responsibility and pressure. There is even the threat of failure-to-predict malpractice suits against actuaries sometime in the near future.[9] However, there are a variety of non-insurance-related uses of life table principles that would be useful to business executives. The requisite probabilities of survival and life expectancies might be calculated by prospective lenders to help determine the creditworthiness of new or prospective businesses that wish to borrow money. The same principles could be applied to the life expectancies of products, for example, automobiles. Those with the most favorable expectancies could use that information in promotional efforts. These same techniques could be used to help direct production of spare parts, as well. Life table calculations in addition could help retailers more effectively measure the turnover of goods sold, including what proportion could be expected to still be on the shelf after one week, two weeks, three weeks, and so on.

Summarizing trends in mortality, the following generalizations can be made. Though age-specific death rates have dropped considerably over the past fifty years, and life expectancies have increased dramatically, the age structure of the U.S. population is such that more deaths are generated each year. While death rates are likely to continue to decline, those reductions cannot halt the aging process. As a result, over the next 100 or so years the number of annual deaths is likely to increase to the point that it equals the number of annual births. Beyond that, the number of deaths will exceed births.

Furthermore, changes in the structure of death have been evident. A decline in the importance of infectious and parasitic diseases has left cardiovascular disease and cancer as the major causes of death in the United States. Together, they account for about 59 percent of all mortality. This cause structure is likely to exist for some time, though the introduction of "new" diseases such as acquired immune deficiency syndrome (AIDS) could bring about changes in this structure.

IMPLICATIONS OF MORTALITY/MORBIDITY TRENDS FOR THE BUSINESS ENVIRONMENT

While a number of business issues have been raised concerning increased life expectancy, an aging of the U.S. population, and the improved health of the elderly, a more detailed discussion of several additional areas for concern should provide the reader with the incentive to examine how the previously discussed mortality trends affect her or his own business environment. While the topics presented focus on national observations, the transition to regional and local markets should be easy to see.

In the presentation about increased life expectancy and the sex differential at the older ages, the term *mature market*—consumers 55 years of age and over—was used. As previously noted, this market has unique product and service needs as well as some interests shared with younger age groups. However, without the ability to purchase goods and services—that is, income—there is no need to segment and target the mature market. There is a fair amount of literature that speaks to the important issues of fixed income and limited purchasing power of older members of U.S. society. Recent data on income, on the other hand, show that the overall purchasing power of the population 55 and over is relatively strong. While average household income peaks at the interval 45–54, average net worth does not peak until the age interval 55–64. And at ages 65–74, net worth still is 96 percent of its peak value.[10] Though household variation in purchasing power must be considered, a substantial amount of wealth exists in the mature market—enough to purchase many of the products and services demanded by this population. The key to tapping this market is to practice basic marketing principles—first learn what the consumers want and then provide it at a price they can afford and in an accessible location.

Another dimension of economic well-being related to mortality patterns is the sex distribution of wealth for the wealthiest people in the United States. Taking data from the annual publication of the *Forbes Four Hundred* (1985), a list of the 458 richest Americans that categorizes persons into age and sex groupings, several interesting observations can be made. While only 19 percent of all of the wealthiest persons are females, the proportion increases as the age groups get older. Starting at 23 percent of all persons 65 years and over, the proportion increases to just under 0.3 to ages 80 and over.[11] Though this increase in percentages is a logical byproduct of the age differences in life expectancy discussed earlier, perhaps more important is the knowledge that older females in the United States have and control a substantial amount of wealth. The sex distribution affects personal consumption and investment patterns. Once again, the major goal of the businessperson must be to find out what the unique needs of this population are and to meet those needs.

Adding labor force participation and retirement to the above discussions, even greater complexity in the mature market is demonstrated. While labor force participation rates for females age 65 and over have remained constant at between 7 and 10 percent over the last thirty years, the proportion for males in the same age group has been more than halved, from about 38 to 16 percent over the same time span.[12] Early retirement is a serious option being faced by many Americans today, and many are selecting that option. Besides the income considerations (and many early retirees are receiving large lump-sum payments which can be spent or invested) are the concerns regarding continued benefits and emotional side effects of early retirement.[13] Early retirement negatively affects consumption patterns through lost wages, but it offers more consumption variation because so many retirees are in good health and have the requisite wealth indeed to maximize the enjoyment of that good health.

Returning to the medical and health care aspects of mortality, treating and preventing the major causes of death in the United States have become big business for a large network of people and organizations. While the cancer and cardiovascular disease "industries" have received a great deal of media attention, other less well known potential medical breakthroughs could affect mortality rates in general, and specifically the physical and mental health of the entire population. A drug designed to block some of the ills of aging, for example, was initially tested in humans in 1986.[14] Clarens USA, Inc. is promoting what it calls double serum anti-aging total skin supplement, which is said to minimize the signs of aging by reducing facial wrinkles.[15] Drugs for the treatment of debilitating diseases such as arthritis are continually being developed and tested. As drug treatment advances are made and breakthroughs occur, the quality of life for the entire population will improve and the business opportunities related to the development and distribution of these drugs will grow.

Given the vast improvements in the general health level of those 55 and over, at least the youngest of the mature market can be expected to purchase goods and services in much different patterns than in the past. They have been characterized as more akin to people in their forties during the 1950's and 1960's, leading active lives and having an orientation toward working to live and not living to work.[16] They are eating lighter foods and are consuming less alcohol than the younger population. They are also a good market for skin care products, vitamins and minerals, and health and beauty aids.

The most recent example of the reaction of the scientific and business community to disease concerns the increasing prevalence and accompanying morbidity and mortality as a result of what is generically called AIDS. Thus far, AIDS has stricken about 22,000 persons in the United States; of those, nearly 12,000 have died. The Center for Disease Control (CDC) projects 270,000 U.S. cases and 179,000 deaths by 1991 ![17] While 73 percent of the AIDS cases in the United States have involved homosexuals, in Africa, where it is estimated that almost 6 percent of the total population is infected with AIDS, the malady is characterized as a heterosexual venereal disease.[18] Its spread in either population will be difficult to halt.

On the business side, several significant developments have already occurred. Diagnostic test kits, although surrounded by controversy, are already big sellers, though the long run goal of medical science is to arrest and perhaps cure the disease. A type of AIDS vaccine being discussed by Dureg Inc., for example, would have to be administered every two weeks for life, though most recent reports are not optimistic about a "cure" for AIDS being available in the near future. Given 300,000 to 1 million estimated vaccine users, the projected profits are enormous.[19] Since AIDS is emerging as a potentially major cause of death in the United States, business opportunities related to its detection and prevention are significant. While the social and moral motivations for entering such a market are important, the profit motive should not be overlooked.

Thus, declining mortality, increased life expectancy, and changing patterns of mortality and morbidity are helping to reshape the business environment. New business opportunities are appearing and the customers are changing as well. Future breakthroughs in medical technology as well as constant progress in combating disease and death will continue to affect the business environment.

NOTES

1. Vicky Cahan, Kathleen Deveny, and Joan Hamilton. 1985. "Health Care Costs: The Fever Breaks." *Businessweek* (October 21): 86–94.

2. Robert Kuttner. 1986. "Where the Free Market Falls Short." *Businessweek* (June 30): 20.

3. Vicky Cahan. 1985. "The Huge Pension Overflow Could Make Waves in Washington." *Businessweek* (August 12): 71–75; Vicky Cahan. 1985. "Tremors in the Pension System Finally Wake Congress Up." *Businessweek* (November 18): 45.

4. For a more detailed discussion of these measures see Chapter 14 in Henry S. Shryock and Jacob S. Siegel (with Edward Stockwell). 1980. *The Methods and Materials of Demography*. Washington, D.C.: U.S. Government Printing Office.

5. U.S. Department of Health and Human Services. National Center for Health Statistics. 1984. *Advance Report of Final Mortality Statistics, 1982*. Monthly Vital Statistics Report, Vol. 33, No. 9. Hyattsville, Maryland: U.S. Public Health Service, table 11.

6. For more detail on multiple-decrement life tables see Nathan Keyfitz. 1977. *Applied Mathematical Demography*. New York: Wiley-Interscience.

7. See Chapter 5 in Mortimer Spiegelman. 1973. *Introduction to Demography*.

Cambridge, Massachusetts: Harvard University Press, for a thorough discussion of life table functions and their derivations.

8. U.S. Bureau of the Census. 1984. *Projections of the Population of the United States by Age, Sex and Race: 1983–2080.* Current Population Reports, Series P–25, No. 952. Washington, D.C.: U.S. Government Printing Office.

9. Richard Morais. 1985. "Faulting the Fortune Tellers." *Forbes* (October 21): 102–104.

10. Courtenay Slater and Christopher Crane. 1986. "The Net Worth of Americans." *American Demographics* (July): 4–6.

11. Forbes Staff. 1985. "Index to the Forbes Four Hundred." *Forbes* (October): 316–330.

12. U.S. Bureau of the Census. 1960, 1986. *Statistical Abstract of the United States.* Washington, D.C.: U.S. Government Printing Office, tables 264 and 660, respectively.

13. Janet Hamford. 1986. "Hang Tough or Take the Gold Watch Early?" *Forbes* (May 5): 158–159.

14. Michael Waldholz. 1986. "Drug to Block Some Ills of Aging Set for Tests in Humans This Year." *Wall Street Journal* (June 20): 17.

15. Christine Dugas. 1985. "Smoothing Baby Boomers' Wrinkled Brows." *Businessweek* (September 23): 68.

16. William Lazer. 1985. "Inside the Mature Market." *American Demographics* (March): 23–49.

17. Omaha World Herald Staff. 1986. "AIDS May Kill 179,000 in U.S. in Five Years." *Omaha World Herald* (June 25): 4.

18. Marilyn Chase. 1986. "AIDS Has Spread Almost Everywhere in Africa, Zaire, Doctor Tells Parley." *Wall Street Journal* (June 24): 10.

19. Marilyn Chase. 1986. "Drug Firms Anticipate Big Market in Products for Immune Disorder." *Wall Street Journal* (June 26): 1, 13.

5

Migration—Geographic Mobility and Change

INTRODUCTION

Migration—geographic mobility—makes up the third element of the population change model shown in Chapter 1. It is the most complex of the three components because it is the hardest to define and, unlike birth and death, fertility and mortality, it can be done more than once. Recall the earlier reference in Chapter 1 to the expected number of residential moves over a lifetime in the United States—more than 20.[1] *Migration*, simply stated, is defined as any permanent change in residence.[2] It involves the "detachment from the organizational activities at one place and the total round of activities to another."[3] And this is just where the complexity begins. While a move from one house to another in the same city block constitutes a permanent change in residence, activities and friendships—the general social and economic surroundings of an individual—are not likely to change much with a move of this type. On the other hand, a migrant worker's trek from home to work is not a permanent move, though this type of change in residence can last for a relatively long period of time. Some temporary moves certainly involve a change in social and economic milieu. As a result of these complexities, demographers have developed several *operational definitions*—ways that migration is measured—that reflect, albeit sometimes in a crude way, the notion of permanency and detachment from organizational activities. Furthermore, two sets of measures have been generated—one for *international migration* (country to country) and the other for *internal migration* (geographic mobility within a given country).

INTERNATIONAL MIGRATION DEFINED

On the surface, international migration seems relatively easy to define because it involves leaving one country to take up residence in another. The nation gaining a person has received an *immigrant* and the country having provided that individual has lost an *emigrant*. The difference in the two is *net migration*, and it is this number that is generally used in calculating the contribution of migration to the change in population size. However simple the definitions may seem, enumerating the immigrants and emigrants is a much more difficult task because it involves having a systematic registry for all persons entering and leaving a given country. Again the notion of permanence must be considered, given that in some cases people do not stay in the country to which they have moved. Maintaining such a registry is quite difficult—especially in a country with many miles of basically unguarded border—because some people will wish to enter or leave the country in question unannounced.

In the case of the United States where (1) the desire to move to the United States at least on a semipermanent basis seems to be fairly high and (2) the number of immigrants is limited by quotas, *illegal immigrants* (undocumented persons who are living in the country illegally through entry without inspection, such as visa abusers, or through the use of fraudulent documents) can emerge as a somewhat large proportion of all immigrants to that country.[4] It must be emphasized, nevertheless, that early guesses at the number of illegals in the United States were exaggerated and more recent estimates put the total of illegal immigrants residing in the United States at around five million. Unfortunately, the number and therefore percentage of total immigrants that should be placed in the illegal entry category in any given year is unknown.

Beyond the terms specified above, there are three others that receive frequent use (and misuse) in the demographic and popular literature. Immigrants are a subcategory of *aliens*—persons who are living in the United States but are not citizens. Also a subcategory of aliens is *nonimmigrants*, or persons who are admitted to the United States for specific and temporary periods of time. They do not normally become U.S. citizens. Examples include tourists, foreign students, and guest workers. Though guest workers number only about 10,000 presently, the number of entrants in previous years was substantial. Each year from 1955 to 1959, for example, over 400,000 guest workers entered the country.[5] During the years 1951–1964, some but not all of the years in which the *Bracero program* (a guest worker agreement with Mexico) was in effect, an average of nearly 318,000 guest workers entered the United States each year. A third subcategory of aliens is *refugees*—conditional entrants who are allowed to live in the United States for an indefinite period of time. Only if the U.S. Congress passes appropriate legislation can these persons become immigrants and eventually qualify for citizenship. While refugees admitted as permanent residents numbered only 484,000 from 1953 to 1970 (1953 marked the passage of the first U.S. refugee act), in the 1970's the number rose to over one-half million; and for 1980 and 1981 alone, nearly 200,000 were admitted.[6]

When one considers immigration either conceptually or as a source of population's growth, the picture is clouded by the contribution of illegal immigrants and refugees. Though illegal immigrants are not citizens and therefore do not enjoy the same rights and privileges that citizens do, they are part of the overall product and service generation and consumption that take place. Furthermore, their (illegal entrants and refugees) legal status can change (it often does in the case of refugees), and as a result many of them eventually will become citizens. Finally, even the legal status of illegal immigrants is in question given congressional immigration reform measures. A further discussion of these issues is presented later in the chapter.

TRENDS IN LEGAL IMMIGRANTS

Numbers

There has been a considerable amount of variation in the number of persons legally immigrating to the United States since nationhood was established. Figure 5.1 presents the number of immigrants by decade from 1831 to 1980 in bar graph form. The range in numbers has been from around one-half million in the 1830's and 1930's decades to over 8.5 million in the 1901–1910 decade. A pattern of increase in numbers from 1831 to 1910 can be seen in the graph followed by a decrease from 1911 to 1940. The numbers began to increase in the 1940's, and for the 1970's the number of immigrants (over 4.5 million) was comparable, though somewhat larger, than that for the 1890's and 1920's. The decline from the 1920's to the 1950's is the result of the Great Depression as well as the initiation of quota laws enacted by Congress in 1921. This quota system, and its first revision which received congressional approval in 1924, greatly reduced the number of immigrants who could legally enter the country.

Origins of Immigrants

Also of great interest is the origin of these immigrants, that is, the countries, continents, and continent groups from where they migrated. Table 5.1 presents the same data from Figure 5.1 cross-classified by continent grouping of origin. As can be seen, immigration to the United States, until recently, has been dominated by Europeans. Even as late as the 1950's, over one-half of all U.S. immigrants came to the United States from some country in Europe. However, beginning as early as the decade 1911–1920, a marked decline in European representation began to be evident. And with the passage of the

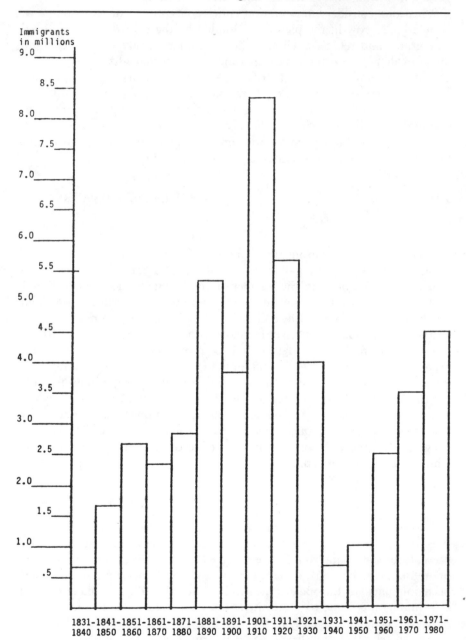

Figure 5.1
Immigrants to the United States: 1831–1980

Table 5.1
Immigrants by Continent Grouping of Origin by Decade: 1831–1984

Decade	Total Immigrants	Continent Grouping of Origin			
		Europe	Asia	America	Africa
1831-1840	599	496 (83)	- (0)	33 (6)	- (0)
1841-1850	1,713	1,598 (93)	- (0)	62 (4)	- (0)
1851-1860	2,598	2,453 (94)	41 (2)	75 (3)	- (0)
1861-1870	2,315	2,064 (89)	65 (3)	167 (7)	- (0)
1871-1880	2,812	2,262 (80)	124 (4)	404(14)	- (0)
1881-1890	5,247	4,722 (90)	68 (1)	426 (8)	- (0)
1891-1900	3,688	3,559 (97)	71 (2)	39 (1)	1 (0)
1901-1910	8,795	8,136 (93)	244 (3)	362 (4)	7 (0)
1911-1920	5,736	4,377 (76)	193 (3)	1,144(20)	8 (0)
1921-1930	4,107	2,478 (60)	97 (2)	1,517(37)	6 (0)
1931-1940	528	348 (66)	15 (3)	160(30)	2 (0)
1941-1950	1,035	622 (60)	59 (3)	355(34)	7 (0)
1951-1960	2,516	1,492 (53)	157 (6)	841(33)	17 (1)
1961-1970	3,322	1,239 (37)	445(13)	1,579(48)	39 (1)
1970-1980	4,493	801 (18)	1,634(36)	1,929(43)	92 (2)
1981-1984	2,294	259 (11)	1,112(48)	849(37)	60 (3)

[a]Numbers in thousand, percentages in parentheses.
-Less than 1,000.

Sources: U.S. Bureau of the Census. 1922. Statistical Abstract of the United States, 1922, Washington, D.C.: U.S. Government Printing Office, table 65; U.S. Bureau of the Census. 1932. Statistical Abstract of the United States, 1932, Washington, D.C.: U.S. Government Printing Office, table 86; U.S. Bureau of the Census. 1953. Statistical Abstract of the United States, 1953, Washington, D.C.: U.S. Government Printing Office, table 105; U.S. Bureau of the Census. 1985. Statistical Abstract of the United States, 1985, Washington, D.C.: U.S. Government Printing Office, table 125; U.S. Bureau of the Census. 1986. Statistical Abstract of the United States, 1986, Washington, D.C.: U.S. Government Printing Office, table 129.

McCarran-Walter Act in 1952, which established a hemispheric and not country-specific quota, European presence was again diminished. By the 1970's, only 18 percent of all immigrants came from Europe. At the same time, immigrants from the Americas began to increase rapidly in the 1940's while those from Asia grew in proportion beginning in the 1960's. Note that in the 1970's, about 80 percent of all immigrants came from Asia or the Americas. Data from the early 1980's indicate that the Asian proportion continues to increase while that for Europeans is still decreasing.

A more detailed breakdown of the above data is possible (data not shown). In the decades 1861 to 1900, 68 percent of the U.S. immigrants came from Northern and Western Europe, 22 percent from Southern and Eastern Europe, 7 percent from North America, and two percent from Asia. By the 1960's, 17 percent came from Northern and Western Europe, 16 percent from Southern and Eastern Europe, 12 percent from North America, 39 percent from Latin America, and 13 percent from Asia. By the late 1970's, Latin America and Asia combined made up over 80 percent of all immi-

Table 5.2

Immigrants and the Proportion of Population Growth Due to Immigration by
Decades for the United States: 1831–1984

Decade	Immigrants (in 1000s)	Population Growth for Decade (in 1000s)	Percent of Population Growth Due to Immigration
1831–1840	599	4,203	14.3
1841–1850	1,713	6,122	28.0
1851–1860	2,598	8,251	31.5
1861–1870	2,315	8,375	27.6
1871–1880	2,812	10,337	27.2
1881–1890	5,247	12,792	41.0
1891–1900	3,688	13,047	28.3
1901–1910	8,795	15,978	55.0
1911–1920	5,736	13,738	41.8
1921–1930	4,107	17,064	24.1
1931–1940	528	8,894	5.9
1941–1950	1,035	19,028	5.4
1951–1960	2,515	27,767	9.1
1961–1970	3,322	23,979	13.9
1971–1980	4,493	23,244	19.3
1981–1984	2,294	8,943	25.7

Source: U.S. Bureau of the Census. 1986. Statistical Abstract of the United States, 1986, tables 1 and 127.

grants, with Europe accounting for only 13 percent. Migrants from other nations in North America declined to 3 percent of the total.[7]

Contribution to Population Growth

As discussed in Chapter 1, population growth can be broken down into contributions made by fertility, mortality, and migration. Table 5.2 presents data on the contribution to overall U.S. population growth that immigration (excluding emigration) has had for each decade since the 1830's. Without question, immigration has contributed greatly to the growth of the population. The pattern of contribution, however, has been one filled with fluctuation. Previous to the 1920's and the introduction of quotas, the pattern was generally one of increase in the proportion of all growth accounted for by immigration from decade to decade, though in the 1890's and the early 1900's there was a significant downturn and upturn, respectively. Beginning in the 1920's, a decline in contribution began that lasted until 1950. In the post–World War II era, the percentage once again began to increase, and in the early 1980's over 25 percent of all U.S. growth was accounted for by immigration. Given present levels of fertility and mortality, the percentage contribution of immigration to all growth is likely to increase in the future.

Middle series population projections for the United States, which assume 450,000 immigrants per year, show that immigration would account for over 25 percent of all population growth during the 1990's if fertility and mortality assumptions hold. Using a higher migration assumption (750,000 per year) a similar series of projections shows that 34 percent of all growth would be due to immigration by the 1990's. In either case, these percentages are much higher than those of the 1940's through 1960's. And they underestimate the growth contribution of immigrants because they do not account for the fertility of immigrants once they arrive in the United States.

Emigration

The effect of emigration on the impact of the country-to-country exchange of persons should not be overlooked. Table 5.3 compares immigrants, emigrant estimates, and net additions to the U.S. population from 1900 to 1979. During that eighty-year period, over 30 million persons immigrated to the United States. At the same time, more than 10 million emigrated. That is, during those eighty years there was only a net addition of 20 million persons through this exchange. The number of emigrants has varied decade by decade from about 3 million in 1900–1909 to 281,000 for the 1940's. Net additions have varied from more than 5 million for 1900–1909 to 50,000 in the 1930's. The table also shows net additions as a percentage of immigrants for each decade. This percentage cannot be viewed as the net outcome of persons who moved to the United States during the decade because emigrants in the 1930's, for example, may have been persons who had immigrated in

Table 5.3
Immigrants, Emigrants, and Net Additions to the U.S. Population: 1900–1979

Decade	Immigrants	Emigrants	Net Addition	Net Addition as a Percent of Immigrants
1900-1909	8,203a	3,008	5,195	63.3%
1910-1919	6,348	2,157	4,191	66.0
1920-1929	4,295	1,685	2,610	60.8
1930-1939	699	649	50	7.2
1940-1949	858	281	577	67.2
1950-1959	2,500	425	2,075	83.0
1960-1969	3,213	900	2,313	72.0
1970-1979	4,334	1,176	3,158	73.0
Total ·	30,450	10,281	20,169	66.2

aNumbers in 1,000s.

Source: Robert Warren and Ellen Kraly. 1985. The Elusive Exodus: Emigration from the United States. Population Trends and Public Policy Series, No. 8. Washington, D.C.: Population Reference Bureau, table 1.

the 1920's. However, the proportion can provide an indication of the percentage impact of net additions accounting for the number of immigrants during the decade. While net additions as a proportion of immigrants have been at least 70 percent since the 1950's, previous to that time it was lower, and during the 1920's and 1930's the figure was less than one-half.

Immigration Law

Several references have already been made to enacted or pending immigration legislation, and in order to provide a better understanding of the historical context in which the figures just presented emerged, a brief history of immigration law is needed. Figure 5.2 provides a summary, in outline form, of the major legislative actions affecting immigration policy in the United States over the past 100 years. Note that before 1875 there was basically no national policy at all.

Immigration law/policy in the United States can be described as restrictive and to a large extent racist, particularly if one compares the pre–1875 time period (no restrictions) with the limiting factors incorporated from 1882 until 1924. Over that period of forty-two years, virtually all Asians and a majority of Southern and Eastern Europeans were barred entry. With regard to Asians, the effect was truly exclusionary. Recalling the data from Table 5.1, not until the 1950's did Asians make up even 5 percent of the total number of immigrants to the United States, though in the early 1980's they were 48 percent of all immigrants. And in the 1880's—the decade of the Chinese exclusion act—they made up only 1 percent. From the 1870's to the 1880's, the total number of Asians immigrating to the United States was reduced 45 percent from 123,000 to 68,000.

Concerning persons from Southern and Eastern Europe, the quota acts of 1921 and 1924—particularly the latter act—truly limited the number of immigrants. With a few exceptions, the 1921 quota put a cap on immigration by limiting the number of persons from a given country to 3 percent of its foreign-born population in the United States according to the census of 1910. The 1924 law limited immigration to 2 percent of the 1890 foreign-born total. Because the Southern and Eastern European population base was much smaller in 1890 (the year of reference for the 1924 act), the effect was to reduce Northern and Western immigration quotas only 2.9 percent, though Southern and Eastern European quotas were reduced 87 percent. For example, the quotas for Italy and Poland were reduced from 42,075 to 3,845 and 30,977 to 5,982, respectively, from 1921 to 1924. Official data show that while in 1921 there were 342,000 immigrants from Southern and Eastern Europe, by 1925 this figure had been reduced 96 percent to 13,000.[8] Comparable data for Northwestern Europe show a smaller decline of 77 percent, from 652,000 to 148,000.[9] In sum, while the passage of the quota acts of 1921 and 1924 significantly reduced the number of immigrants

Figure 5.2
Selected Congressional Legislation and Court Action Affecting the Number and
Origin of U.S. Immigrants

Year	Legislative or Court Action
1875	Denial of entry to persons suffering from certain mental or physical weaknesses.
1882	Chinese Exclusion Act (not repealed until 1943)--prohibited entry of virtually all Chinese.
	Headtax (50¢) imposed.
	Barred immigration of convicts, mental incompetents and persons otherwise deemed likely to become public charges.
1891	Aliens barred from U.S. if suffering from a loathsome or dangerous contagious disease.
1892	Immigrant Processing Center moved to Ellis Island, New York.
1897, 1913, 1915, 1917	Congress passes literacy test legislation four times-- vetoed by Presidents Cleveland, Taft, and Wilson. "Gentlemen's Agreement"--refused passports to the U.S. for Japanese laborers.
1917	Creation of "Asiatic Barred Zone"--any native of Burma, India, Siam, the Malay States, East Indies, or Polynesian Islands barred from entry to the U.S. (not repealed until 1943).
1921	First Quota Act--limited the number of aliens of any nationality to 3 percent of foreign-born persons of that nationality who lived in the U.S. in 1910. Result was a total quota of 358,000--200,000 for Northern and Western Europe and 158,000 for Southern and Eastern Europe.
1924	Second Quota Act--limited the number of aliens of any nationality to 2 percent of foreign-born persons of that nationality who lived in the U.S. in 1890. Also imposed 150,000 person limit, though countries in the Western Hemisphere were not part of the quota system.
1929	National Origins Quota established. Developed complex procedure of determining what proportion of 150,000 person ceiling each country was allotted.

entering the United States overall, the proportional decline for Southern and Eastern European nations was greatest.

The obvious question emerging from this discussion is, Why did the U.S. Congress pass these exclusionary acts? The answer to the question is very complex and has its probable root cause in a combination of pressure from organized labor (in the case of Chinese and Japanese in particular) as well as the desire for maintaining a racial/ethnic composition that was less threaten-

Figure 5.2 Continued

1952	McCarran-Walter Act--maintained approximately 150,000 person hemisphere limit and national origin quota system, but developed a preference hierarchy for allowing persons to enter. Abandoned "Asiatic Barred Zone" and continued to exclude Western Hemisphere countries as part of the quota.
1965	Immigration Act of 1965--abolished national quota system which applied to Eastern Hemisphere nations. Increased ceiling on Eastern Hemisphere immigrants to 170,000 and placed a ceiling (120,000) on those immigrants from the Western Hemisphere. Reprioritized the preference hierarchy of 1952. Placed a 20,000 person per country limitation on immigrant limit from Eastern Hemisphere countries.
1976	Immigration Act of 1976--maintained the overall ceiling (290,000) as well as Eastern and Western Hemisphere divisions (170,000 and 120,000, respectively). Placed 20,000 per country limit on Western Hemisphere nations and made slight adjustments in the preference hierarchy.
1986	Immigration Reform

Sources: Charles Keeley. 1979. "The United States of America." pp. 51-64 in Daniel Kubat (ed). The Politics of Migration Policies. New York: Center for Migration Studies; Leon Bouvier. 1977. International Migration: Yesterday, Today and Tomorrow. Population Bulletin Vol. 32, No. 4. Washington, D.C.: Population Reference Bureau, pp. 23-25; John Weeks. 1981. Population. Belmont, CA: Wadsworth, pp. 165-169.

ing to the majority population. The same general arguments can be heard today in proposed legislation and accompanying discussion to modify existing immigration and guest worker laws. One of the first issues voiced concerns whether or not immigrants (both legal and illegal) are taking jobs that U.S. citizens would. The second major issue, though not stated in blatant terms, focuses on the *desired* racial/ethnic composition of state and local populations.

Post–1929 legislative activity, although at first recertifying the 1924 quota system, had the basic intent of (1) establishing a within-country preference system for immigrants and (2) removing the element of bigotry from the previous immigration acts. A *preference system* refers to what priority visa applicants are assigned within countries. In many instances, there are many more visa applicants than the quota allows, so a method of determining the priority of each applicant must be devised. By 1965 immigration law contained both a hemisphere person limit (170,000 Eastern; 120,000 Western), as well as a 20,000-person country limit for Eastern Hemisphere countries. The preference structure had changed from one that offered first preference to skilled laborers to one favoring family re-formation.[10] The 1976 act, with a few changes, reaffirmed the 1965 preference structure and placed 20,000 country-specific limits for nations in the Western Hemisphere.

Recent Legislation

Since 1976, many immigration law changes have been proposed, and an immigration reform bill was passed by the Congress in October 1986. Each proposed revamping of the immigration system, from the proposal by President Carter in 1978 to the Simpson-Mazzoli and Simpson-Rodino bills of 1984 and 1986, has attempted to address several issues deemed important by both elected leaders and the American public. The immigration legislation offered by Senator Alan K. Simpson (R., Wyoming) and Representative Romano L. Mazzoli (D., Kentucky), which died in the House-Senate Conference Committee in 1984, contained the essential elements of reform sought since 1976. However, there was a great deal of disagreement about just what "reforms" should include. The proposed act had three major provisions: (1) control of illegal immigration, (2) legalization of alien status, and (3) reform of legal immigration. Concerning control of illegal immigration, the bill made it unlawful to hire, recruit, or refer any unauthorized alien for employment in the United States. Employers would have been required to verify U.S. employment authorization. Fines and/or six-month prison terms were provided as punishment. With regard to legalization, aliens who could prove continued domicile in the United States from January 1, 1977, on could have their migration status adjusted to permanent resident and could eventually become U.S. citizens. Finally, the proposed law would have raised the world quota ceiling from 290,000 to 425,000 and would have increased the country limit for Canada and Mexico to 40,000 per year. Furthermore, the unused visas of Mexico or Canada could be used by the other country. In effect, this would have increased Mexico's country limit to around 70,000 per year.[11]

The bill was criticized on a variety of grounds ranging from the feeling that employer fines were too large to the claim that the legalization provision was too liberal. The recently passed Simpson-Rodino bill incorporates many elements of the earlier bill. It essentially provides for (1) fines to employers who knowingly have undocumented workers, (2) an amnesty program for persons who immigrated illegally to the United States before 1982, and (3) a ban of employment discrimination on the basis of national origin or citizenship. The bill has been both applauded and criticized by a variety of groups. Supporters contend that the bill will provide better control of illegal immigration. The criticisms range from the possible negative effect on non-Anglo workers whom employees may fear to hire because of the concern over the workers' legal status to the concern that employers will not be able to assess the legal status of workers.

Internal migration, as previously stated, focuses on residential mobility within a given country. A series of definitions have been generated in order to identify not only migrants in general, but types of migrants. Once again, internal migration refers to permanent changes of residence, and therefore daily commuting and seasonal changes are not considered migration.

Initially, all persons who change residence permanently are classified *movers*. In order to be a *migrant* a person must cross a political boundary—in the United States a county boundary. Therefore, all migrants are movers, though not all movers are migrants. The mover-migrant distinction is useful and makes intuitive sense if the reader recalls the two components of the migration definition: (1) permanent change of address and (2) change in social surroundings. A mover satisfies (1) but likely not (2)—he or she has moved a short distance and maintains the same social contacts. On the applied side, the mover-migrant dichotomy is sometimes less useful because anyone who has moved within a county—for example, from one corner of a country to another—can testify that social contacts change markedly at the new address.

Within the migrant category are *in-migrants* (persons moving into an area), *out-migrants* (persons who have moved out of an area), and *net migration* (the net sum, positive or negative, of the two flows). Net migration is the migration component used to arrive at population change figures for subnational populations. *Gross migration* adds, without regard to sign, both in-migrants and out-migrants and is a measure of total geographic mobility. *Migration efficiency* measures how efficiently the net figure was arrived at and is calculated by dividing net migration by gross migration. Values close to 1 signify the most efficient movement. A *migration stream* refers to a group of migrants who have a common origin and destination. For example, Oklahomans who moved to common areas of California during the "dust bowl" years made up a stream of migration. Movement in the opposite direction is known as a *counterstream*. *Return migration* is the return of migrants to the area of their former residence. Using the Oklahoman example again, the movement back to Oklahoma during the 1970's of persons who had moved to California during the "dust bowl" years is defined as return migration.

Calculating migration rates is much more difficult than establishing rates for fertility or mortality because identifying the population at risk is much more difficult. In the case of fertility, females approximately 15–44 years of age are at risk of having children. Mortality measures have their bases in age-specific mortality rates because the risk of dying increases greatly with age. However, demographers have developed no analogous measures of migration. In fact, most often migration rates are not really true rates—generally they are measures of population or population growth attributable to migration. So, for example, net migration rates are usually calculated as follows:

$$\text{Net migration rate} = \frac{\text{Number of net migrants to Area X over time period}}{\text{Population of Area X at beginning of time period}}.$$

That is, net migration over a certain time interval is expressed as a proportion of the total population at the beginning of the internal. Conceptually, however, the population at risk of moving into Area X is everyone outside Area X, though the probability of moving to Area X drops considerably with distance and fluctuates markedly by a host of other factors. Persons at risk to moving out of Area X are only those persons who live in Area X. Moreover, people are at risk starting at the beginning of the time period in question, though over long intervals (for example, ten years) the population figure at the beginning of the time period would (1) exclude people born during the interval (they too could have moved during the ten-year period), (2) exclude persons who died during the ten years, and (3) include or exclude net migrants. (Depending on whether an area was experiencing net in- or out-migration, some persons would have been included or excluded in the population at risk.) Frequently, demographers use the population in the middle of the time interval in question as the rate base. Selecting bases and determining populations at risk for the calculation of migration rates is a difficult task (not all the complexities have been introduced here) and so demographers have turned to other measures, though these too are not without their problems.

Recognizing the limitations stated above, migration rates can be calculated. In the example below, the midpoint population is used as the base for rate calculation because it "adjusts" for fertility, mortality, and migration taking place during the five-year period. The migration rate of the North Central (Midwest) region of the United States (an area of slow growth) between 1975 and 1980 is produced as follows:

$$\text{Net migration rate} = \frac{1{,}380{,}000 \text{ (net migrants 1975--1980)}}{58{,}285{,}000 \text{ (midpoint population estimate---1977½)}}$$

$$= -.0236, \text{ or } -23.6 \text{ per 1,000 persons.}$$

Focusing on in, out, and gross migration for the North Central states between 1975 and 1980:

$$\text{In-migration rate} = \frac{2{,}125{,}000}{58{,}285{,}000} = .0365, \text{ or } 36.5 \text{ per 1,000 persons;}$$

$$\text{Out-migration rate} = \frac{3{,}505{,}000}{58{,}285{,}000} = .0601, \text{ or } 60.1 \text{ per 1,000 persons;}$$

Gross migration rate $= \dfrac{5,630,000}{58,285,000} = .0966$, or 96.6 per 1,000 persons;

Migration efficiency $= \dfrac{1,380,000}{5,630,000} = .245$.

By comparison, the South—a region of high percentage growth during the 1975–1980 period—had a net migration rate of 27.5, an in-migration rate of 65.6, an out-migration rate of 38.1, a gross migration rate of 103.7, and .265 migration efficiency. The Midwest region had a smaller in-migration, larger net migration (negative), and comparable gross migration rate than that for the South. Migration efficiency was also comparable.

DATA SOURCES

While some discussion of migration data was presented in Chapter 2, a somewhat more detailed presentation is required at this point. Unlike the calculation of fertility and mortality rates, for which vital registration and population counts (sometimes estimates) provide the numerators and denominators for the rates desired, the data sources for deriving migration rates are more diverse. In the case of international migration, the Immigration and Naturalization Service (INS), a U.S. government agency, is responsible for collecting and tabulating data on immigration, emigration, visas applied for, and the like, while the U.S. Department of Health and Human Services furnishes registration data on refugees. However, the number of emigrants must be estimated. Illegal immigrants, of course, must be estimated as well.

In the case of internal migration, a variety of data sources exist. The U.S. Bureau of the Census with its tabulation of state of birth by present state of residence allows one to measure *lifetime* migration. That is, one can ascertain where persons are presently living (most recent year for which census data are available) versus the state in which they were born (another question asked in the census of population). Table 5.4 shows native-born Americans (born in the United States) categorized by state of birth and residence. As can be seen, about two-thirds of all native Americans lived in their state of birth in 1980. However, this marks a decline since 1900, when nearly four-fifths of all native-born Americans lived in the state in which they were born. This measure has limited use because it only taps state-to-state movement and not migration as it was defined earlier.

A question asked on the population censuses of 1960, 1970, and 1980 focused on a person's residence five years earlier. In other words, persons filling out questionnaires on April 1, 1980, for example, were asked where they were living on April 1, 1975. These data were then tabulated into nonmover and mover categories, and among movers further subdivided within-a-county (mover) and different-county (migrant) change of residence

Table 5.4
Place of Birth of Native Persons: 1870–1980

Year	Total	Born in State of Residence		Born in Different State	
1980	212,466[a]	144,871	(68)	65,452	(31)
1970	193,591	131,718	(68)	50,639	(26)
1960	169,588	119,293	(70)	44,691	(26)
1950	139,869	102,788	(74)	35,284	(25)
1940	120,074	92,610	(77)	26,906	(22)
1930	108,571	82,678	(76)	25,388	(23)
1920	91,790	71,071	(77)	20,274	(22)
1910	78,456	61,185	(78)	16,910	(22)
1900	65,653	51,902	(79)	13,501	(21)
1890	53,372	41,872	(78)	11,093	(21)
1880	43,475	33,883	(78)	9,593	(22)
1870	32,991	25,321	(77)	7,657	(23)

[a]Numbers in 1,000s, percentages in parentheses, percentages do not always add to 100 because of excluded category (born abroad).

Sources: U.S. Bureau of the Census. 1983. 1980 Census of Population and Housing. Volume 1, General Social and Economic Characteristics, U.S. Summary. Washington, D.C.: U.S. Government Printing Office, table 78; and U.S. Bureau of the Census. 1975. Historial Statistics of the United States, Colonial Times to 1970, Bicentennial Issue, Part I. Washington, D.C.: U.S. Government Printing Office, series C 1-14.

categories. Among migrants, the data were additionally categorized as within and out-of-state migrants. Table 5.5 presents these data from the censuses of 1960, 1970, and 1980, though to make the table easier to read a few categories have been deleted. As can be seen, a little more than one-half of the total population five years old and over lived in the same house for each time period in question, though a slight increase in the proportion is evident from 1960 to 1980. Within-county residence changes (moves) make up 25 percent of all persons in 1980—down from 30 percent in 1960. Among different-county movers (migrants), a relatively even split between same-state and different-state migrants is evident. No trend appears for these categories since 1960.

Over a five-year period slightly less than one-half of the population five years old and over changes residence; 25 percent move, but in the same county, and about 10 percent move out of the state. Regional and divisional differences in geographic mobility can also be ascertained from similar data (data not shown). Between 1975 and 1980, while only 39.3 percent of persons in the Northeast changed residences, 56.2 percent in the West did—a difference of 17 percent! The divisional range is even greater from a low of

Table 5.5
Residence Five Years Ago: 1960–1980

Year	Total Population	Same House	Different House		
			Same County	Different County	
				Same State	Different State
1980	210,323	112,695 (54)	52,750 (25)	20,588 (10)	20,358 (10)
1970	186,095	98,564 (53)	43,357 (23)	15,656 (8)	16,081 (9)
1960	159,004	79,331 (50)	47,387 (30)	13,668 (9)	14,141 (9)

[a]Based on residence five years ago census question; numbers in 1,000s; population five years old and over, percentages are in parentheses; percentages do not add to 100 because of excluded category (born abroad).

Source: U.S. Bureau of the Census. 1983. 1980 Census of Population and Housing. Volume 1, General Social and Economic Characteristics, U.S. Summary, table 80.

37.4 percent in the Middle Atlantic states to 57.3 percent in the Mountain states.

An additional source of migration data is the Current Population Survey, where in March of every year a national representative sample of respondents are queried about their residence one year earlier. So, for example, persons in the March 1984 survey were asked where they were living in March 1983. These data are then categorized by the same groupings utilized for the five-year question discussed above. These data provide detailed information at the national and regional levels on year-to-year trends in residential mobility. Between March 1983 and 1984, 17 percent of the population changed residences—were classified movers—a percentage comparable to recent years, but somewhat smaller than the roughly 20 percent per annum during the 1960's.[12]

CORRELATES OF RESIDENTIAL MOBILITY

Similar to the fertility difference correlates discussed in Chapter 2, differences in geographic mobility exist among various social and economic groups. While an exhaustive list and presentation of residential mobility is not possible for this type of presentation, the following discussion shows the major categorical differences by mover categories.

Table 5.6
Percentage Distribution of Residence One Year Earlier by Age: 1983–1984

Age	Percent Nonmover	Percent Mover
Total	82.7	16.8
1–4	74.5	24.8
5–9	80.5	19.0
10–19	84.6	14.9
20–24	64.8	34.1
25–29	69.2	30.0
30–34	78.2	21.2
35–44	85.5	14.1
45–54	91.1	8.7
55–64	93.5	6.4
65 years and older	95.4	4.6

Source: U.S. Bureau of the Census. 1986. Statistical Abstract of the
          United States, 1986, table 16. Percentages do not add up to 100
          because movers from abroad are excluded.

Age

As stated earlier, about 17 percent of the population changed residences between March 1983 and March 1984. But as Table 5.6 shows, the age-specific percentages differ greatly. The peak years of mobility are 10–34 and the age group with the lowest incidence of mobility is 65 years old and over. Beyond age 29, the percentage of persons who move in a given year drops considerably, from 30 percent at ages 25–29 to around 5 percent at ages 65 and above. Under age 20, residential mobility is low, though under age 5 it is higher. (Many are children of those persons 20–34.)

Race/Ethnicity

Differences by race and ethnicity are also apparent. The data in Table 5.7 show that Spanish-origin persons are most mobile (movers), followed by whites and blacks. The same order prevails for migration; that is, Spanish-origin persons exhibit the highest percentages of migrants followed by whites and then blacks. However, if one looks merely at persons who moved to

Table 5.7
Percentage Distribution of Residence Five Years Ago by Race and Ethnicity: 1980

Race/Ethnic Group	Total Population	Same House	Different House, Same County	Different County Same State
White	176,526,656	53.9[a]	24.3	10.4
Black	24,000,883	56.8	29.4	5.7
Spanish Origin	12,883,674	44.8	32.2	7.7

[a]Population five years old and over; percentages do not sum to 100 percent because of overlapping and deleted categories.

Source: U.S. Bureau of the Census. 1983. 1980 Census of Population and Housing. Volume 1, General Social and Economic Characteristics, U.S. Summary, tables 122 and 132.

different counties and the focus is on out-of-state movers, a different pattern emerges. Of all persons moving out of their 1975 county, 49.3, 46.1, and 40.8 percent of the whites, Spanish-origin, and blacks, respectively, lived in a different state altogether in 1980 (data not shown). In sum, while overall geographic mobility is highest in the Spanish-origin population, longer distance movement is most prevalent in the white population.

Educational Attainment

Table 5.8 shows the same mover/nonmover categories (five-year question) subdivided by education level for the population 30–34 years of age. This age group was selected for presentation because it is old enough to have allowed for the continuation of education that was either postponed or took a long time to complete.

There is clearly a pattern of increase in the proportion of persons who move as level of education increases. Starting with a low of 53.9 percent for elementary school completion (0–8 years of school), the proportion rises to three-quarters of the population with five or more years of college. Furthermore, the median number of years of school completed is greater for movers than it is for nonmovers.

Occupation

Differences in geographic mobility by occupational groups are exhibited in Table 5.9. Married males whose spouses are living with them serve the group

Table 5.8

Percentage Distribution of Residence Five Years Earlier for Persons 30—34 Years
of Age by Education Level: 1975—1980

Education Level		Percent Nonmovers	Percent Mover
All Education Levels		32.5[a]	64.8
Elementary:	0 to 8 years	37.8	53.9
High School:	1 to 3 years	36.1	62.2
	4 years	38.2	59.9
College:	1 to 3 years	30.5	67.5
	4 years	26.0	71.6
	5 years or more	20.2	75.3
Median Education (years)		12.7	13.2

[a]Percentages do not add to 100 percent because of deleted small category
(movers from abroad).

Source: U.S. Bureau of the Census. 1981. Geographic Mobility: March 1975
          to March 1980. Current Population Reports, Series P-20, No. 368.
          Washington, D.C.: U.S. Government Printing Office, table 22.

of description, though the decision to use this group was somewhat arbitrary. Overall, the proportion having moved over the five-year period is
high—47 percent for all employed persons. Nevertheless, the employed/un-
employed comparison is noteworthy because unemployed persons are much
more likely to change residences than employed persons—60 versus 47
percent. Among occupational groupings with the highest mover percentages
are sales workers, laborers (except farm), and professional workers. Those
with the lowest proportions are farm workers (only 32 percent), crafts, and
service workers. No clear generalizations other than the employed/unem-
ployed distinction and the low farm worker percentage can be drawn.

Income

The final social/economic characteristic to be considered is income category. Data for mover/nonmover statuses are presented in Table 5.10. Again,
married males with a spouse present is the category described. Overall,
geographic mobility increases as income increases, though a slight drop in
the proportion is evident in the last two income groups. The range is rela-

Table 5.9
Percentage Distribution of Residence Five Years Earlier for Married Males (Spouse Present) 16 Years Old and Over by Occupational Group: 1975–1980

Occupational Group	Percent Nonmover	Percent Mover
Employed Persons	51.1	47.4
Professional, Technical, and Kindred	47.0	51.3
Managers and Administrators (except farm)	51.9	46.8
Sales Workers	46.4	52.7
Clerical and Kindred Workers	54.9	44.8
Crafts and Kindred Workers	53.6	44.7
Operatives (except transportation equipment)	47.3	50.1
Transportation Equipment Operatives	49.4	49.8
Laborers (except farm)	45.9	52.6
Farm Workers	66.8	32.0
Service Workers	53.1	45.0
Unemployed Persons	36.5	60.4

Source: U.S. Bureau of the Census. 1981. Geographic Mobility: March 1975 to March 1980. Current Population Reports, Series P-20, No. 368, table 28.

tively large, over 12 percent, though the median income difference is quite mall—less than $25.

MODELS OF GEOGRAPHIC MOBILITY

There are a host of geographic mobility models—many of them inter-reated—designed to provide an explanation regarding why people move. Surveys of movers and potential movers, in general, indicate that economic considerations are clearly the major reason that individuals give for changing residences.[13] Other reasons include climate, family life cycle considerations (for example, getting married and having children), and neighborhood quality (for example, housing and schools). However, these reasons, while interesting, do not provide a useful mechanistic framework needed for understanding why people move. The following models are both interesting and informative.

Lee's explanation focuses on factors that enter directly into the decision-making process of the potential migrant and are categorized as:

1. Factors associated with the migrant's area of origin.
2. Factors associated with the migrant's potential area of destination.

Table 5.10

Percentage Distribution of Residence Five Years Earlier for Married Males (Spouse Present) 16 Years Old and Over by Income Category: 1975–1980

Income Category	Percent Nonmover	Percent Mover
Total With Income	54.4	43.9
$1 to $2,999 or Loss	60.4	36.1
$3,000 to $4,999	64.5	33.8
$5,000 to $6,999	58.9	38.8
$7,000 to $9,999	52.8	44.7
$10,000 to $14,999	49.0	49.1
$15,000 to $24,999	52.8	46.0
$25,000 or more	57.1	41.7
Median	$15,489	$15,510

Source: U.S. Bureau of the Census. 1981. Geographic Mobility: March 1975 to March 1980. Current Population Reports, Series P-20, No. 368, table 32.

3. Intervening obstacles.

4. Personal factors.[14]

The factors at the origin and destination are objective characteristics, subjectively interpreted, that the potential migrant takes into account when a move is considered. Intervening obstacles are factors that stand in the way of moving, such as moving costs or legal barriers. Personal factors make up the individual variations, objective and subjective, that account for differences in interpreting the factors at origin and destination and the obstacles at both locations. The migration stream from Oklahoma to California during the 1930's discussed earlier provides a good example through which to see how this model works.

During the 1930's, Oklahoma was plagued with severe drought, and factors (economic) at the area of origin were evaluated to be poor. Factors (economic, lifestyle) at the potential destination (California), though not good (this was also the middle of the Great Depression) were perceived to be much better than those in Oklahoma—so much so that intervening obstacles (economic costs) could be overcome. Another intervening obstacle, the separation of friends and family members, was to a great extent avoided because of the stream nature of the migration. People who moved from the same area tended to settle in the same new areas.

Lee's theory is consistent with cost-benefit models that depict individuals as making rational migration decisions given economic conditions at the origin and potential destinations. Included in these economic considerations

Figure 5.3
Stress-Threshold Model of Residential Mobility

is the cost of moving, which is in a sense an intervening obstacle.[15] Migration is treated as an investment from which one expects to receive a return large enough to offset the cost of moving. In other words, persons assess their present and projected future economic well-being where they are presently living versus that in places to which they might move. If the economic future at some place(s) of destination is greater than that where they presently live (moving expenses included), then a move is likely to result.

Stress and stress-threshold models also fit well with Lee's theory as well as the cost-benefit approach.[16] Stress and stress-threshold models view migration as a process that requires several events to occur before a move results. Figure 5.3 shows these steps. First, an individual must develop a desire to move. In a sense, one must begin to feel dissatisfaction with regard to where one lives either because of the conditions at the place of residence or because the way in which these conditions are evaluated have changed. The conditions can include job, neighborhood, and/or social relationships, and together they determine the relative level of satisfaction with where one lives. Once dissatisfaction is at a sufficient level, a search for alternative locations takes place. It is here that a person seeks to identify potential areas of destination that do not have the characteristics that are causing her or his present level of dissatisfaction. The third state, evaluation, is really a cost-benefit analysis, and noneconomic costs and benefits are considered. If the expected level of satisfaction at the place(s) of destination exceeds that regarding where the person presently lives (moving costs considered as well), then a move is likely to take place.

While the above models are individual decision-making-based, there are a few macro or aggregate models of migration that view migration from a different perspective. They include factors at the origin and destination considerations, but they focus mainly on what structural changes occur that result in large numbers of persons moving from one area to another. One such theory views migration as basically a process that returns populations back to an equilibrium when disequilibrium has occurred.[17] When the socioeconomic structure of an area changes, a migration response is illicited. For example, when jobs are lost because factories in the area are no longer competitive, out-migration can be expected because of the overabundance of labor supply (disequilibrium). Migration to another area where an employee shortage exists can be expected, once again, because the system is seeking equilibrium. While on the surface this theory may seem overly simplistic, studying the types and mechanisms of social change that can occur is important, and linking these to variations in geographic mobility is useful.

THE IMPACT OF MIGRATION ON THE UNITED STATES—BUSINESS ENVIRONMENT CONSIDERATIONS

The impact that migration has had on the United States is almost impossible to overstate. From the more than 49 million people who moved to the United States from other nations between 1831 and 1980 to the extensive redistribution of the population already here, migration has affected virtually every aspect of society. Future immigration as well as internal migration promises to play a significant role in change until at least well into the next century. In the following paragraphs, several thoughts are offered on the likely impact of immigration and interval migration for the remainder of the century.

Immigration

Though the proportion of all U.S. population growth attributable to immigration was low by historical standards from the 1930's through the 1960's, a return to higher levels is evident in the 1980's, and this trend is not likely to be altered any time soon. Furthermore, if current fertility rates remain low, there may be long-term pressure to increase immigration flows in order to supply the labor required in certain industries. This labor-need pressure is certainly not new to many nations. Western European nations, for example, have experienced labor shortages for several years. The shortages have in part been overcome by increasing immigration flows.

Assuming that the immigration flow to the United States continues, one question raised concerns what the impact will be on persons already residing in the United States. First, the United States is again returning to an era where foreign-born citizens are a higher proportion of the total population. Though in 1910 14.8 percent of the U.S. population was foreign-born, by 1970 this proportion had declined to 4.7 percent. However, an increase to 6.2 percent occurred between 1970 and 1980, and a further increase, albeit not a large one, is almost certain to occur between now and the end of the century.[18] In addition, these new immigrants are much more likely to be culturally different from (and to speak a different language than) the native population when compared with earlier immigrants (recall earlier data on origin of migrants). They will contribute to creating a population at the turn of the century that is nearly 30 percent black, Hispanic, and Asian. The "new"

Table 5.11
Percentage Distribution of U.S. Population by Region: 1860–1980

		Region		
Year	Northeast	Midwest	South	West
1980	21.7	26.0	33.3	19.0
1960	24.9	28.8	30.7	15.6
1940	27.2	30.4	31.5	10.9
1920	28.1	32.1	31.2	8.7
1900	27.6	34.6	32.2	5.6
1880	28.9	34.6	32.9	3.6
1860	33.7	28.9	35.4	2.0

Sources: U.S. Bureau of the Census. 1975. Historical Statistics of the United
States, Colonial Times to 1970, Bicentennial Issue. Part 1, series
A 172-194; U.S. Bureau of the Census. 1981. 1980 Census of
Population and Housing. Volume 1, General Social and Economic
Characteristics, U.S. Summary, table 238.

American will contribute significantly to cultural diversity, though some social and economic costs will be incurred as they are assimilated into society.

Internal Migration

Internal migration, the percentage of persons moving in any given year, has been relatively constant (17–21 percent) for the last thirty-five years. However, the lowest percentages have been exhibited most recently, and to the extent that the age/migration relationship holds, an older population could well bring about a significant reduction in residential mobility. Furthermore, among the most likely to move age group (20–29 years), the incidence of year-to-year mobility has been declining. Though nearly 41 percent of the 20-to-29-year-olds changed residence between 1960 and 1961, only 35 percent of the same age group did so between 1980 and 1981. This proportion dropped even further to below 33 percent in the 1982–1983 time period.

Past streams of migration have significantly changed the geographic distribution of population in the United States. The data in Table 5.11 show the distribution of the population by region since 1860. As can be seen, the movement, or redistribution, has been away from the Northeast and Mid-

west to the South and West. While the South and West together made up only
a little over one-third of the total in 1860 (37.4 percent), it made up over 52
percent just 120 years later.

The contribution of migration to the redistribution described above is
evident from the region-specific net migration figures available for an intercensal time period. For example, between 1970 and 1980 northeastern
and midwestern states experienced a net out-migration of 2.9 and 2.7 million
persons, respectively. And these figures are a conservative measure of loss
because they also include some gain garnered through immigration. Between
1970 and 1975, the northeastern states had a net 1.2 million–person loss to
the southern and western states, while the midwestern states lost 1.3 million
to the same receiving states.[19] Table 5.12 shows the migration streams for the
latter half of the 1970's. Between 1975 and 1980, for example, the Northeast
received 654,000 migrants from the South, though it lost 1.8 million in the
counterstream, for a net loss of 1.1 million persons (see column 3). Net

Table 5.12

Migration Streams for Regions of the United States: 1975–1980

	Region of Origin				
	Northeast	North Central	South	West	Total
Region of Destination					
Northeast					
In	x	360[a]	654	261	1,275
Out	x	465	1,817	777	-3,059
Net	x	-105	-1,163	-516	-1,784
North Central					
In	465	x	1,029	630	2,124
Out	360	x	1,878	1,267	-3,505
Net	105	x	-849	-637	-1,381
South					
In	1,817	1,878	x	1,044	4,739
Out	654	1,029	x	1,069	2,752
Net	1,163	849	x	- 25	1,987
West					
In	777	1,267	1,069	x	3,113
Out	261	630	1,044	x	1,935
Net	516	637	25	x	1,178

[a]Numbers in 1,000s.

Source: U.S. Bureau of the Census. 1983. 1980 Census of Population and
          Housing. State of Residence in 1975 by State of Residence in 1980.
          Supplementary Report. Washington, D.C.:   U.S. Government Printing
          Office, table 2.

person losses amounted to 1.8 and 1.4 million persons, respectively, for the Northeast and Midwest. Furthermore, the Northeast and Midwest experienced a net loss of 1.7 and 1.5 million persons, respectively, to the southern and western states alone. All in all, a redistribution to the South and West appears to be continuing.

The impact of this redistribution is felt at both the origin and the destination of the migrants. For the sending regions, states, and communities, the loss of persons is symptomatic of economic hard times that have affected many parts of the United States. Continued population loss, given that it is frequently the most economically productive people who do move, only exacerbates the problem at the origin as tax bases shrink while the demand for service does not.

On the other hand, areas receiving migrants—and the job opportunities that precede them—are economically fortunate. These areas are experiencing increasing tax bases and general financial health. However, growth is not without disadvantages. Municipalities are not always able to meet the service requirements of rapidly growing areas. Also, the physical environment of some of these areas has probably suffered (Houston, Texas, added 2,000 cars per week between 1975 and 1978) as the rapid increase of persons brings about environmental demands.

From now until the end of the century, it appears that redistribution will continue, though the pace will slow. The end result is that by the end of the century nearly 60 percent of the U.S. population is likely to live in the South and West, and areas losing people will experience undesirable economic hardship.

Given low levels of fertility and slowly declining mortality rates, migration—both immigration and internal migration—has become the major component of population change in the United States. And the changes resulting from the trends outlined above are creating a different business environment in which organizations must function. At the national level, the population is becoming less homogenous, thus creating new markets for products and services both in the private and public sectors. Existing markets are changing as well, in part because the source of population growth is now adults and not children, as was the case during the post–World War II baby boom.

Internal migration has brought about a redistribution of the population and significant changes in regional and local business conditions. Areas experiencing population gain are quite different from places losing persons both in the goods and services demanded and in the ability to purchase those goods and services. Organizations providing goods and services in growing and declining regions must either adapt to these new environments or move to places where the environment is seen as friendlier. In the public sector (for example, city government), organizational geographic mobility is not possible. In cases where mobility cannot occur, adjustments to the new environment must occur even if it means significant change in the way functions are performed.

NOTES

1. Mohamed Bailey and David F. Sly. 1985. "Metropolitan-Nonmetropolitan Migration Expectancy in the United States, 1965–1980." Paper presented at the annual meeting of the Southern Regional Demographic Group. Austin, Texas.

2. John Weeks. 1981. *Population*. Belmont, California: Wadsworth, p. 150.

3. Calvin Goldscheider. 1971. *Population, Modernization, and Social Structure*. Boston: Little, Brown and Company.

4. Robert Weller and Leon Bouvier. 1981. *Population: Demography and Policy*. New York: St. Martin's Press, p. 214.

5. U.S. Bureau of the Census. 1985. *Statistical Abstract of the United States, 1985*. Washington, D.C.: U.S. Government Printing Office, table 133; S. M. Tomasi and C. B. Kelly. 1975. *Whom Have We Welcomed*. New York: Center for Migration Studies, p. 31.

6. Population Reference Bureau Staff. 1982. *U.S. Population: Where We Are; Where We're Going*. Population Bulletin Vol. 37, No. 2. Washington, D.C.: Population Reference Bureau, figure 10; U.S. Bureau of the Census. 1985. *Statistical Abstract of the United States, 1985*, table 126.

7. Leon Bouvier. 1981. *Immigration and Its Impact on U.S. Society*. Population and Public Policy Series No. 2. Washington, D.C.: Population Reference Bureau, figure 1.

8. William Barnard. 1950. *American Immigration Policy*. New York: Harper and Row, p. 27.

9. U.S. Bureau of the Census. 1975. *Historical Statistics of the United States, Colonial Times to 1970*. Bicentennial Issue, Part 1. Washington, D.C.: U.S. Government Printing Office, series C 89–119.

10. For more detail on preference systems see Charles Keely. 1979. "The United States of America." Pp. 51–64 in Daniel Kubat (ed.), *The Politics of Migration*. New York: Center for Migration Studies, chart 1.

11. Michael Greenwood and John McDowell. 1984. "U.S. Immigration Policy: Issues and Analysis." Unpublished manuscript, p. 4.

12. U.S. Bureau of the Census. 1983. *Geographic Mobility: March 1981 to March 1982*. Current Population Reports, Series P–20, No. 384. Washington, D.C.: U.S. Government Printing Office, table 1.

13. Larry Long and Kristen Hansen. 1979. *Reasons for Interstate Migration*. Current Population Reports, Series P–23, No. 64. Washington, D.C.: U.S. Government Printing Office; John Lansing and Eva Mueller. 1967. *The Geographic Mobility of Labor*. Ann Arbor, Michigan: Institute for Social Research; Alden Speare, Sidney Goldstein, and William Frey. 1975. *Residential Mobility, Migration and Metropolitan Change*. Cambridge, Massachusetts: Ballinger Publishing Co.

14. Everett Lee. 1966. "A Theory of Migration." *Demography* 3: 47–57.

15. Larry Sjaastad. 1962. "The Cost and Return of Human Migration." *Journal of Political Economy* (Supplement on Investment in Human Beings) 70 (Part 2): 80–93.

16. Julian Wolpert. 1966. "Migration As an Adjustment to Environmental Stress." *Journal of Social Issues* 22: 92–102.

17. Amos Hawley. 1950. *Human Ecology: A Theory of Community Structure.* New York: Ronald; Otis D. Duncan. 1959. "Human Ecology in Population Studies." Pp. 678–716 in P. Hauser and O. D. Duncan (eds.), *The Study of Population.* Chicago: University of Chicago Press; David Sly and Jeff Tayman. 1977. "Ecological Approach to Migration Reexamined." *American Sociological Review* 42: 783–794.

18. U.S. Bureau of the Census of Population. 1981. 1980 Census of Population. Vol. 1, Characteristics of the Population. *General Social and Economic Characteristics, U.S. Summary.* Washington, D.C.: U.S. Government Printing Office, table 77.

19. Jeanne C. Bigger. 1979. *The Sunning of America.* Population Bulletin Vol. 34, No. 1. Washington, D.C.: Population Reference Bureau, figure 2.

6

Geographic Concepts: Why Knowing about the Geographic Availability of Data Is Important

INTRODUCTION

In the discussion of data sources in Chapter 2, it should have been apparent that there is marked variation in the geographic availability of data sources, and that availability significantly affects if and how data can be used. For example, because of its relatively small sample size, the Consumer Expenditure Survey reports and aggregations contain only national-level summaries. Small-area estimates from the survey would be too unreliable to be of any value. On the other hand, data from the 1980 census of population and housing include characteristics for small areas such as census tracts and blocks. Any local area use of national-level data sets for which there are no reliable local area estimates must be accompanied by the assumption that national-level characteristics are at least good approximations for local area factors. Depending on which locality is being studied, this may be a good or a poor assumption.

Even data available for subnational geographic areas can be limited in use. For example, the County Business Patterns data set described in Chapter 2 contains a wealth of valuable economic information for all U.S. counties in every year. However, if the need for data is subcounty in nature (that is, for a zip code or census tract, for example), then the data set geography can only approximate the areal unit for which information is needed. Such an approximation many times results in biased decision making because the link between subnational and smaller area characteristics is not clear. Any assumptions and linkages made must be based on a thorough understanding of

delineated using the same basic considerations and that the boundaries do not overlap. When more than one type of geographic unit is used for analytical purposes, caution with regard to boundary overlap must be stressed. For example, zip code and census tract boundaries do not correspond well, and it is usually the case that any zip code area will contain one or more complete census tracts *and* several fractional tracts. Therefore, if a businessperson decides to use data for both levels of aggregation and, for example, and the market area is approximated by a zip code, data from the complete census tracts will overbound the market area. If the fractional tracts are eliminated from consideration, complete tract data will underbound the market area. Fortunately, many of the geographic units that are usually used are based on the same general considerations over time, and while tracts may be contiguous, their boundaries do not overlap.

If an organization is interested in the analysis of change in the business environment, then it is important that geographic unit boundaries remain constant over time. Political boundaries such as those for states and counties almost always remain constant. However, the boundary areas for many metropolitan areas, most cities, and some census tracts and blocks have changed over time, presenting serious problems for those wishing to document change. While it is certainly functional to change some boundaries over time (for example, if a group of census tracts grow substantially over a decade, it may be necessary to redraw boundaries), longitudinal analysis may become virtually impossible if boundary redrawing is particularly extensive. In many urban and suburban fringe areas that were initially tracted in the 1960's and 1970's, 1960–1970 and 1970–1980 population growth was so great that those area boundaries had to be substantially redrawn. In many instances, existing census tracts were merely split, and for those tracts an aggregation of the fractional parts reconstitutes the original boundaries. In other areas, radically different growth patterns occurred, and a simple splitting of existing census tracts was not done. Because of the problems inherent when boundary changes occur, it is extremely important that the user of demographic data look closely at geographic boundaries to assure that they are consistent over time, and if changes have occurred, he or she must determine whether or not an aggregation of fractional parts can be accomplished. It is important to maintain geographic boundary consistency as often as possible when comparing one time period with another. If consistency is not possible, then it should be noted and an evaluation of the effect of comparing different areas undertaken.

As the discussion of specific geographic delineations proceeds, the considerations presented above should be kept in mind. Specifically, the reader should consider what the boundaries of her or his market area are; how well these boundaries correspond with the geographic areas discussed; whether or not the market area has changed; if significant change has accrued, can the change be reflected in looking at data for the same geographic area for two or more time periods; and are the data available for each of the geographic areas presented.

GEOGRAPHIC DELINEATIONS

Regions and Divisions

Perhaps the easiest geographic delineations to understand are those labeled *census regions and divisions*. Figure 6.1 presents the regions and divisions of the United States, and as can be seen they comprise state groupings. The nine divisions in the figure have been used since 1910 and the four regions since 1942. When initially created, the division and region boundaries were drawn to reflect homogeneous populations with regard to both the physical characteristics of the land and the social and economic characteristics of the people. While the physical features have changed little in the seventy-seven years since their initial creation, the characteristics of the people have. Many analysts have found it more useful to create their own boundaries based on aggregations of state data, though there can be problems with proceeding in this fashion. For example, the areas of the United States that have come to be labeled the snowbelt or frostbelt and sunbelt—which are aggregations of states—are defined differently by a variety of authors. There is no commonly agreed-on definition for either area. The major advantage of regions and divisions is that their boundaries are precisely specified and they do not change. Their major disadvantage is their loss of homogeneous populations over time.

Metropolitan, Urban, and Urbanized Areas

Metropolitan Statistical Areas (MSAs), which were formerly Standard Metropolitan Statistical Areas (SMSAs) from 1960 through 1980, Standard Metropolitan Areas (SMAs) in 1950, and Metropolitan Districts in 1940, were first delineated in 1910, though before 1940 criteria for metropolitan designation were very different. From 1910 to 1940 only cities with at least 200,000 persons were designated as the core area of a Metropolitan District. Metropolitan Districts included the city as well as contiguous minor civil divisions and adjacent unincorporated places with a population density of at least 150 persons per square mile. Unlike later metropolitan delineations, the geographic unit that comprised Metropolitan Districts was *not* the county. Beginning in 1940, the minimum city size was reduced to 50,000 persons. In 1950, the SMA was defined as a county that contained a city of at least 50,000 persons as well as adjacent counties that had "metropolitan character" and were socially and economically integrated with the central county. The central county was the county that contained the large city. With some modification, the minimum 50,000-person city core criteria and county unit

Figure 6.1

Census Regions and Geographic Divisions of the United States

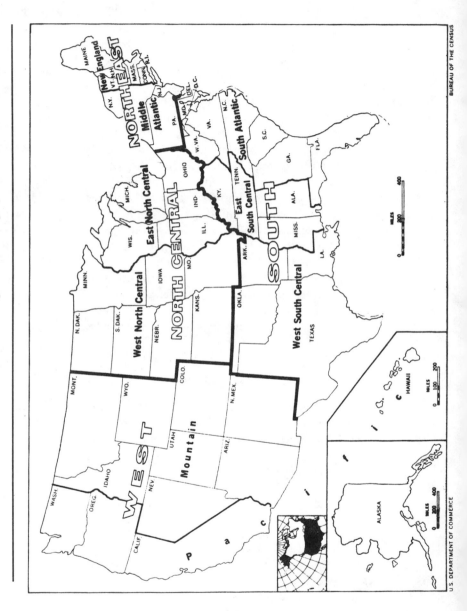

building blocks have been maintained since 1950. The number of metropolitan areas has grown from 169 in 1950 to 212 in 1960, 243 in 1970, 288 in 1980, and 323 in 1981.[1]

While the official standards for establishing MSAs are quite lengthy and detailed, it is possible to reduce the detail and still capture the essential elements. For the entire list of criteria, the reader should examine the U.S. Bureau of the Census' *State and Metropolitan Area Data Book*.[2] Overall, it should be remembered that an MSA comprises a city with a minimum population size, the county containing that city—designated the central county—and any other adjacent counties that are socially and economically integrated with the central county. There can be multiple central cities, multiple central counties, and more than one tier of adjacent counties. The terms discussed below, Metropolitan Statistical Area (MSA), Primary Metropolitan Statistical Areas (PMSAs), and Consolidated Metropolitan Statistical Areas (CMSAs) went into effect June 30, 1983.

Basic Standards

Size

1. Each MSA must contain a city, which when combined with its contiguous densely settled territory (Hereafter called an urbanized area), contains a population of 50,000 or more persons.
2. If the city contains fewer than 50,000 persons, the entire MSA must have a population of at least 100,000.

Central Counties—A MSA can contain more than one central county. In general, this is the county(ies) containing the central city(ies). To be a central county a county must have

1. At least 50 percent of its population residing in the urbanized area, or
2. At least 2,500 of its population residing in a central city of the MSA.

Central Cities—The following cities are designated central cities:

1. The city with the largest population in the MSA.
2. Each additional city with at least 250,000 persons or at least 100,000 persons working within its city limits.
3. Other cities based on a minimal size criterion and the ratio of employees to residents.[3]

Adjacent Counties—Adjacent counties are included as part of the MSA if they meet any of four conditions:

1. At least 50 percent of the employed persons in the county commute to the central county and the population density of the county is at least 25 persons per square mile.

2. Between 40 and 50 percent of the counties' workers commute to the central county(ies) and the population density is at least 35 persons per square mile.

3. Between 25 and 40 percent of the counties' workers commute to the central county(ies) and the county must contain at least one of the following:

   a. a population density of at least 50 persons per square mile.

   b. a population which is at least 35 percent urban (urban is defined below).

   c. at least 10 percent of the population of the county, or 5,000 persons, live in the urbanized area.

4. Between 15 and 25 percent of the counties' workers commute to the central county(ies) and at least two of the following:

   a. a population density of at least 60 persons per square mile.

   b. a population which is at least 35 percent urban.

   c. population growth between the last two decennial censuses of at least 20 percent.

   d. at least 10 percent of the population of the county, or 5,000 persons, live in the urbanized area.

Combining Adjacent MSAs

MSAs, as defined above, may be consolidated into a single MSA if they meet the following conditions:

1. At least 15 percent of the workers in the smaller MSA commute to the larger MSA, or

2. At least 10 percent of the workers in the smaller MSA commute to the larger MSA, and

   a. The urbanized areas of at least one central city in each MSA(s) are contiguous or

   b. A central city in one MSA is included as part of the same urbanized area as a central city in the other MSA.

3. At least 60 percent of each (all) MSA's populations must be urban.

4. The total population of all MSAs combined is at least one million persons.

Differentiating MSAs

Recent changes in metropolitan area classifications have resulted in the creation of size categories, or levels, or MSAs. Table 6.1 presents the minimum population size required to be placed at each level.

In addition to changes regarding population-size differentiation, two other categories of MSAs have emerged, Primary Metropolitan Statistical Areas (PMSAs) and Consolidated Metropolitan Statistical Areas (CMSAs). While PMSAs must meet certain criteria for designation, local political support is requisite to establishing new PMSAs.[4] Only level A MSAs may qualify as a

Table 6.1
Minimum Population Size Comprising MSA Level Hierarchy

Level	Minimum Population Size
A	MSA with at least one million persons
B	MSA of 250,000 to 999,999 persons
C	MSA of 100,000 to 249,999 persons
D	MSA of less than 100,000 persons

PMSA; CMSAs are groupings of two or more PMSAs. Any county or group of counties recognized as a separate MSA on January 1, 1980, is recognized as a PMSA. Any additional county or groups of counties may be designated a PMSA if the county(ies) has a population of at least 100,000 persons, at least 60 percent of the population is urban, and less than 50 percent of resident workers commute to jobs outside the county. If part of a MSA has been recognized as a PMSA, then the balance of the MSA is also regarded as a PMSA. Each level A MSA in which PMSAs have been defined is designated as a CMSA.

New England County MSAs

MSAs in New England are defined in terms of cities and towns rather than counties. The substitution occurs because cities and towns are administratively more important than counties in New England. New England County MSAs, NECMAs, are based for the most part on density and commuting patterns. First, a central core population is defined—which corresponds to the central counties discussed earlier—and then commuting patterns are established to determine additional areas to be added to the MSA. NECMAs are delineated through the establishment of two zones, and when combined these zones make up the central core. The first zone comprises

1. The largest city in the urbanized area.
2. Other places in the urbanized area, or an adjacent urbanized area, that qualifies as a central city, though at least 15 percent of the resident-employed workers are employed in the largest city of the urbanized area.
3. Each other city or town with at least 50 percent of its population living in the urbanized area or a contiguous urbanized area with the same 15 percent resident population stipulated in point 2.

The second zone is made up of the following:

1. A city or town that has at least 50 percent of its population living in the urbanized area or adjacent urbanized area.

2. A city or town with at least 15 percent of its resident-employed workers employed in the first zone.

Outlying cities and towns that are contiguous to the central core are included in the MSA if at least one of the following criteria is met:

1. They have a population density of 60 persons per square mile and at least 30 percent of its resident workers are employed in the central core.

2. They have a population of 100 persons per square mile with at least 15 percent of its workers employed in the central core.

Overall, the area qualifies as an MSA if it contains a city of at least 50,000 persons or contains a total population of 75,000.

Urbanized Areas

The *urbanized area*, first designated in 1950, is made up of an incorporated place and contiguous surrounding area that together have a population of at least 50,000 persons.[5] That is, within MSAs, urbanized areas consist of a central city or cities as well as the surrounding densely settled territory. The densely settled area comprises the following:

1. Adjacent incorporated or census designated areas with
   a. a population of at least 2,500 persons, or
   b. a population of less than 2,500 persons, but having a density of 1,000 persons per square mile, a densely settled area containing 50 percent of the population, or a cluster of at least 100 housing units.
2. Adjacent unincorporated area which has a population density of 1,000 persons per square mile and is connected by roads.
3. Other adjacent unincorporated area with a density of less than 1,000 persons per square mile if
   a. it allows the inclusion of an enclave of less than five square miles surrounded by a densely inhabited area.
   b. it encloses an indentation in the urbanized-area boundary which is less than one mile across the open end and comprises no more than five square miles.
   c. it links an outlying area of qualifying density to the main body providing:
      (1) the outlying and main areas are connected by road and no more than 1.5 miles apart.
      (2) the outlying and main areas are separated by water or other undevelopable land but are connected by road and no more than five miles apart.

4. Large concentrations of nonresidential-urban area (for example, major airports and industrial parks), as long as at least one-quarter of the boundary is adjacent to the urbanized area.

Urban and Rural Distinction

Urban areas are made up of all persons living in urbanized areas as well as those residents living outside urbanized areas but in places of 2,500 or more persons. These places of 2,500 or more persons can be incorporated, such as villages or cities, census-designated places of at least 2,500 persons, or unincorporated areas of 2,500 or more inhabitants within an urbanized area. The population not defined urban is considered *rural*.

Only one basic change in the rural-urban distinction has occurred over the last four decades. Prior to 1950, unincorporated areas of 2,500 or more persons were not defined urban, thereby eliminating many densely inhabited areas from consideration. These areas have been named *census designated places*. A census designated place (CDP) must meet a minimum size standard, though this standard is not constant across all geographic units. In Alaska and Hawaii a CDP must have population of 25 and 300 persons, respectively. In other states, agglomerations within urbanized areas that contain at least one city of 50,000 or more persons must contain at least 5,000 persons. In urbanized areas without a city of 50,000 as well as outside urbanized areas, the minimum population size is 1,000 persons. In comparing the 1940 and 1950 urban population, it was found that reclassifying persons in unincorporated areas as urban dwellers had a noticeable effect on the size and proportion of all persons classified urban. However, post–1950 changes in the urban definition have had very little impact on the number of persons defined as urban. As is the case in any of the definitions presented here, the reader is urged to examine definitional changes if the analyses being considered are longitudinal. Only then can an understanding of the impact of definitional changes on the phenomena of interest be determined.

Census Tracts, Blocks, and Block Groups

Census tracts are statistical divisions of MSAs and usually range in population from 3,000 to 6,000 persons. The average population size is approximately 4,000 persons. They are intended to include homogeneous populations with regard to social and economic characteristics, though as discussed earlier some homogeneity may be lost over time. Census tracts within each MSA are numbered and data with accompanying maps are made available.

In order to obtain census tract–specific data, first the tract must be identified on a tract map. Once the tract is identified and the tract number ascertained (numbers are assigned on the maps), the census tract data book

can provide information classified under that specific tract number. Figure
6.2 presents a portion of the area tracted in the Omaha, Nebraska, MSA in
1980. The area represented in the figure is within two miles of the downtown
area. The areas within the tracts are *census blocks* which are discussed a few
paragraphs from now. Assuming that the market area of interest is tract 50,
all that remains is looking up the tract-specific data for the Omaha MSA in
1980. Table 6.2 presents selected characteristics, and as can be seen, the tract
contains about 4,100 persons, 736 families, and 2,069 housing units, of
which 510 (24.6 percent) are owner-occupied. The second column of data
presents some of tract 50's social and economic characteristics. As can be
seen, the total population of the tract declined between 1970 and 1980,
though the black population grew. Other tract-specific characteristics are
available and it is up to the data user to determine which are the most
relevant to the situation at hand. Though the initiation of the tracting of
cities with large populations can be traced back to 1910 in seven U.S. cities,
it was not until 1940 that more than fifty cities were tracted.

Beginning in 1940, *blocks* in cities of 50,000 or more inhabitants were
numbered and data and maps were made available for use. Block statistics

Table 6.2
Social and Economic Characteristics for Omaha MSA Census Tract 50:
1970 and 1980

Characteristic	1980	1970
Total Population	4,097	5,173
Black Population	194	14
Number of Persons 65 Years Old and Over	547	759
Number of Families	736	1,046
Total Number of Employed Persons	2,149	2,675
Number of Housing Units	2,069	2,188
Owner-Occupied Housing Units	510	554
Median Value of Owner-Occupied Housing Unit	$29,700	$13,600
Median Contract Rent	$ 164	$ 98
Median Family Income	$17,500	$ 9,274

Source: U.S. Bureau of the Census. 1983. Census Tract Data for the Omaha,
Nebraska, Iowa MSA, 1970 and 1980. Washington, D.C.: U.S. Government
Printing Office.

Figure 6.2
Selected Census Tracts and Blocks in the Omaha MSA

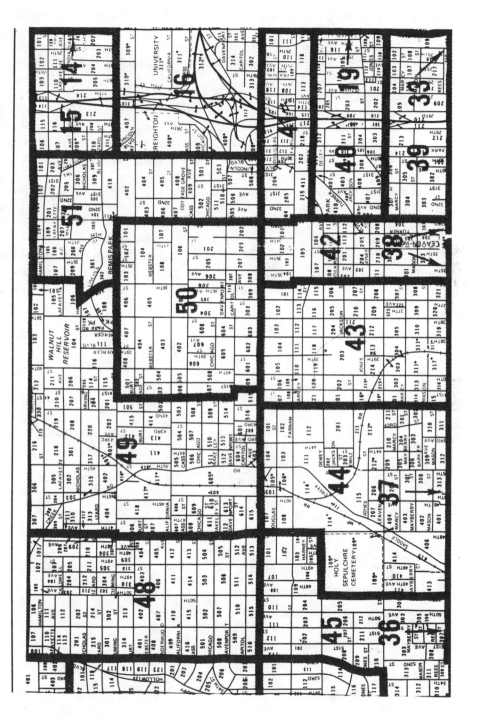

are now tabulated for each urbanized area, all incorporated places of 10,000 or more persons, and other areas that have contracted with the U.S. Bureau of the Census to provide those data. *Block groups* are aggregations of blocks, and the major advantage of using block groups over blocks is that more data are available for block groups.

Selecting block-specific data from MSAs is procedurally the same as selecting census tract data. Initially the block in question is located on a map and then data for that block are found in the block statistics data book. For example, if the area of greatest interest within tract 50 in the Omaha MSA was block 508, data for that block can be found. Table 6.3 presents such data, which are specific to block 508 (seen in Figure 6.2). The table shows that there are 166 persons residing in the block, of which 37 (22.3 percent) are under 18 years of age and 44 (26.5 percent) are 65 years of age and over. Out of eighty-nine housing units only twenty-two (24.7 percent) are owner-occupied. The second column in the table presents the same characteristics for block 508 for 1970. Comparison of the two columns indicates that the population is declining and that the number of housing units has fallen. Once again, as in the case of the census tract example, the data specific to block 508 are available and the user must decide which figures are most useful.

Table 6.3

Social and Economic Characteristics for Block 508 and Tract 50, Omaha MSA: 1970 and 1980

Characteristic	1980	1970
Total Population	166	270
Number of Persons Less Than 18 Years of Age	37	21
Number of Housing Units	89	98
Number of Housing Units with 10 or More Units (Apartments)	29	34
Owner-Occupied Housing Units	22	27
Median Value of Owner-Occupied Housing Units	$32,300	$14,800
Median Contract Rent	$ 166	$ 114

Source: U.S. Bureau of the Census. 1983. Block Statistics for the Omaha, Nebraska, Iowa MSA, 1970 and 1980. Washington, D.C.: U.S. Government Printing Office.

Counties and County Subdivisions

In most states primary divisions are known as *counties*. In Louisiana the divisions are known as parishes and in Alaska, which has no counties, boroughs and census areas are the statistical equivalents. In four states (Maryland, Missouri, Nevada, and Virginia), there are one or more cities that are independent of any county organization and are considered to be primary divisions.

Statistical subdivisions for counties are *Minor Civil Divisions* (MCDs) in twenty-nine states, *Census County Divisions* (CCDs) in twenty states, and census subareas in Alaska. MCDs have a variety of names such as townships, towns, precincts, and Indian reservations, among others. CCDs are geographic areas that have been defined by the U.S. Bureau of the Census in cooperation with state and county officials. CCDs have been defined in states where there are no legally established MCDs, where MCD boundaries change frequently, and/or where MCDs are not generally known to the public. CCDs are usually designed to represent community areas focused on trading centers or to represent major land use areas.

Summary of Metropolitan Area Geography

Geographic subdivisions within MSAs are hierarchical in nature in that each level of sub-MSA geography (PMSAs and CMSAs can be disaggregated as well) can be aggregated to produce a higher-level geographic unit. Beginning at the block level, aggregations of blocks produce block groups and census tracts. An aggregation of all tracts results in a MSA, and an aggregation of MSAs yields a CMSA. With regard to other geography, cities are combined with densely inhabited areas to generate urbanized areas. Urbanized areas, in addition to the balance of counties, make up MSAs. The addition of county-level data for more than one county yields an MSA if a multicounty MSA has been specified.

One of the major advantages of this hierarchical relationship is that market areas do not exist in a vacuum, and because aggregations of smaller geographic visits can be conceptually justified in the MSA hierarchy, market-area contexts can be ascertained. That is, while it is important to ascertain small-area business conditions, the larger economic context in which the smaller area exists is important as well. A second major advantage is that the ability to disaggregate a larger areal unit enables a business to document the variation in consumer characteristics or business conditions within a market area. Small areas can be either targeted for greater market penetration or identified as places where the business environment is not conducive to promoting activity for a particular product or service. A third advantage results from the combination of the hierarchical nature of the geographic units and the fact that unit boundaries remain constant over time.

boundaries (or boundary approximation) contain business environment characteristics that should be monitored. Income, age structure, and racial/ethnic composition are but three factors that can have considerable interdivisional and interregional differences, indicating that different business strategies may be required. When combined with purchasing behavior and psychographic data, the combination of demographic and other factors can demonstrate the large interareal business environment differences that exist.

NOTES

1. See Charles P. Kaplan and Thomas L. Van Valey. 1980. "Geography for a Changing Society." Pp. 129–158 in Kaplan and Van Valey (eds.), *Census '80: Continuing the Factfinder Tradition*. Washington, D.C.: U.S. Government Printing Office; U.S. Bureau of the Census. 1982. *State and Metropolitan Data Book, 1982*. Washington, D.C.: U.S. Government Printing Office; and Richard Forstall and Maria Elena Gonzalez. 1984. "Twenty Questions." *American Demographics* (April): 22–42, for more MSA detail and history.

2. U.S. Bureau of the Census. 1982. *State and Metropolitan Area Data Book, 1982*, pp. xv-xxiii.

3. See U.S. Bureau of the Census. 1982. *State and Metropolitan Area Data Book, 1982*, p. xx, for detail with regard to size and ratio criteria.

4. See Richard Forstall and Maria Elena Gonzalez. 1984. "Twenty Questions," for answers to frequently asked questions concerning PMSAs and CMSAs.

5. A more detailed definition of urbanized areas is presented in U.S. Bureau of the Census. 1982. 1980 Census of Population. Vol. 1, Characteristics of the Population. *General Population Characteristics*. Washington, D.C.: U.S. Government Printing Office, appendix A.

6. Additional detail on a variety of geographic units can be found in Henry S. Shryock and Jacob S. Siegel (with Edward Stockwell). 1980. *The Methods and Materials of Demography*. Washington, D.C.: U.S. Government Printing Office, chapter 5.

7

Population Composition

INTRODUCTION

Population composition for many of those interested in demographic phenomena is a term almost synonymous with demographics; that is, the descriptive characteristics of a population. Howver, population composition (in other words, what types of people the population comprises) takes on an important dynamic dimension when the factors leading to compositional change are known and the processes responsible for the changes understood. Just as demography is the study of the size, distribution, composition, and change in human populations, business demography focuses on these four elements with an emphasis on how they affect the business environment. Compositon tells the businessperson what the market is like by providing information on the following types of comsumer characteristics: age, sex, race/ethnicity, marital status, employment status, and income. Combined with psychographic and behavioral data, information on compositional characteristics contributes a great deal of insight into buying patterns of current and potential consumers. Observed changes in consumer characteristics provide the businessperson with important information about changing markets, and the ability to anticipate future compositional change puts the businessperson at a competitive advantage.

The importance of compositional considerations go well beyond the need to know more about individual consumers. In the industrial market, production, distribution, and technological change are greatly affected by the composition of the end users of products and services. From a personnel perspective, the composition of the available work force is important in planning the staffing needs for individual businesses as well as for entire industries. And these needs are greatly affected by the composition of customers, who in turn must be served by that work force. Concerning accounting issues, for example, the composition of taxpayers has substantially increased the complexity of tax returns prepared by CPAs and received by the IRS. The IRS's staffing needs have been altered by this increased complexity, at times leaving the agency with personnel shortages in some locales. With regard to finance and insurance areas, the changing needs of consumers, in part brought about by compositional shifts, have led to the expansion of many services and the creation of several others. For example, women and the elderly are being targeted for insurance programs as never before. And some financial institutions are offering financial services geared mainly to what have been labeled upscale women.

This chapter discusses the types of compositional issues that are generally considered by demographers, and it shows how recent compositional change has affected the business environment. Specific examples of how compositional change has altered markets or business strategy are offered, with a special emphasis on prospective compositional changes likely to affect the business environment in the future. The reader should keep in mind the earlier fundamental issues from the chapters on fertility, mortality, and migration. Once again, while it is these three population processes that bring about increases or decreases in population size, they are also responsible for alterations in composition. The connection should become clearer as the discussion proceeds.

Data with regard to most compositional factors are generally found in publications from the decennial censuses and the Current Population Survey, although special surveys often contain information on a number of demographic dimensions. Recent data concerning the age, sex, and race structure of the U.S., broken down by states, counties, and selected local areas, can be obtained from population estimates and projections. The key to documenting the compositional factors of any population is first to identify the compositional variables that can be of use and then to determine in what data sources those variables can be found. Of course, geographic considerations such as those discussed in Chapter 6 must be kept in mind.

Finally, it should be noted that business compositional characteristics, while perhaps lying outside the more narrow domain of demography, provide important information about both the market and the business environment. These characteristics, which include a number of compositional qualities of competitors such as the number of employees, employee composition, the age of the business, production capacity, and distribution activities, provide valuable data on the other business entities in the marketplace. In the industrial market, where businesses are the purchasers of goods and services, these data become most valuable.

COMPOSITIONAL CHARACTERISTICS

Age

The *age structure* of a population, that is, the number and proportion of persons alive at various ages, is perhaps the most important compositional element. Generally speaking, a population of a county or local area is subdivided into five- or ten-year age intervals, with the exception of the youngest and oldest ages, and the number of persons and proportion of the total population in each age group is presented. However, the importance of age structure goes beyond the simple descriptive nature of determining the size and proportion of the population at various ages to ascertaining how the age structure of a population affects other demographic as well as nondemographic factors. Recalling the chapters on fertility and mortality, the reader should remember the major impact age structure has not only on the number of births and deaths but also on birth and death rates. The standardization techniques discussed in Chapter 4 make mortality rate comparisons only after the age structure has in a sense been held constant. As was reported in Chapter 4, the unstandardized death rate (CDR) of Mexico is lower than that of the United States because the age structure of Mexico is much younger. A comparison of age-standardized death rates shows the U.S. rate to be lower.

Aside from subdividing the population into five- or ten-year age intervals, several other age-compositional measures are used. One such measure, median age, summarizes an age distribution into one index. While median age is useful for general descriptive purposes, it cannot provide the detailed information often sought by an owner or manager. The *median age*, the age that divides in one-half the distribution of ages when they are listed from lowest to highest, has varied considerably throughout U.S. history. While the median age was about 28 years in 1970, middle series population projections show it rising to over 37 years by the year 2000.[1] Putting this all in a historical perspective, the median age for the United States in 1900 was 22.9 years, and even younger before that time. Racial differences in median ages are also evident in the United States: In 1984 the black population of the United States was about six years younger than the white, or 32.2 versus 26.3 years.[2]

An additional measure of age composition is labeled a dependency ratio. A *dependency ratio* is designed to reflect the proportion of persons in the population who are economically dependent on the remainder of the population. The measure, which certainly oversimplifies reality, takes the sum of the populations under age 18 and 65 and over and divides that figure by the total population aged 18–64. Though the measure does not account for the employment status of anyone, it can approximate shifts in the age structure, which in turn generate the ratio of nonworkers to workers. This measure, also known as the *total dependency ratio*, can be decomposed. The *youth*

Table 7.5
Population of the United States by Race and Spanish-Origin: 1950–2000

	Total[a]	Black	Spanish-Origin[b]
2000	267,955	35,753 (13.3)[c]	23,706 (8.8)
1985	238,631	29,074 (12.2)	17,025 (7.1)
1980	226,546	26,683 (11.8)	14,609 (6.4)
1970	203,235	22,581 (11.1)	10,500 (5.2)
1960	179,323	18,872 (10.5)	6,927 (3.9)
1950	151,325	15,045 (9.9)	4,012 (2.7)

[a]Numbers in 1,000s.

[b]Spanish-origin may be of any race.

[c]Percentages in parentheses; do not add to 100 due to rounding and excluded racial categories.

Sources: U.S. Bureau of the Census. 1986. Statistical Abstract of the United States, 1986, tables 26 and 28; Development Associates, Inc. 1982. The Demographic and Socioeconomic Characteristics of the Hispanic Population of the United States 1950-1980. Arlington, Virginia: Development Associates, Inc., table I-2; Leon Bouvier, Cary Davis, and Robert Haupt. 1983. Projections of the Hispanic Population in the United States, 1990-2000. Arlington, Virginia: Development Associates, Inc., table A-1.

sumption unit in the United States, has changed over the last forty years and to document what today's household/family is like.

When household/family change is discussed, almost immediately there is a reference to the decline in size for both units since the end of World War II. Table 7.6, which measures households and families in terms of median persons per unit, shows the substantial decline in both between 1940 and 1985. Households declined .98 persons, or nearly 27 percent. Families declined .43 persons, or 11 percent, over the interval. In other words, given a community of 100,000 households, there would be 98,000 fewer persons now when compared with 1940 as a result of simply the decrease in household size. Assuming that 90 percent of these households were family households, the decline in family size would mean a loss of about 48,000 family members. Whichever way these data are viewed, the decline in unit size results in many fewer potential customers, and a different structure for the households and families that do exist.

Several factors have contributed to the decline in size. The decrease in fertility, documented in Chapter 3, has resulted in smaller families, and

Table 7.6
Median Household and Family Size in the United States: 1940–1985

	Household	Family
1985	2.69	3.23
1980	2.76	3.29
1970	3.14	3.58
1960	3.33	3.67
1950	3.37	3.54
1940	3.67	3.76

Sources: U.S. Bureau of the Census. 1986. Statistical Abstract of the United
States, 1986, table 54; U.S. Bureau of the Census. 1975. Historical
Statistics of the United States, Colonial Times to 1970, series A
288–319.

therefore smaller households. Other factors have contributed as well. The
percentage of males and females 18 years old and over who are married has
decreased from 76.4 and 71.6 percent, respectively, to 65.8 and 60.8 percent.[7] Single-person households increased from 6.9 percent of all households
in 1960 to 20 percent of the total in 1984.[8] One- and two-person households
now make up nearly 55 percent of all households.

Table 7.7 presents data for households and family composition within
households from 1940 to 1984. As can be seen, the growth in households
was substantial over the forty-four-year period—an increase of over 50
million households (a 144 percent increase). Large increases appear for all of
the categories shown with the exception of male-headed families. The proportion of all households that are families declined by nearly 20 percent over
the interval. Nonfamily households (data not shown) increased from 2.8
million in 1940 to 23.4 million—an 836 percent increase! Traditional husband-wife families have also markedly declined as a percent of total households. Female-headed families now constitute 11.6 percent of all households
and nearly 16 percent of all families.

Cross-classifying family size by race/ethnicity illustrates the large differences in size exhibited by white, black, and Spanish-origin families. Looking
at Table 7.8, the 1984 average family size varied from 3.18 for whites to 3.87
for Spanish-origin, a difference of 0.71 persons per family. That is, 100,000
white families result in 318,000 persons, while 387,000 persons are contained in the same number of Spanish-origin families. Since 1960, white
families have decreased an average of .4 persons and black families declined
by .7 persons.

Table 7.7
Household/Family Composition in the United States: 1940–1984

	Households	Family Households	Husband-Wife Families	Other Male Head Family	Female Head Family
1984	85,407[a]	61,997(72.6)[b]	50,090(58.6)[b]	2,030(2.4)[b]	9,878(11.6)[b]
1980	80,776	59,550(73.7)	49,112(60.8)	1,733(2.1)	8,705(10.8)
1970	63,401	51,456(81.2)	44,755(70.6)	1,239(2.0)	5,591(8.8)
1960	52,799	45,111(85.4)	39,329(74.5)	1,275(2.4)	4,507(8.5)
1950	43,554	39,303(90.2)	34,440(79.0)	1,184(2.7)	3,679(8.4)
1940	34,949	32,166(92.0)	26,971(77.2)	1,579(4.5)	3,616(10.3)

[a]Numbers in 1,000s.

[b]Percent total households.

Sources: U.S. Bureau of the Census. 1986. Statistical Abstract of the United States, 1986, table 59; U.S. Bureau of the Census. 1975. Historical Statistics of the United States, Colonial Times to 1970, series A 288-319.

Finally, looking at the presence of children by type of family for racial and ethnic groups in Table 7.9 provides another view of family units. While more than four out of five white families and seven out of ten Spanish-origin families with children under 18 contain both parents, about four out of ten black families are classified as such. Fifty percent of the black families with children under 18 are mother-only types.

Social and Economic Characteristics

In addition to the characteristics discussed above, social and economic factors are frequently used to describe populations. Though many different measures may be used to summarize these data, in general median, mean, and percentage figures are disclosed. However, as with any summary measure, one number does not provide any information on the range of characteristics found, and readers are urged to look at distributions any time they wish to profile a population. That is, for example, though a median income value may be $20,000 or $25,000, it could be the case that the distribution contains many incomes over $75,000 and under $10,000, indicating a great deal of income diversity in the population in question. Another population containing a median value of $20,000–$25,000 may contain no incomes above $35,000 or under $12,500, owning much less variation. Certainly, there are very different business implications for the two populations.

Table 7.10 contains selected social and economic characteristics of the U.S. population cross-classified by race and ethnicity. While two measures of education, one measure of labor force status, two measures of income, and one measure of housing status are used as descriptors, other measures and other dimensions could have been used. For example, median years of educa-

Table 7.8

Average Family Size for Whites, Blacks, and Persons of Spanish Origin: 1960–1984

	White	Black	Spanish-Origin[a]
1984	3.18	3.61	3.87
1980	3.23	3.67	3.90
1970	3.52	4.13	b
1960	3.58	4.31	b

[a]May be of any race.

[b]Not available.

Source: U.S. Bureau of the Census. 1986. Statistical Abstract of the United States, 1986, table 64.

Table 7.9

Children under 18 Years Old by Presence of Parents for Whites, Blacks, and Spanish-Origin Persons in the United States: 1984

	White	Black	Spanish-Origin[a]
Percent of children under 18 living with both parents	81.0	41.0	70.2
Mother only	15.1	50.2	24.9
Father only	2.1	2.9	2.0
Neither Parent	1.8	5.9	3.0

[a]May be of any race.

Source: U.S. Bureau of the Census. 1986. Statistical Abstract of the United States, 1986, table 66.

Table 7.10
Selected Social and Economic Characteristics of the White, Black, and Spanish-
Origin Populations of the United States: 1984

	White	Black	Spanish-Origin[a]
Percent With 0-8 Years of Education	13.3	22.5	37.7
Percent College Graduate	19.8	10.4	8.5
Unemployment Rate	6.5	15.9	11.3
Median Family Income	$25,757	$14,506	$18,833
Percent Persons Below Poverty Level	12.1	35.7	28.4
Percent Owner-Occupied Housing Units	67.3	45.5	41.1

[a]May be of any race.

Source: U.S. Bureau of the Census. 1986. Statistical Abstract of the United
States, 1986, tables 33, 34, and 38.

tion or the percentage of the population with high school or greater education could have been presented to describe educational attainment. Users of
these data must first determine their data needs and then seek out the
measures of greatest value, keeping in mind the potential or actual advantages and disadvantages of using a given measure.

The table indicates substantial variation in all measures among the three
populations. With regard to education, the white population is best educated
and the Spanish-origin worst. Over one-third of the Spanish-origin population has an education attainment of eight or fewer years. Unemployment,
while nearly 16 percent in the black population, is 11.3 and 6.5 percent,
respectively, in the Spanish-origin and white populations. Concerning income, white median family income is 177 percent of black income and 137
percent of Spanish-origin income—a considerable disparity. Over one-third
of the black and nearly 30 percent of the Spanish-origin populations live at
or below the official poverty level. Finally, while nearly two-thirds of the
housing units occupied by whites are owned by those persons, less than half
of the black and Spanish-origin housing units claim the same status. Overall,
the above descriptive characteristics indicate that black and Spanish-origin
social and economic levels are far less than that of the white population.

The compositional snapshot presented thus far is characterized by both diversity and change. Substantial compositional change will continue to mark the U.S. population well into the future. Overall, the population is aging, and though the impact of additional persons reaching retirement age is important, the aging of baby boomers is likely to have the greatest effect on the U.S. business climate until at least early in the next century. As the population ages and more deaths and a relatively constant number of births are generated, population growth rates will become even smaller than they are at present. Given the aging of the population coupled with the sex difference in life expectancy, a substantial imbalance of males and females (more females) at the older ages has developed. Though there is some evidence to suggest that life expectancy differentials are narrowing, the imbalance is likely to continue for a long period of time. As the total population ages and persons 65 and over become proportionately larger, the sex ratio for the entire population (for all ages) will become smaller.

Racial/ethnic differentials in population growth are substantial. As a result of younger age structures, some differences in fertility rates, and substantial immigration (for Spanish-origin and Asian populations), racial and ethnic minorities are growing much faster than the Anglo population. Before this century ends, blacks, persons of Spanish origin, and Asian Americans will make up more than 25 percent of the total population. In several states this percentage is already exceeded. For example, in Texas and California the percentages are 33.8 and 31.9, respectively.[9]

Changes in household structure and family composition are also evident. A combination of increases in one- and two-person households, fewer children, and more one-parent families has resulted in a marked decline in household and family size. The percentage of all households that contain families has also dropped considerably. Furthermore, substantial racial/ethnic differences in family structure exist, with black families far more likely to be female headed.

Finally, considerable variation in social and economic characteristics exist among racial and ethnic groups, though it should be noted that substantial differences in characteristics exist within groups. While blacks receive the lowest incomes and experience the highest levels of unemployment, Spanish-origin persons have the lowest level of education and are least likely to live in a home they own. Implications of these patterns and changes for the business environment are discussed in the next section.

IMPLICATIONS FOR THE BUSINESS CLIMATE

Compositional structure and change have a wide range of effects on markets as well as the ways in which business is conducted. Population segments that are increasing in size represent new and expanding opportunities while those segments experiencing population decline offer challenges to existing businesses. Though demographic trends do not give the entire picture of the way markets change (psychographic and behavioral data are needed as well), they do provide some hard information on the size and many of the important characteristics of market segments such as aggregate purchasing power. Population projections furnish some of the requisite data for anticipating change.

With regard to changing age structure, the tendency on the part of most businesses has been to follow the aging of the baby boom cohort. Given the roughly 45 million persons born between 1954 and 1964, this strategy has a great deal of appeal. Some researchers argue that by the end of this century baby boomers will account for over one-half of consumer expenditures. Evidence of baby boomer targeting can be seen in the creation of minivans as well as the reintroduction of convertibles in the automobile market, the expansion of resort services to accommodate interests in physical fitness, and the expansion of menus at fast food restaurants catering to concerns over health.[10] The baby boomer market is changing, however, and changes call for new business strategies. In ten years three-quarters of baby boomers will be married and two-thirds will be home owners. Coupled with an aging of this population, Cheryl Russell, editor of *American Demographics* magazine, argues that the United States is in the process of becoming a nation of homebodies.[11] At the same time, homemaking has taken on a new set of priorities with housekeeping chores becoming less important, and home entertainment (VCRs and physical fitness equipment) emerging as more important. These intra–baby boomer changes have marked implications for businesses manufacturing and selling home entertainment (expanding market) as well as for those businesses manufacturing and selling cleaning and cooking devices (the emphasis is on convenience), for example.

Nevertheless, other age segments should not be ignored, and there is much evidence that the teen, baby, and mature markets have been targeted by a number of businesses. Even though the size of its population is shrinking, annual teenage spending is estimated to be between $30 and $50 billion, and teen savings are estimated at about $9 billion each year.[12] Certainly, this is a market worth targeting! The market is a diverse one, though, with substantial sex differences in the way money is spent. While movies, dating, entertainment, gasoline, and auto expenditures make up more than 40 percent of the money spent by teenage boys in an average week, clothing, cosmetics, and fragrances account for over 55 percent of what girls of the same age spend.[13] Markets such as that for cosmetics are greatly affected by the number of teens because they make up a substantial proportion of persons most likely to use perfume, nail polish, shampoo, and creme rinses.[14] Employment among teens is increasing, and coupled with their projected population increase starting in the late 1990's, they represent a substantial market for a broad variety of goods and services.

From a baby and young infant perspective, several markets are evident. Recalling the discussion in Chapter 3, the increase in the number of births from the mid–1970's to the mid–1980's has offered a marked expansion in the market for baby goods and services. Forecasters are predicting that in 1990 more than $20 billion will be spent on children—$11 billion on clothes alone.[15] Because today's families are smaller, a larger proportion of births are first births. An increase in the proportion of first births serves as a boom to the baby market because parents spend much more on first births.[16] Along with the general increase in goods and services sold for babies has come specialized markets for "upscale babies" and children whose parents wish to purchase designer clothes and expensive furniture. In addition, having a first child has been linked to the increased consumption of other goods and services such as appliances and homes.

In reference to the mature market, a number of considerations are important. First, the mature market, those 55 and over, should be divided into at least four segments: 55–64, "older persons"; 65–74, "elderly persons"; 75–84, "aged persons"; and 85 and over, "very old persons." Each market is distinctly different, and therefore distinguishing among the groups is important. Per capita discretionary income is greatest for households headed by someone 55 and over, and it actually increases from the ages 55–59 ($3,500) to 65 and over ($4,100).[17] Persons 55–64 are seen as clearly interested in appearing youthful and are therefore prime markets for diets, health programs, sports clothing, cosmetic surgery, and health equipment. Furthermore, 65-to-74-year-olds resemble far younger people of past generations in their attitudes, income, health, and use of leisure time, again distinguishing them as a separate market.[18] It is really persons in the 75–84 age group that best fit the image of senior citizen, with regard to the limits of their physical activities and the requirement of greater amounts of health care. People aged 85 and over, the true elderly, require the most support on an everyday basis. However, even the two oldest groups contain considerable intra-group variation.

In sum, the mature market is highly fragmented. Younger members of the mature market resemble much younger persons of years past in terms of health and interests, and given their relatively sound economic status, they demand and purchase a wide variety of goods and services. Many of these purchases are in conjunction with maintaining a younger lifestyle. Persons in the middle years of maturity, though for the most part retired, still retain a good deal of younger activities and interests. The eldest of the matureds have significant health care needs, which range from increased in-home care to a rise in demand for nursing home services. Since this is the second fastest growing age group in the United States, demand for goods (for example, drugs) and services (for example, health care) specific to these individuals will grow rapidly.

Racial and ethnic structure and changes in that structure are important to the extent that purchasing and other business behavior can be identified as varying among the groups targeted. It should be noted at the outset that although consumer differences by race and ethnic group have been isolated, those generalizations should be interpreted with caution. All groups, regardless of identifying characteristics, are made up of relatively heterogeneous individuals, households, and families, and these differences result in a wide range of business-related behavior. For example, Asian Americans are seen by some businesspersons as a homogeneous group. However, while nearly one-half of all Asian Indians are managers or professionals, only 13 percent of Vietnamese Americans work in those occupations. Japanese Americans have a median family income of $27,000, while that for Vietnamese is $13,000.[19] Nevertheless, if there are general racial and ethnic differences in business behavior, then the changes in racial and ethnic structure noted above have serious implications for the business climate.

Several differences in black business behavior have been noted in the literature. Blacks tend to listen to radio more overall, as well as with greater frequency on evenings and weekends, than whites, though blacks listen to FM radio less.[20] Radio stations programming to blacks, for example, do quite well in the deep south. Black-programmed stations have a combined market share of 35.6 percent in Memphis, 33.9 percent in Savannah, and 27.6 percent in New Orleans.[21] Information such as this is important for advertisers who wish to target blacks in the marketplace.

With regard to marketplace behavior, blacks spend two to three times as much per capita as whites on hair and skin-care products.[22] Blacks are also much more likely to buy music albums or tapes and to make artwork or crafts than whites.[23] Blacks are also known to be very loyal to specific brands.[24] Overall, the reader should keep in mind that even with a low median family income of $14,506 the nearly 6.7 million black families have over $93 billion in purchasing power annually!

A variety of efforts at targeting a black market segment have been undertaken. Kraft Inc., for example, has developed a specialized promotional campaign for its brand of barbecue sauce because of its popularity among black consumers. Other products, Crest toothpaste, Revlon's Creme of Nature, and Smirnoff vodka, and services such as Eastern and United Airlines, have advertising specially targeted to black audiences.

Buying behavior of Spanish-origin consumers has also been documented: Hispanics are more likely to shop at smaller stores, to dislike impersonal stores more, to be more ecologically minded, and to be more cautious about unknown brands than whites. They are also less skeptical of advertising and are more likely to be impulse buyers.[25] Products marketed directly to

Spanish-origin persons include Bulova watches, Ford automobiles, and Revlon's La Solucion, a line of shampoos and hair coloring.

There are several special considerations that must be noted in targeting the Hispanic market. Most of these considerations are related to the language/subculture differences of Hispanics. About one-half of the Spanish-origin population is bilingual and care must be exercised in translating advertising from English to Spanish. Common translation errors often cited include one automobile name which translated as "no go," a cigarette's message which originally read "less tar" became "less asphalt," and one chicken processor who had the message "it takes a tough man to make a tender chicken" was translated as "it takes a sexually excited man to make a chick sensual."

Smaller households and families and fewer family households have serious implications for the ways in which consumers spend their money. For example, a two-person household spends $2,548 per person on housing-related expenses each year, while the per capita cost for three- and four-person households is $1,896 and $1,605, respectively.[26] Furthermore, single-person households spend 50 percent of their food dollars dining out, versus 37 percent by two-person households.[27] Businesses that have grown as a result of the increase in single persons including dating services (an estimated 5,000 agencies now versus the 300 or so that existed 10 years ago); travel services targeted to singles; and rent-a-wife and maid services, which provide options from house or apartment cleaning to unpacking and laundry assistance. Buying a condominium in a certain Memphis, Tennessee, development includes one-year free maid service.

While there are proportionately fewer families with children in the United States, families with children still represent a sizable market. In 1982, for example, there were 32.1 million families with children, and the mean income for these families was a little over $25,000. Together those families represented over $1 trillion in purchasing power! The unique needs of families with children range from child-care services to educational systems. As labor force participation rates for women with children increase, there will be a growing pressure on employers and the state and federal governments to provide child-care services.[28] Supplying such services is and will continue to be a lucrative business.

Finally, though many businesses are targeted to upscale consumers, the markets within what can be labeled downscale consumers should not be overlooked.[29] About 67 million Americans, about 28 percent of the entire population, live in families who make $25,000 or less each year, and that represents a substantial market. Many companies have entered the market for a variety of products and services, and a number of these have become quite profitable. Dollar General, with 1,300 stores in 23 states, had $600 million in net sales in 1985, double the sales realized in 1982. Family Dollar's sales for the first three-quarters of 1985 totaled $307 million. The typical Family Dollar customer has an income of $17,000. Wal-Mart, the retailing giant that still emphasizes the downscale (but with a growing emphasis on the upscale), had estimated sales of $6.4 billion in 1985.

In sum, it should be remembered that compositional structure, and particularly change, are important only if they are good indicators of differential behavior in the marketplace. The evidence offered in this chapter documents well the connection between compositional characteristics and market activities. Compositional change, therefore, is important as it carries the substantial shifts in overall activity that are occurring. Furthermore, the fact that different compositional groups are growing faster than others (for example, racial and ethnic minorities and persons aged 85 and over) means that several markets are in the process of showing substantial growth. Finally, given the wealth of data available and the ease in obtaining these data, population composition is something that can be monitored by most businesspersons.

NOTES

1. U.S. Bureau of the Census. 1984. *Projections of the Population of the United States by Age, Sex and Race: 1983–2080*. Current Population Reports, Series P–25, No. 952. Washington, D.C.: U.S. Government Printing Office, table C.

2. U.S. Bureau of the Census. 1986. *Statistical Abstract of the United States, 1986*. Washington, D.C.: U.S. Government Printing Office, table 27.

3. U.S. Bureau of the Census. 1984. *Projections of the Population of the United States by Age, Sex and Race: 1983–2000*, table D.

4. More specifically, the labor force comprises those persons who are (1) presently employed, (2) temporarily absent from work for noneconomic reasons, and (3) not presently working but have made specific efforts (for example, applying for a job and registering with an employment service) to find work in the last four weeks.

5. U.S. Bureau of the Census. 1986. *Statistical Abstract of the United States, 1986*, tables 25 and 39.

6. Paul Glick and Arthur Norton. 1977. *Marrying, Divorcing and Living Together in the U.S. Today*. Population Bulletin Vol. 32, No. 5. Washington, D.C.: Population Reference Bureau; Arland Thornton and Deborah Freedman. 1983. *The Changing American Family*. Population Bulletin Vol. 38, No. 4. Washington, D.C.: Population Reference Bureau.

7. U.S. Bureau of the Census. 1986. *Statistical Abstract of the United States, 1986*, table 44.

8. U.S. Bureau of the Census. 1986. *Statistical Abstract of the United States, 1986*, table 55.

9. U.S. Bureau of the Census. 1986. *Statistical Abstract of the United States, 1986*, table 32.

10. Abigail Trafford. 1984. "Marketplace Aims at New Breed of Burgers." *U.S. News and World Report* (November 5): 71–72.

11. Cheryl Russell. 1985. "The New Homemakers." *American Demographics* (October): 23–27.

12. Doris Walsh. 1985. "Targeting Teens." *American Demographics* (February): 21–41.

13. Doris Walsh. 1985. "Targeting Teens," p. 25.

14. William Dunn. 1985. "The Changing Face of Cosmetics." *American Demographics* (March): 40–51.

15. Paul Brown, Ellyn E. Spragins, Peter Engardino, Kirvin Ringe, and Steve Klinkerman. 1985. "Bringing Up Baby: A New Kind of Marketing Boom." *Business Week* (April 22): 58–65.

16. Brad Edmondson. 1985. "How Big Is the Baby Market?" *American Demographics* (December):23–48.

17. William Lazer. 1985. "Inside the Mature Market." *American Demographics* (March): 23–49.

18. William Lazer. 1985. "Inside the Mature Market," p. 24.

19. Bryant Robey. 1985. "Asian Americans." *American Demographics* (May): 23–29.

20. Gerald Glasser and Gale D. Metzger. 1975. "Radio Usage by Blacks." *Journal of Advertising Research* (October): 39–45.

21. Michael Hedges. 1986. "Radio's Lifestyles." *American Demographics* (February): 32–35.

22. William Dunn. 1985. "The Changing Face of Cosmetics," p. 42.

23. Roger Blackwell, Lee Mathews, and Carolyn Randolph. 1979. *Living in Columbus* Columbus, Ohio: Nationwide Communications, Inc.

24. Alphonzo Wellington. 1981. "Traditional Brand Loyalty." *Advertising Age* (May 18): 5–12.

25. Danny Bellinger and Humberto Valencia. 1982. "Understanding the Hispanic Market." *Business Horizons* (May-June): 49.

26. U.S. Bureau of the Census. 1985. *Consumer Expenditure Survey: Interview Survey, 1980–81.* Bulletin 2225. Washington, D.C.: U.S. Government Printing Office.

27. Joann Lublin. 1986. "Staying Single." *Wall Street Journal* (May 28): 1, 18.

28. Albert Hunt. 1986. "What Working Women Want." *Wall Street Journal* (June 6): 20.

29. William Dunn. 1986. "In Pursuit of the Downscale." *American Demographics* (May): 26–33.

8

Population Distribution—Where They Live Is Also Important

INTRODUCTION

While size and composition are important factors in describing populations, the *distribution*—knowing where people live—is crucial to a demographic perspective in business. Simply stated, data on the geographic distribution of people tells a business owner or manager where actual and potential customers are located, while historical and projections data provide the comparison figures to measure customer redistribution. Information on population distribution and redistribution is particularly important to enterprises whose sales and other business activities are tied to clearly delineated market areas, though ascertaining the characteristics of prospective locations is important for business expansion and business relocation considerations. Even large organizations, whose markets are national and/or international in nature, require distribution data in order to make regional or local decisions about advertising, transportation systems, and allocation of resources. Furthermore, data on distributional change are extremely important because, coupled with size and compositional factors, they indicate whether a geographically defined market is changing in ways important to business concerns.

Population distribution is generally analyzed in human terms, that is, the focus is on where *people* live. Though that information is quite useful, the concept geographic distribution can be generalized to include the location of businesses and other organizations to provide information on both competitors and industrial consumers. A population profile of an area for businesses should include both population data from the various census and survey sources along with enterprise data from many of the economic censuses. Interarea comparisons can be made to determine the best markets to enter and intra-area differentials in demographic characteristics sought out if, for example, a business is confined to a very small market area. Distributional change is important for the measurement of growth or decline in a market.

In addition, distributional considerations include the geographic location of where people work. The resident and daytime workplace populations are quite different in most locales, and businesses must account for both totals (size and composition) in order to properly evaluate a market area. Data on daily commuting totals can be found in U.S. Census Bureau publications or can be obtained through special tabulations.

Population distribution literature is really nothing new to most readers. Articles and newscasts have been appearing for quite some time on population movement from the "snowbelt" or "frostbelt" (a more recent term is the "rustbelt") to the "sunbelt," the rapid growth of suburbs and concomitant decline of cities, and the revitalization (growth in population) of certain nonmetropolitan and rural areas. At the international level, many of the issues focus on the distribution of persons between what is called the more developed and the less developed nations of the world along with the concerns for trade flows, the uneven distribution of food and wealth, and the location of the highest levels of technology. Within other nations, distributional data are important to local and international business concerns. Fortunately for persons interested in these and related issues, there is a relatively large amount of accessible information from which to measure distribution and distributional change. Some of these data are presented in Chapter 13, which focuses on international business issues.

There has been and continues to be a great deal of population-distributional change for regions in the United States as was mentioned in the discussion of migration in Chapter 5. In general, the change has been from lesser population concentrations (although continued growth) in the Northeast and Midwest to a greater concentration in the West. The pattern for the South has been one of an increase, but only in the most recent years. However, these data mask the more complex patterns at the subregional level. A breakdown of population distribution by census divisions and MSAs, along with projected distributional change, is presented later in this chapter.

Population redistribution results through the interaction between (1) migration differentials and (2) variations in the level of natural increase (the difference between fertility and mortality). Though migration is the quickest response that a population can have when environmental conditions change (for example, job opportunities grow or decline), migration, as was shown in Chapter 5, tends to be very selective with regard to age and other compositional characteristics. In many large cities in the United States, for example, the population composition is highly skewed because this selectivity has left behind the poor, the racial and ethnic minorities, the very old, and the very young. Present compositional characteristics of each of these cities will to a great extent determine future growth and therefore distribution patterns. While net out-migration continues in many cities, overall population growth results because the positive impact of natural increase is greater than the negative impact of migration. In some other cities, migration actually overcomes the population-depleting effect of negative natural increase. The point to this discussion is that population distribution and redistribution are the product of several processes, and before any business decisions are made, the impact that each of these factors is having on the markets in question should be carefully studied. Therefore, while population distribution data provide a first look at the size of markets, compositional differentials contribute the detail required to measure market potential.

The general purpose of this chapter is to describe in some detail population distribution and redistribution in the United States. Population projections to the year 2000 allow for a view toward the future. Furthermore, some distributional data on employees, businesses, and consumption patterns are presented to provide a more complete picture on interarea differences in population and business factors. Together, these factors are responsible for creating a substantial part of the regional- or local-business environment. Finally, the owner or manager implications for population and business redistribution are discussed.

POPULATION DISTRIBUTION AND REDISTRIBUTION PATTERNS

Various patterns of distribution and redistribution are to some extent tied to the geographic units that have been chosen for comparison. The users of distributional data must decide which units are most important for their purposes. The choice is usually determined by the extent of an actual or potential market area (for example, county, city, MSA, division, or region), though other considerations may dictate the need for additional comparisons. As was noted in Chapter 6, sometimes market areas must be approximated using established geographical boundaries in order to use the data available. For the purposes of this chapter, distribution is discussed with regard to a host of geographic areas in order to present different dimensions of variation, and to show how the selection of one geographic unit over another can affect an owner's or manager's conclusions about distribution and redistribution patterns.

Table 8.1 presents population-size data cross-classified by census region and division for 1950, 1970, 1984, and 2000. Regions and divisions were defined in Chapter 6. The data reconfirm the observation in Chapter 5 that the Northeast and Midwest (formerly North Central) regions are gaining population slowly while the South and West are increasing much more

Table 8.1
Population Distribution for Regions and Divisions of the United States: 1950–2000

	1950	1970	1984[a]	2000[b]
Northeast	39.5[c]	49.1	49.7	46.4
New England	9.3	11.8	12.6	12.8
Middle Atlantic	30.2	37.2	37.2	33.6
Midwest	44.5	56.6	59.1	59.7
East North Central	30.4	40.3	41.6	41.6
West North Central	14.1	16.3	17.5	18.1
South	47.2	62.8	80.6	98.8
South Atlantic	21.2	30.7	39.5	49.0
East South Central	11.5	12.8	15.0	17.2
West South Central	14.5	19.3	26.1	32.7
West	20.2	34.8	46.7	62.5
Mountain	5.1	8.3	12.6	20.1
Pacific	15.1	26.5	34.2	42.4

[a]Population estimate.

[b]Population projection.

[c]Population in millions.

Source: U.S. Bureau of the Census. 1986. Statistical Abstract of the United States, 1986. Washington, D.C.: U.S. Bureau of the Census, table 10.

rapidly. Specifically, the gain over the fifty-year period in the Northeast and Midwest is nearly 22 million persons, while the increase in the West and South is about 94 million. However, the pattern of increase among divisions shows even more variation. While New England increases by 3.5 million persons over the fifty-year interval, the West South Central and Pacific divisions increase by nearly 18 and 27 million, respectively. All three divisions had similar population bases in 1950. Presented as percentage change, the New England, West South Central, and Pacific divisions grew 38, 126, and 181 percent, respectively, over the fifty-year period.

Table 8.2
Percent Population Distribution for Regions and Divisions of the United States:
1950–2000

	1950	1970	1984[b]	2000[c]
Northeast	26.1[a]	24.1	21.1	17.4
New England	6.2	5.8	5.3	4.8
Middle Atlantic	19.9	18.3	15.7	12.6
Midwest	29.4	27.8	25.0	22.3
East North Central	20.1	19.8	17.6	15.6
West North Central	9.3	8.0	7.4	6.8
South	31.2	30.9	34.1	37.0
South Atlantic	14.0	15.1	16.7	18.3
East South Central	7.6	6.3	6.4	6.4
West South Central	9.6	9.5	11.1	12.2
West	13.3	17.1	19.8	23.4
Mountain	3.4	4.1	5.3	7.5
Pacific	10.0	13.1	14.5	15.8

[a]Percentages may not add to 100 due to rounding.

[b]Population estimate.

[c]Population projection.

Source: U.S. Bureau of the Census. 1986. Statistical Abstract of the United States, 1986, table 10.

Table 8.2 presents data from Table 8.1 in percentage form. The West and South regions gain 16 percent of the total distribution, while the Northeast and Midwest lose the same percentage. While all divisions in the Northeast and Midwest are percentage losers, not all divisions in the South and West are gainers. The East South Central division is projected to gain 5.7 million persons between 1950 and 2000, though it will lose 1.2 percent in terms of its share of total population. Significant increases—greater than 4 percent—can be seen in the Pacific and South Atlantic divisions, while large decreases—a loss of 4 or more percent—are found in the Middle Atlantic and East North Central divisions.

The same divisional differences in growth are evidenced in the change in the number-of-households data for 1981–1984. States experiencing the smallest increase in households—less than 3 percent—are for the most part located in the East and West North Central divisions (Ohio, Michigan, Iowa), though one state, West Virginia, is in the South Atlantic division. On the other hand, all of the states exhibiting a large increase in households—greater than 14 percent between 1980 and 1984—are located in the South Atlantic, West South Central, Mountain, and Pacific divisions (Florida, Texas, Arizona, Nevada, Alaska).[1]

Recent interregional comparisons of migration data in part explain why the pattern of growth seen in Tables 8.1 and 8.2 emerge. From 1980 to 1985 the net exchange (in-migrants versus out-migrants) was −1.0, −1.5, 1.9, and .6 million persons, respectively, in the Northeast, Midwest, South, and West regions. Of particular note is the loss of 1.1 and 0.7 million persons from the Northeast and Midwest, respectively, to the South.[2]

In sum, the data from both of these tables demonstrate that there is a large and ongoing redistribution of the population and, therefore, consumers in the United States. However, in order to better measure the change in the geographic distribution of consumption, additional information about intraregional and divisional compositional changes are required. For example, data on the 1975–1980 net exchange (in-migrants versus out-migrants) of persons cross-classified by income and education for the state of New York indicate that while the entire state experienced net out-migration during the interval, a disproportionate number of persons came from upper-income households and from the highest educational attainment categories.[3] That is, the population residing in New York in 1980 had a somewhat lower income and was less well educated than the 1975 population. Therefore, the population's buying power and its needs and interests in certain products and services were lessened. Continued patterns of this type can significantly alter aggregate purchasing behavior—a factor of extreme importance to the businessperson. This point is further elaborated on in the last section of the chapter. Furthermore, trade association and economic census data specific to the industry/business of interest and cross-tabulated by geographic area are needed along with salient social and economic factors from census of population sources in order to complete the distribution picture. The reader is encouraged to seek out such data which are important to the specific business/market under consideration.

Another factor important to distributional concerns is urban/rural residence. Table 8.3 presents population distribution data classified by urban/rural residence and size of urban place for 1960, 1970, and 1980. As can be seen, the percentage of the total U.S. population living in urban areas increased somewhat over the twenty-year period. However, a greater change

Table 8.3
Percent Urban/Rural Residence by Size of Place: 1960–1980

	1960	1970	1980
Urban	69.9	73.5	73.7
Places 1,000,000 or more	9.8	9.2	7.7
Places 250,000-999,999	12.2	11.5	10.2
Places 50,000-249,999	14.2	15.2	16.2
Places 10,000-49,999	18.1	19.3	22.5
Places 2,500-9,999	9.7	10.4	10.9
Places under 2,500	0.4	0.4	0.6
Other urban	5.5	7.5	5.6
Rural	30.1	26.5	26.3
Places under 2,500	5.8	5.2	4.8
Other rural	24.3	21.3	21.4

Source: U.S. Bureau of the Census. 1986. Statistical Abstract of the United States, 1986, table 17.

in the distribution among urban places of various size has occurred. The general trend has been a deconcentration of population living in large places (250,000 persons and over) and an increase in the concentration of persons residing in smaller urban places. Of particular note is the 4.4 percent increase in the concentration of persons living in places of 10,000–49,999. More than one in five Americans now lives in such locations. With regard to rural areas, both size categories experienced losses over the twenty-year period, though the absolute decline was greatest in the smallest category of rural areas.

The population of the United States is subdivided by metropolitan and nonmetropolitan status in Table 8.4. Between 1950 and 1984, there was an increase of 111 metropolitan areas as the size of the population classified metropolitan increased from 85 to 180 million persons, or 112 percent. At the same time the size of the nonmetropolitan population decreased by 10 million persons. Nevertheless, when comparing data for 1980 and 1984, an interesting observation can be made. During that time, the nonmetropolitan population grew by nearly 2 million persons, reversing a pattern of loss for every decade since at least 1950. This phenomenon, first identified in the

Table 8.4
Metropolitan and Nonmetropolitan Population: 1950–1984

	1950	1960	1970	1980[a]	1984[a]
Number of Metropolitan Areas	169	212	243	280	280
Population (in millions)	84.9	112.9	139.5	172.2	179.9
Percent of total U.S. Population	56.1	63.0	68.6	76.0	76.2
Nonmetropolitan population (in millions)	66.5	66.4	63.8	54.4	56.2

[a]MSAs and CMSAs.

Source: U.S. Bureau of the Census. 1986. Statistical Abstract of the United States, 1986, table 20.

1970's when it was observed that nonmetropolitan areas were growing faster than metropolitan areas and labeled "nonmetropolitan turnaround," seems to be reversing direction again back in the direction of more rapid metropolitan growth. However, the absolute size of the nonmetropolitan population could well continue to show modest gains and at least will probably not experience decline before the end of the century. Row 3 of the table demonstrates the rapid rate of metropolitanization—from 56 to 76 percent of the total—the U.S. population has experienced over the last thirty-five years.

Table 8.5 reclassifies the data from Table 8.4 for 1980 by including the

Table 8.5
Racial/Ethnic Differences in Metropolitan Residence: 1980

	White	Black	Spanish-Origin
Inside MSAs	74.5%	82.0%	88.1%
Central Cities	27.0	59.7	53.1
Outside Central Cities	47.5	22.3	35.0
Outside MSAs	25.5	18.0	11.9

Source: U.S. Bureau of the Census. 1986. Statistical Abstract of the United States, 1986, table 22.

factors race/ethnicity and central city/noncentral city status. While non-central city residents are often referred to as suburbanites, this category actually includes a host of resident categories that make up the noncentral city portion of the MSA. Row 1 of the table indicates that blacks and persons of Spanish origin are much more likely than whites to be residing in MSAs. Moreover, when the central city/noncentral city dichotomy is considered, it can be seen that blacks and Spanish-origin persons are at least twice as likely to be living in central cities. While blacks and persons of Spanish origin made up 11.7 and 6.4 percent of the total U.S. population in 1980, they made up 21.8 and 10.8 percent, respectively, of the central cities' population (data not shown). In sum, both minority populations are heavily concentrated in MSAs, with the majority residing in central cities.

Population redistribution is the product of differences in growth rates among geographic areas. Tables 8.6 and 8.7 present interarea growth rate differentials which are radically changing the business climates of regions, divisions, and perhaps more importantly, local areas. Population growth is measured for selected states and the District of Columbia for the decades of the 1970's and 1980's in Table 8.6. The upper panel of the table presents population increase percentages for the ten fastest growing states, while the bottom panel presents data for the slowest (or negative) growing states. As can be observed, outside the state of Florida, each of the high-growth states is located in the West region. Furthermore, out of this list only Florida is among the ten largest states in the United States. During the decade of the 1970's, each of these states grew by at least one-fourth and Nevada's population increased by nearly 64 percent! For the 1980's, only one state, New Mexico, is not projected to grow by at least 20 percent.

Data in the second panel show a much different pattern. Each of the sates in this list is located in the Northeast or Midwest regions and five of the ten are among the ten largest states in the United States (New York, Pennsylvania, Ohio, Illinois, and Michigan). Two states, in addition to the District of Columbia, exhibited population loss during the 1970's and an additional two are projected to join the list during the 1980's. During the 1980's, all but two of these states are growing at less than 1 percent per decade. All of these states are projected to be losing population by the year 2000, with the loss in New York during the 1990's nearing 9 percent.[4]

Table 8.7 examines growth data but in the context of cities with 100,000 or more population, and only for 1980–1984. The top panel shows the ten fastest growing cities, and with the exception of four cities in the South, they are all located in the West. Furthermore, those four cities are located in two relatively high-growth states, Florida and Texas. Each city grew at least 19 percent in the four-year period and two—Tallahassee, Florida, and Arlington, Texas—grew by more than one-third.

The bottom panel of the table presents the slowest growing cities (in this case all negative growth); each is located either in the Northeast or Midwest. All experienced at least a 5 percent population loss over four years; Detroit

Table 8.6
Percentage Growth for Selected States in the United States: 1970–1980, 1980–1990

	State	1970-1980	1980-1990[a]
Largest Growth			
	Nevada	63.8	59.1
	Arizona	53.1	46.5
	Florida	43.5	36.6
	Wyoming	41.3	48.3
	Utah	37.9	38.7
	Alaska	32.8	29.7
	Idaho	32.4	28.0
	Colorado	30.8	29.5
	New Mexico	28.1	17.7
	Oregon	25.9	25.7
Smallest Growth			
	District of Columbia	-15.6	-21.4
	New York	- 3.7	- 6.5
	Rhode Island	- 0.3	0.2
	Pennsylvania	0.5	- 1.4
	Massachusetts	0.8	- 0.8
	Ohio	1.3	- 0.6
	Illinois	2.8	0.5
	Iowa	3.1	2.1
	South Dakota	3.7	0.9
	Michigan	4.3	1.2

[a]Population projection.

Source: U.S. Bureau of the Census. 1986. Statistical Abstract of the United
States, 1986, tables 11 and 14.

lost nearly 10 percent of its population during this interval. Worthy of note
is the concentration of cities in the contiguous six-state area running from
western New York (Buffalo) to Illinois (Peoria).

Table 8.7

Percentage Growth for Selected Cities with 100,000 or More Population: 1980–
1984

	City	Percentage
Largest Growth		
	Tallahassee, FL	37.8
	Arlington, TX	33.6
	Anchorage, AK	29.9
	Mesa, AZ	27.2
	Bakersfield, CA	23.3
	Fresno, CA	22.9
	Aurora, CO	22.8
	Odessa, TX	20.7
	Ontario, CA	19.7
	Laredo, TX	18.8
Smallest Growth		
	Detroit, MI	-9.5
	Flint, MI	-6.6
	Youngstown, OH	-6.5
	Dayton, OH	-6.4
	Gary, IN	-5.8
	Peoria, IL	-5.7
	Warren, MI	-5.6
	Buffalo, NY	-5.3
	St. Louis, MO	-5.2
	Pittsburgh, PA	-5.0

Source: U.S. Bureau of the Census. 1986. Statistical Abstract of the United
States, 1986, table 19.

In sum, Tables 8.3–8.7, which present population growth data for
urban/rural, metropolitan/nonmetropolitan, and selected state and city classifications, demonstrate the tremendous variance in growth being exhibited
by a wide range of geographic areas. The population of the United States has
become more concentrated in urban and metropolitan areas over the past

Table 8.8
Employees in Selected Nonagricultural Establishments Classified by Census
Division: 1975–1984

Division	Manufacturing			Wholesale Retail Trade			Services		
	1975	1980	1984	1975	1980	1984	1975	1980	1984
New England	1,312[a]	1,523	1,497	1,018	1,167	1,333	946	1,203	1,417
Middle Atlantic	3,479	3,562	3,179	2,876	3,134	3,397	2,709	3,278	3,825
East North Central	4,605	4,715	4,195	3,314	3,765	3,811	2,560	3,122	3,440
West North Central	1,225	1,379	1,325	1,463	1,709	1,742	1,080	1,361	1,512
South Atlantic	2,632	3,042	3,071	2,591	3,229	3,752	2,062	2,731	3,406
East South Central	1,226	1,364	1,332	887	1,074	1,161	658	823	930
West South Central	1,308	1,662	1,566	1,695	2,214	2,457	1,190	1,601	1,925
Mountain	416	564	601	795	1,055	1,175	685	964	1,149
Pacific	2,042	2,560	2,563	2,366	3,040	3,323	2,036	2,793	3,234

[a]Numbers in 1,000s.

Sources: U.S. Bureau of the Census. 1976. Statistical Abstract of the United States, 1976,
table 596; U.S. Bureau of the Census. 1981. Statistical Abstract of the United
States, 1981, table 668; U.S. Bureau of the Census. 1986. Statistical Abstract of
the United States, 1986, table 693.

thirty years, though the rates of urbanization and metropolitanization have
slowed considerably over the last few years. These data should be seen in the
context of the business environment presently existing and projected in each
of these places, though as stated earlier, additional information is required to
truly understand a market area.

DISTRIBUTION AND REDISTRIBUTION OF EMPLOYEES, EMPLOYMENT, AND CONSUMPTION PATTERNS

As discussed earlier, population is but one distribution dimension of potential importance to the businessperson. The location and changing locations of jobs, competitors, and resources can be crucial to the development
of any business strategy. In Table 8.8, the numbers of employees in three
establishment categories—manufacturing, wholesale and retail, and service
industries—are presented for 1975, 1980, and 1984 for each of the nine
census divisions. These data are presented for the purpose of illustration, as
a variety of other employment categories could have been selected.

Overall, growth in the number of employees in all three categories took
place in all divisions, though growth was substantially greater in the divisions making up the South and West. The increase in *all* nonagricultural
employees was from about 4.7 to 5.9 million in New England between 1975
and 1984 (data not shown in table), or 26 percent. The increase in nonagricultural employees in the West South Central division was from 7.2 to 10.0

million, or 38 percent. Furthermore, substantial growth differences are shown for different industry categories. Nationwide, manufacturing employees increased from 18.3 to 21.4 million—5.8 percent—during the interval, while service workers increased 48 percent from about 14 to nearly 21 million. Divisional differentials are also evident within industry categories. Though manufacturing employees decreased from 3.5 to 3.2 million, or − 8.6 percent in the Middle Atlantic division, an increase from 2.0 to 2.6 million—26 percent—occurred in the Pacific division. Within the service industry, an increase of 62 percent in service employees occurred in the West South Central division, while the increase in New England was smaller at about 50 percent. Not surprisingly, these data are consistent with the population figures presented earlier, and once again they illustrate the large amount of geographic unit variation.

Extending these data by looking at projections from 1985 to 2030 and focusing on comparisons for three regions—South, West, and North (Northeast and Midwest combined)—several interesting patterns emerge.[5] Employment growth in the South and West is projected to increase by over 40 percent, though in the North the increase is about 10 percent. In the North, losses in primary and secondary jobs are projected, which are offset by modest increases in finance-related and service positions. In the South and West, only the South is projected to lose primary jobs, and both regions are projected to experience at least an 80 percent rise in finance-related positions.

While Table 8.8 provides data on employees within selected industries, Table 8.9 shows the figures for the number of establishments in one industry, manufacturing. The industry data are classified by census division, and information for three enumerations—1972, 1977, and 1982—are provided. The reader is reminded that analogous tables for other industries and for other geographic areas of interest (for example, states) can easily be constructed. Substantial divisional differences in the growth of manufacturing establishments were evidenced between 1972 and 1982. As has been the case with population and employee growth, the greatest increases are in the divisions making up the South and West regions. However, growth in the West South Central, Mountain, and Pacific divisions far surpass increases in any other division. On the other hand, growth in the New England and East North Central divisions are less than 10 percent, and the Middle Atlantic division exhibited an 11.4 percent loss in establishments!

Additional information of importance to the businessperson concerns geographic area differences in the Consumer Price Index (the cost of living index, or CPI) and consumer expenditures. The CPI variations provide another dimension of the business environment, and when coupled with population and establishment growth, they can indicate the relative health of an actual or potential market. Table 8.10. provides CPI differences for selected cities and expenditure categories for 1985. As can be observed, only

Table 8.9
Divisional Distribution of Manufacturing Establishments: 1972–1982

Division	1972	1977	1982	Percent Change 1972-1982
New England	23,731	25,737	25,659	8.1
Middle Atlantic	73,872	71,009	65,443	-11.4
East North Central	64,667	69,237	67,378	4.2
West North Central	21,467	24,321	23,940	11.5
South Atlantic	41,533	47,692	48,855	17.6
East South Central	16,525	19,187	18,573	12.4
West South Central	24,012	29,796	31,876	32.8
Mountain	10,119	13,808	14,854	46.8
Pacific	46,829	59,106	61,483	31.3

Source: U.S. Bureau of the Census. 1986. Statistical Abstract of the United States, 1986, table 1336.

the CPI for Denver is greater than that for the United States as a whole. The figure for Denver (357.8) is 13 percent higher than the U.S. figure, while that for Detroit is 6 percent lower. City-to-city variations by specific category are substantial. The housing index, for example, is 432.8 for Denver and only 311.3 for Detroit—a difference of 121.5 points. Conversely, fuel and other utilities in Detroit show an index of 437.6 versus 354.4 in Denver—an 83.2 point difference in indices. In general, the table provides evidence of CPI differentials large enough to demonstrate yet another dimension of the wide range of business environments existing among geographically defined areas.

Table 8.11 presents data on regional differences in urban household consumption (dollars spent) for a variety of product categories. Information on the number of households and average size of household is provided as background information. Per capita figures were derived by dividing category-specific dollars by average household size. For example, the per capita food at home figure for the Northeast region is the result of dividing $1,925 (the average dollar amount per household) by 2.6 (average household size). As a note to the reader, even small dollar differences in average regional expenditures can result in large aggregate differences in total dollars spent in a category. For example, Midwest regional expenditures on food exceed those in the West region by $76 per household ($1,826 versus $1,749). However, given that there are 4.1 million more households in the Midwest than in the West, the aggregate spending difference is $312 million. House-

Table 8.10
Consumer Price Differences for Selected Cities: 1985

	U.S. City Average	Detroit	Los Angeles[a]	New York[a]	Denver[a]	Boston
All Items	317.3	298.6	312.1	306.4	357.8	311.9
Food and Beverages	300.8	282.6	300.8	303.8	294.1	285.4
Housing	340.5	311.3	332.3	312.7	432.8	329.1
Fuel and Other Utilities	393.8	437.6	366.2	404.0	354.4	383.3
Household Furnishings and Operation	243.6	209.0	220.0	249.7	246.7	243.7
Apparel and Upkeep	204.2	165.7	177.2	190.0	222.1	223.6
Transportation	323.3	306.3	335.7	347.4	323.9	344.5
Medical Care	397.7	417.9	416.0	391.1	377.7	392.7
Entertainment	258.9	220.8	204.9	266.5	270.0	259.0

1967 = 100

[a]Includes surrounding urban area.

Source: U.S. Bureau of Labor Statistics. 1985. CPI Detailed Report. Washington D.C.: U.S. Government Printing Office, tables 21(OS)and 22(OS).

hold expenditures on electricity in the South exceed those in the West by $205 per household, and overall the 6.4 million difference in households (South is larger than West) results in $1.3 billion more being spent in the South than in the West on electricity.

Overall, substantial differences in consumption by region can be observed for most categories of expenditures. Per capita differences range from $27 for personal care to $82 for electricity. The natural gas differential is also large. Relatively small differences are evident for food away from home and alcoholic beverages. Coupled with data on population growth, these data indicate that spending on energy, exclusive of gasoline products, will grow even faster than population in the South and West when compared with the remaining two regions.

An examination of regional differences in projected aggregate consumption of food reveals that wide variation in increases and decreases occur. Between 1977–1978 and 2000, aggregate consumption loss is projected for the Northeast in the categories cereal and bakery (−22%), dairy products (−29%), pork (−9%), and poultry (−4%). On the other hand, substantial

Table 8.11
Regional Differences in Urban Household Consumer Expenditures: 1980–1981

	Northeast	Midwest[a]	South	West
Number of Households[b]	17.2	18.2	20.5	14.1
Household Size	2.6	2.7	2.5	2.5
Food at Home	$1925($740)[b]	$1826($676)	$1624($650)	$1749($700)
Food Away From Home	850(327)	818(303)	823(329)	898(359)
Alcoholic Beverages	287(110)	258(96)	228(91)	329(132)
Personal Care	190(73)	196(73)	201(80)	217(87)
Natural Gas	222(85)	305(113)	138(55)	172(69)
Electricity	406(156)	406(150)	509(204)	304(122)
Gasoline, Motor Oil, Additives	785(302)	945(350)	923(369)	884(354)

[a]Formerly North Central.
[b]In millions.
[c]Per capita figures in parentheses.

Source: Consumer Research Center. 1984. How Consumers Spend Their Money. New York: The Conference Board, Inc.

increases—greater than 80 percent—are projected for the South in the categories fresh fruits, beef, fish, and fats, and oils.[6]

A summary of the data from Tables 8.8 to 8.11 indicates that divisional increases in the number of employees for wholesale, retail, and service jobs as well as manufacturing establishments are larger in the South and West than in the remaining regions. Differences in consumer price indices and household expenditures, however, show no regional trend, indicating that the "favored status" of the South and West may be limited along certain dimensions.

WHAT IS IMPORTANT ABOUT THESE TRENDS?

While the data presented thus far illustrate the large differences in the geographic distribution and redistribution of people, businesses, and consumption patterns, the underlying value in the knowledge is in understanding how the overall business environment, and thus strategic planning, is affected by the changes. As evidenced by the data in Tables 8.10 and 8.11, measuring the business environment of census regions, divisions, or local areas can be complex because trends in population are not necessarily mirrored by patterns in other factors. The following discussion supplements the data already presented with information that shows more specifically how additional considerations may alter an owner's or manager's evaluation of a market area.

The population distribution data presented earlier take on additional meaning if compositional differentials are introduced. Differences in age, education, and income as well as other factors have all been shown to affect how customers behave in the marketplace. With regard to age, reasonably large regional, divisional, state, and local age differences demonstrate the wide range in market potential for specific goods and services. Focusing on the population at or above retirement age—the segment in greatest need of health care and general living assistance—large state and local area differences in the percentage of the total population that is 65 years of age and over indicate the range in demand for such services. At the state level, western states—particularly Alaska (3.1%), Utah (7.7%), and Wyoming (8.2%)—show the lowest concentration of older persons. On the other hand, Florida (17.6%), Rhode Island (14.3%), and Pennsylvania and Iowa (14.1% each) have the greatest market potential for geriatric services.[7] With regard to smaller markets, MSAs for example, even more variation is evident in the percentage of population age 65 and over. The largest markets are in West Palm Beach (23.3%), Daytona Beach and Fort Myers (22.3% each), Miami–Fort Lauderdale (22.0%), and Tampa–St. Petersburg (21.5%).[8]

Educational attainment, specifically the percentage of adults who have completed four years of college, has been linked to differences in product/service interest, media habits (for advertising), and method of purchase (cash versus credit card) among other factors. Large areal unit differences in the percentage of adults in this educational category exist. At the state level, Colorado (23.3%), Alaska (21.1%), and Connecticut (20.7%) demonstrate the highest concentration of college graduates while Arkansas (10.8%), Kentucky (11.1%), and Alabama (12.2%) have the lowest percentages.[9] MSA differentials are much larger, with Iowa City, Iowa (38.6%); Lawrence, Kansas (35.1%); and Columbia, Missouri (34.7%), having the highest percentages, and Altoona, Pennsylvania (8.1%); Cumberland, Maryland–West Virginia (8.7%); and Gadsden, Alabama (8.9%) having the lowest percentages.[10]

Income variation represents aggregate differences in purchasing ability. The range in interregional per capita income is about $900 between the Northeast ($5,992) and the South ($5,027). Divisional differences are somewhat larger, with the highest figure in New England ($6,099) and the lowest in the East South Central ($4,299). States show even greater variation—nearly $4,200 between Alaska ($8,023) and Mississippi ($3,827). Projections to the year 2000 show that these same patterns (region, division, and state) of difference continue.[11] The same per capita figures exhibit even a wider range when the focus is on the fifty largest cities in the United States—$12,116 for San Francisco and $7,018 in El Paso.[12]

In sum, while the population and the industry data imply that the markets in the Northeast and Midwest are shrinking and therefore are at risk, the compositional factors that are part of this last section provide qualifying information. For example, while it is true that the Northeast and its divisional components are experiencing slowing population and employment growth, the region also contains many of the areas of the United States with the highest education and income levels. Conversely, the South, with its higher population growth, also contains the areas with the lowest in education and income levels. So for certain goods and services, markets in the Northeast and Midwest are superior to those in the South and West. Though population growth and decline are important and determine compositional characteristics at a later time, they sometimes mask other interarea differences. The businessperson must decide which demographic dimensions are most salient to her or his business and then must evaluate alternative areas.

NOTES

1. U.S. Bureau of the Census. 1985. *Estimates of Households for States: 1981–1984.* Current Population Reports, Series P–25, No. 974. Washington, D.C.: U.S. Government Printing Office.

2. John D. Kasarda, Michael D. Irwin, and Holly L. Hughes. 1986. "The South Is Still Rising." *American Demographics* (June): 33–70.

3. Richard Alba and Michael Batutis. 1985. "Migration's Toll: Lessons from New York State." *American Demographics* (June): 38–42.

4. U.S. Bureau of the Census. 1986. *Statistical Abstract of the United States, 1986.* Washington, D.C.: U.S. Government Printing Office, table 14.

5. John D. Kasarda, Michael D. Irwin, and Holly L. Hughes. 1986. "The South Is Still Rising."

6. Patricia Guseman and Stephen Sapp. 1986. "Fords of the Future." *American Demographics* (April): 4.

7. U.S. Bureau of the Census. 1986. *Statistical Abstract of the United States, 1986,* table 29.

8. U.S. Bureau of the Census. 1986. *Statistical Abstract of the United States, 1986,* table 24.

9. U.S. Bureau of the Census. 1986. *Statistical Abstract of the United States, 1986,* table 217.

10. U.S. Bureau of the Census. 1986. *Statistical Abstract of the United States, 1986,* table 246.

11. U.S. Bureau of the Census. 1986. *Statistical Abstract of the United States, 1986,* table 736.

12. U.S. Bureau of the Census. 1986. *Statistical Abstract of the United States, 1986,* table 760.

9

Population Estimates and Projections

As reported in Chapter 2, population estimates and projections are synthetically produced data for demographic phenomena that are not directly measured. An *estimate* is a population total—perhaps dissaggregated into its age, race, and sex components—for a date that has already occurred after the most recent census. A *projection* concerns population totals, and possibly dissaggregated figures, for some date in the future. Population estimates and projections are derived through a combination of existing information (for example, the age, race, and sex structure of a population in the most recent census) and assumptions about population change since the last complete enumeration.

With regard to population estimates, it is most often the case that fewer assumptions are required because some actual data exist to determine the change in population between the last census and the estimate year. So, for example, if the goal is to estimate the population of the United States on July 1, 1987, the population enumerated on April 1, 1980 (census), becomes the base figure. To that base, births (birth registration data) between 1980 and 1987 are added, deaths (death registration data) subtracted, and net in- or out-migrants (legal immigrants added from Immigration and Naturalization Service records, emigrants, and illegal immigrants estimated) added or subtracted. In generating projections, heavy reliance on assumptions is necessary, though these assumptions are grounded in historical trends.

As the discussion in this chapter proceeds, recall that a population changes through births and in-migration additions and death and out-migration losses. The task of the demographer is to determine (actually measure, estimate, or project) the number of births, deaths, and in- and out-migrants between two time periods. Furthermore, methodologies have been developed to capture the joint effect of fertility, mortality, and migration.

While the demographer's task is usually centered on estimating and projecting populations and their component parts, estimating and projecting business-related phenomena is certainly not new to the business community. While the activities (sales or economic growth, for example) to be projected, in other words forecasted, are different, the same basic principles apply in that a good business or demographic forecast relies on sound historical data and a set of reasonable assumptions. It is not unusual for business forecasts to be grounded in part on demographic factors. Parker and Segura, for example, created an equation based on historical data that viewed sales as a function of population characteristics such as new marriages, new housing starts, and disposable income. The equation was then used to forecast sales for a year beyond the historical data base.[1]

Though the terms *projection* and *forecast* are frequently used interchangeably, there is, or at least should be, some difference in their use and meaning. Whereas a forecast is a best prediction of events likely to occur in the future, projections generally come in sets where the effect of varying assumptions on future demographic events can be seen. Because future events cannot be known, it is best to examine a range of possible population figures in order to better understand the variety of scenerios that could occur. For example, the Bureau of the Census produces thirty different population projections for the United States, each with a different set of assumptions with regard to future fertility, mortality, and immigration. Though it is typical to use one of these projections for planning purposes, good planners will also ascertain the effect of varied assumptions by examining alternative projections. Good business forecasters actually produce projection series because they begin with constant base figures and alter assumptions about future events in order to better understand a variety of planning scenerios.

In addition, population estimates and projections frequently serve as base figures for business forecasts in that incidence or prevalence rates are multiplied by population figures in order to generate data for planning purposes. That is, an estimated incidence rate (for example, the number of new cars purchased in a year per 10,000 population) can be multiplied by a population projection or forecast in order to predict future new car sales. A new car projection series can be generated by using different population projections for the base figures and/or altering the assumptions concerning the incidence rate. In this way, the effect of an increasing or decreasing demand for new cars can be examined jointly with the effect of varying population growth rates. Uses of incidence and prevalence rate-based projections are discussed more fully later in this chapter.

The value of strictly demographic estimates and projections should not be overlooked. Population estimates and projections provide a great deal of information about growing or declining market size. Recall, for example, the discussion in Chapter 7 about the changing age structure of the United States. The size of the population 20–24 years of age (for the middle series projection) is in the process of shrinking and is expected to decline by about 4 million persons by the year 2000. Therefore, unless incidence rates for the purchased goods and services specific to that population change, sales can be expected to decline. On the other hand, the rapid growth in the population age 65 and over (an increase of more than 6 million persons by the end of the century) brings with it a rapidly growing market for health care services most heavily concentrated in this age group.

Concerning products and services sold to broader age, sex, and race groupings, the assessment of the effect of changing structure becomes more complex. Given different incidence rates by age cohorts, the automobile example from above becomes somewhat more complicated as the impact of the growth and decline in the size of multiple age groupings is determined. If the incidence rate for 20-to-29-year-olds is 150 new cars purchased per 10,000 population each year and the incidence rate for 30-to-39-year-olds is 250, then even though the size of the population 20–39 may not change, a shift in concentration from one age group to another could significantly alter sales. For example, if a population contained 100,000 20-to-29-year-olds and 100,000 30-to-39-year-olds, 4,000 new car purchases could be expected. Expected car sales would be derived by the following simple formula:

$$\text{Expected new car sales (4,000)} =$$

$$\frac{150}{(10,000)} \times 100,000 + \frac{250}{(10,000)} \times 100,000.$$

However, if incidence rates remain constant (they probably will not and therefore should be adjusted) and the population 20–29 declines by 30,000 persons in the next 14 years while the population 30–39 increases by 30,000, then expected car sales would be:

$$\text{Expected new car sales (4,300)} =$$

$$\frac{150}{(10,000)} \times 70,000 + \frac{250}{(10,000)} \times 130,000.$$

The aggregated population size (200,000) would not have changed, yet expected sales would have increased by 300 cars, or about 7 percent.

Aside from providing information on total market and market-segment size, population estimates and projections also lend insight into other structural and cultural dimensions of the market. The expected aging of the population and increased minority representation in the marketplace brings about significant cultural changes that will most certainly alter aggregate spending behavior. Chapter 7 addresses differential consumption behavior by age, race, and ethnicity as well. A more middle-aged, less race/ethnicity majority-dominated population, such as that projected for the year 2000, will certainly exhibit different spending habits than the present population. Also, the U.S. population in the year 2000 will be 29 million persons larger than it is today.

Projections of other demographic phenomena are useful to business planners. The income projections that were introduced in Chapter 2 are useful in that they provide guidelines concerning consumers' ability to buy goods and services in the future. The labor force projections, also introduced in Chapter 2, allow personnel administrators to plan for the age-specific labor force shortages and gluts that will affect the selling, maintenance, and replacement of goods and services sold.

Before a discussion of various estimates and projections methodologies is initiated, two additional population estimates and projections issues should be presented. Many businesspersons are accustomed to making planning decisions based on short- and long-term forecasts without much attention being paid to alternative scenerios that might come about if the assumptions prove incorrect. The temptation with regard to population estimates and projections is the same. The tendency is to take a projection and treat it as a forecast without asking about what would happen if only two out of three or three out of five assumptions are met. The advice of this writer is to look at alternative projections and do not behave as if the middle series (Series 14) U.S. Bureau of the Census population projection, or any other middle series projection, is written in stone. It is not, and there is already evidence that the immigration component of the Series 14 projection is too low. If the focus of the projections is to determine the size of the market in several age groupings, then an assessment of the impact of lower or higher fertility, mortality, and/or immigration on those projections can be measured. The data user may in fact find that the range of lowest to highest in projections for particular age groups is relatively narrow, giving her or him confidence that the figures obtained reflect what will in fact occur. If the range is large, then looking at two or three most-likely-to-occur scenerios could narrow the range.

The second issue concerns the length of time for which projections are made. Many businesspersons make forecasts for only a few quarters ahead and so the issue of how far in the future to forecast never becomes important. However, other businesses and industries require longer range forecasting for planning purposes, and a question frequently arises with regard to how far in the future projections are "good." There is no one answer to the question and it must be emphasized that as projection years pass and estimates or actual enumerations of populations become available, the measurement of error, comparing projections with actual figures, should take place. The U.S. Bureau of the Census makes projections for up to 100 years, though many of the numbers only illustrate what would happen if certain combinations of fertility, mortality, and migration levels were attained. There is some evidence that population projections of up to twenty years are useful but that beyond twenty years the numbers lose their value quickly.[2] Furthermore, the work presently being done to attach confidence intervals to population projections is providing valuable information about the range of figures in which projections are likely to fall.[3] However, because confidence intervals must be constructed out of distribution errors that can only be assumed, there are limitations concerning this work.[4]

Data needed for generating population estimates and projections come from a variety of sources. Population-base data are available from census counts or special censuses that are sometimes conducted. If information on the components of change is required, birth, death, and immigration registration data can be obtained from registration systems. The population of older persons can be determined via social security records. The population of school-aged children can be estimated by examining school enrollment records and making assumptions about the proportion of persons in those age groups who are enrolled in school.

However, other surrogate measures for population totals are available. Knowing the number of occupied housing units and the average number of persons per unit (housing unit method of population estimation) yields a population estimate that reflects change resulting from the effects of all three components (births, deaths, and migrants). Data for determining the number of occupied housing units come from census enumeration baseline data and administrative records that contain information on new housing, demolitions of existing housing, and utility hook-ups which indicate whether or not a household is occupied. Estimates for the number of persons per household are derived from census counts and are updated by recent national-level data from the Current Population Survey.

Finally, both the U.S. Census Bureau and the Bureau of Economic Analysis produce population estimates and projections for the nation as well as smaller geographic areas. There are interagency differences in estimates and projections figures due to variations in methodologies and assumptions. Some users take an average of the two totals when applying the data, though in certain instances one number is better than another.

In this chapter the reader should first gain a basic understanding of how population estimates and projections are produced. Readers wishing to develop specific skills in these areas should consult other publications and/or consider attending any number of seminars conducted for training purposes.[5] The reason for describing the techniques utilized is to assist the reader in becoming a better consumer of these data. Second, understanding the techniques, data requirements, and underlying assumptions for any estimate or projection should allow the user to evaluate the quality, and therefore dependability, of the available figures.[6] Third, consumers who wish to purchase data from vendors should be in a better position to assess the accuracy of those data. Once the techniques are presented, general uses of population estimates and projections data are presented. Additional specific applications are also discussed in Chapters 11 and 12.

POPULATION ESTIMATES

Population estimates can be derived via a number of methodologies. Each method requires different data, various assumptions, and the users and producers of the estimates frequently must decide on the methods to be used based on the data that are available. As discussed earlier, some methods require data for each component of change (fertility, mortality, and migration), while others utilize surrogate measures that capture the effects of all three components at once. The simplest method uses only historical data on population counts. Population estimates, as mentioned in Chapter 2, are produced for the nation, states, counties, and local areas by various public and private organizations.

Mathematical Extrapolation

The simplest of estimation techniques is *mathematical extrapolation* because it requires only historical data for total population counts. If a demographer wishes, for example, to estimate the population of the United States for April 1, 1985, all that is required are the population figures for April 1, 1970 (next most recent census), and April 1980 (most recent census) *and* the assumption that the 1970–1980 growth rate remains constant from 1980 to 1985. Procedurally, the following steps are required to obtain an estimate:

1. Population on April 1, 1970 (next most recent census)   203,302,000
2. Population on April 1, 1980 (most recent census)   226,546,000
3. Ratio of (2) and (1)   1.1143
4. Natural log of line 3   0.1049
5. Average annual growth rate (line 4 ÷ 10)   0.0105
6. Years between most recent census and estimate years   5
7. Product of annual growth and years between most recent
   census and estimate year (line 5 × line 6)   .0525
8. Exponential for line 7   1.055
9. Population estimate (line 8 × line 2)   239,006,000.[7]

The baseline data for two time periods, the most recent and next most recent censuses, and a knowledge of how to manipulate natural logarithims are necessary to produce such an estimate.[8] More recent independent estimates of the U.S. population placed its size at 238,816,000 in 1985—within 200,000 persons of the estimate using mathematical extrapolation. The discrepancy, though very small, occurred because population growth rates declined in the 1980's, and applying 1970's growth rates to the 1980 population thereby overestimated the population. The basic procedure of mathematical extrapolation is quite simple and can be applied to virtually any area for which census data are available. The error rate, less than 1 percent for this example, can be small enough for most data users. Exceptionally high error rates can occur, especially in small area applications, and this technique should be used and evaluated with caution.

Vital and Migration Events/Rates Procedures

Another way to derive an April 1, 1985, population estimate for the United States is to begin with the April 1, 1980, population base and add the births and immigrants between 1980 and 1985 and subtract the deaths and emigrants for the same time interval. This method is called the *component method* because each of the components—fertility, mortality, and migration—is measured independently and then aggregated to derive an overall estimate. Immigration figures can be adjusted to reflect illegal immigrants, and emigrant figures have to be estimated. A major disadvantage of this procedure is that while it works well for national-level estimates, local-area estimation is sometimes problematic because in- and out-migration data are not available and must be estimated separately. Frequently, estimates of net migration are produced as residuals of the population equation after an independent estimate for the total population has been generated.

However, when requisite data are available, net migration can be estimated by comparing actual school enrollments with expected enrollments, with the difference being attributed to net migration. In other words, the population of children enrolled in school in the most recent census year is brought forward to the estimate year with allowances made for child mortality and dropping out. The number of grade/age–specific expected enrollments from bringing forward census year enrollment data is then compared with the actual grade/age enrollments measured in the estimate year, and the difference becomes the numerator for a grade/age–specific net migration rate. The denominator is the total enrollment in the base year for that grade/age. The grade/age–specific net migration rate is translated into a net migration rate for all ages by assuming that the ratio of the age/grade–specific net migration to the total net migration rate remains constant over time.

An alternative estimates procedure, utilizing birth and death data, relies on what has already been discussed about birth and death rates. As outlined in Chapters 3 and 4, birth and death rates (CBRs and CDRs) are derived in the following fashion:

$$CBR = \frac{\text{Births in year X}}{\text{Midyear population in year X,}} \quad \text{and}$$

$$CDR = \frac{\text{Deaths in year X}}{\text{Midyear population in year X.}}$$

If demographers assume that birth and death rates remain constant over a short period of time (a reasonable assumption in some instances), then knowing the number of births and/or deaths in a given year can allow them to produce a population estimate for that year. All that is required is to solve the equation for the midyear population in year X since everything else is known. At the subnational level it is possible to adjust birth and death rates up or down by assuming that the ratio of rates (local rate ÷ national rate), remains constant over time. While national-level birth and death rates are produced each year, local rates are not, and being able to account for rate changes at the local level is a real advantage.

Because the 1980 CBR and CDR are known along with the number of births and deaths in 1985, solving for the missing midyear U.S. population produces the desired population estimate:

The U.S. CBR for 1980 was $\dfrac{3,598,000}{226,546,000}$ = .01588, or 15.88 births per 1,000 persons.

The U.S. CDR for 1980 was $\dfrac{1,990,000}{226,546,000}$ = .00878, or 8.78 deaths per 1,000 persons.

Knowing that there were 3,709,000 births and 2,080,000 deaths in 1985 yields the following population estimates:

Birth-derived population estimate = $\dfrac{3,709,000}{.01588}$ = 233,564.000.

Death-derived population estimate = $\dfrac{2,080,000}{.00878}$ = 236,902,000.

Both of these estimates fall within about 3.5 million persons (about 1 percent of the independently derived estimate discussed earlier). Each estimate is low because the CBR and the CDR have increased somewhat since 1980.

The major advantage of this method is that it requires only six pieces of information, is easy to compute, and local-area estimating is possible to the extent that birth and death data are available. Furthermore, estimates for specific age intervals can be produced by utilizing age-specific birth or death rates and solving for the population denominators. A major disadvantage can be that in some local areas year-to-year fluctuations in births and deaths, brought about by yearly abberations or rapid increases or decreases in birth and death rates, can result in widely varying population estimates. Three-year averages of births and deaths can provide one solution to this problem, and adjusting for national-level trends accounts for overall change in fertility and mortality rates.

Housing Unit Method

The *housing unit method* of estimating population measures aggregated change resulting from fertility, mortality, and migration by taking advantage of a very simple relationship. Furthermore, the method can be used to produce small-area population estimates when fertility and mortality data are not available. The simple relationship is as follows:

Population estimate = Occupied housing units × Average number of persons per occupied housing unit.

The estimate must be adjusted for the number of persons living in group quarters, for example, nursing homes and army barracks; and the key is to determine both the number of occupied housing units and the average number of persons per unit for the estimate year. In 1985, there were 86.8 million households averaging 2.69 persons per housing unit. The product of the two figures, in addition to the approximately 5.5 million persons living in group quarters, makes up the roughly 239 million persons estimated in 1985.[9] The Current Population Survey (CPS) collects yearly data on the number of persons in group quarters, the number of occupied housing units, and the average number of persons per unit for the nation as a whole. Local-area data on the average number of persons per household are not available, but they can be estimated.

Local-area data for determining housing units, occupied housing units, and the average number of persons per unit are derived by combining census data, CPS figures, and administrative records. Administrative records include building permits, demolition records, certificates of occupancy, and utility connection data. First, however, the group quarters population must be known and this can be determined by conducting an actual census of institutions. This census is not difficult to conduct in many local areas due to the small number of group quarters that exist. Once the group quarters population is known, the number of housing units must be estimated. The number of housing units in the most recent census becomes the baseline figure and to it is added new housing units while at the same time demolished housing units are subtracted.

Procedurally, the estimated number of housing units is derived by the formula:

Estimated housing units = Housing unit count for most recent census

+ Number of residential certificates of occupancy issued since most recent census

− Number of residential demolition permits issued since the most recent census.

An alternative way to estimate housing units is to add or subtract the net change in metered housing units since the last census to the baseline housing unit figure. To estimate vacancy rates, the number of active residential meters is divided by the total number of meters (active + inactive) and adjustments made for meters that contain multiple housing units. The product of housing units and the vacancy rate yields the number of occupied housing units.

To generate an estimate of the average number of persons per occupied housing unit, the baseline figure from the most recent census is initially used. However, the rate is adjusted by assuming that national- or regional-level trends are mirrored at the local level (not always a good assumption). A ratio of rates is calculated for the most recent census (local-area rate ÷ national-level rate) and in the estimate year the local-area rate is adjusted by assuming that the ratio remains constant. Therefore, if the national-level persons per household declines 10 percent, the local-area figure is assumed to decline by the same proportion.[10]

Ratio Correlation (Regression)

In addition to the techniques discussed above, there is a procedure which in a modified form is often used to project population. The technique requires considerable data and additional skill in data manipulation. The *ratio correlation*, or *regression*, method of population estimation establishes an equation where the ratio of the population of a local area to a larger area (for example, a county population to a state population) is seen as a function of other symptomatic indicators also expressed as ratios of the local area to the larger area. Symptomatic variables can be actual events such as school enrollments, sales tax records, and voter registration. A ratio of ratios is established, generally taking the ratio of the most recent census population count (for example, county to state ratio) and dividing it by the ratio for the next most recent census, and the resulting figure is designated the dependent variable. The independent variables are the ratio of ratios of the symptomatic variables (again county to state ratio), dividing the ratio for the estimate year by the ratio for the most recent census. Regression coefficients are estimated over all local units, in this example counties, and are assumed to remain constant through the estimate year. The estimated population is the product of the predicted ratio times the proportion at the most recent census (reflecting change) times the total population (in this example, for the state) for the estimate year. In sum, an independently derived state estimate is disaggregated into county totals by multiplying it by various ratios—one for each county.[11]

Population Estimates—Summary

There are a wide range of population estimation techniques, each with its own data requirements and level of calculation complexity. No one method is best and the consumer of estimates data should understand the potential shortcomings of each method. For example, if the consumer knows that a component estimating procedure was used to derive a population estimate for a small area, and yet there really was no good way to estimate net migration (either data or procedural shortcomings), then the confidence placed in those estimates should not be very great. If, on the other hand, good data and sound techniques were utilized, then there is good reason for having confidence in the estimates. Again, this section has not been written to train the reader to generate population estimates. By presenting the various methodologies in modest detail, it is hoped that a better understanding *and* evaluation of the estimates will occur.

POPULATION PROJECTIONS

There is a certain degree of overlap in population estimates and projections methodologies. Recalling mathematical extrapolation, there is nothing to prevent a demographer from going beyond the estimate year to a projection year by assuming a continuous constant growth rate. Instead of assuming that 1970–1980 growth rates remain the same for the first five years of the 1980's decade, the rate could be applied for the entire ten years, producing a population projection for 1990. More sophisticated curve fitting techniques can be applied to a more extensive series of historical data. For example, census data for 1960, 1970, and 1980 can be combined with population estimates for 1965, 1975, and 1985 to construct a curve to project the population for 1990 and beyond. Once again, however, the assumption of constant growth, or even growth adjusted for other historical data points, can be a poor one, and this technique should be used with caution.

The data requirements for producing population projections are basically the same as those used for generating population estimates, though the administrative records needs are more limited because there are no analogous projection techniques to the housing unit method for population estimation. The general data needs are a population base by age, and perhaps race and sex, from the most recent census. Fertility, mortality, and migration/immigration data are also required, though once again surrogate measures for migration are required for subnational projections. Because assumptions must be made about future demographic events, a good set of historical data is quite helpful for making the most accurate projections of the components of population change.

Cohort Component Procedure

An extension of the component method for population estimation, the *cohort component procedure*, is one of the most frequently used techniques for projecting populations. While more detailed discussions of this technique appear in a variety of sources, a more general presentation of the procedures, assumptions, and data requirements will help the reader to understand how many national, state, and local population projections are produced.[12] A census-enumerated population, with its age, sex, and race structure, serves as the baseline data, and to that population fertility, mortality, and migration rates are applied until a projection for any given year is produced. Alternative projections—projection series—are generated by varying the assumptions with regard to fertility, mortality, and migration. Each age, sex, and race grouping (for example, black women aged 20–24) is treated separately, and all cohorts summed in order to produce a total projection. Each component—fertility, mortality, and migration—is allowed to vary independently of the other two components.

If the reader wished to produce a projection series for 1990 for the United States, the following general procedure would be followed. Starting with the April 1, 1980, population, or a more recent population estimate, the 1990 population would be a product of the base population, the addition of births, subtraction of deaths, and the addition or subtraction of net immigrants. However, since the desire is to retain the detail of the base population, age, sex, and race-specific change to fertility, mortality, and immigration must be accounted for.

The population already alive on April 1, 1980, can change only through mortality and migration. Therefore, the population aged ten years and above in 1990 is a product of the natural aging of the 1980 population and the accompanying mortality and net immigration or emigration. Each age, sex, and race cohort is carried forward ten years, either adding or subtracting the net difference between deaths and net migrants. But because the actual death and migration rates are unknown, assumptions with regard to both components be made. The population projection series for the United States produced by the U.S. Census Bureau has a low, middle, and high assumption with regard to mortality and immigration.[13] Since these projections are carried out to the year 2080, the mortality assumptions are in a sense prorated for intervals shorter than the roughly 100 years between the census and the projection year. The low, middle, and high mortality assumption are

translated into life expectancies (all races and both sexes) of 85.9, 81.0, and
77.4 years, respectively, in the year 2080. Low, middle, and high net immigration is 250,000, 450,000, and 750,000 net immigrants per year.
Concerning both mortality and immigration, each assumed figure must be
dissaggregated into its age-, sex-, and race-specific portions, that is, age-,
sex-, and race-specific mortality rates and numbers of net immigrants. The
population of black females aged 20–24 in 1990 (the earlier example re-
peated again) is then the sum of the survivors of the cohort 10–14 in 1980
based on assumed mortality rates plus or minus net migrants for the same
cohort over the ten-year period. An aggregation of all age, sex, and race
cohorts provides a total projected population ten years and over in 1990.

The population under 10 years of age in 1990 is the product of births
between 1980 and 1990, deaths to those births, and immigration. Therefore,
the younger age group must be projected separately. Mortality and net
immigration data for the under 10 years of age population are based on the
assumptions discussed in the previous paragraph. Fertility is projected independently, and the average numbers of lifetime births per women for the
low, middle, and high scenerios are 1.6, 1.9, and 2.3 births, respectively.
These data must also be disaggregated into their age and race components.

In all, there are twenty-seven possible combinations for the low, middle,
and high fertility, mortality, and immigration assumptions when aggregated
by sex and race, that is, projection totals without regard to sex and race.
These twenty-seven and an additional three, which assume zero net immigration, yield the thirty series of population projections produced by the U.S.
Bureau of the Census. In evaluating which series to rely on for strategic
planning purposes, each assumption should be carefully examined, and, once
again, strict reliance on the middle series (middle fertility, mortality, and
immigration) is not suggested. While middle fertility and mortality assumption seem "reasonable," recent net immigration totals have been in
excess of 450,000 persons yearly when immigrants and refugees are accounted for.

Ratio Techniques

Beyond extrapolation and component procedures comes a methodological
series called *ratio techniques*. These techniques begin simply by assuming
that the ratio of a local or regional population to a parent population (for
example, the total United States) remains constant over time. That is, if the
U.S. population (denominator of the ratio) increases 10 percent, so does the
local population (numerator of the ratio). While this can be a questionable
assumption, short-term projections based on constant ratios require little
data and may be "reasonable." Because U.S. projections are updated frequently, no new data for the local-area population are required.

A more sophisticated adaptation of this general principle does not assume constant ratios across time but fits a least-squares regression line (another type of curve may be fit) through the historical data, and the line is allowed to predict the ratio at some time in the future (the projection year). All that remains is to multiply the predicted ratio by the projected U.S. population and the local-area projection results. The amount of historical ratio data required varies, though data that go back too far in time can in fact bias ratio predictions because the most recent trends are not mirrored in the earlier information.

Additional Projections Techniques

Two other projections procedures less often used are economic-based and land-use methods. *Economic-based methods* attempt to tie population growth, particularly increases or decreases resulting from net migration, to economic activity.[14] Changes in an area's population are treated as a function of total employment, and total employment is regarded as a function of earnings. The major problem with the procedures is that before population projections can be generated, economic activity projections are needed. Instead of one set of assumptions attached to the projection activities, as is the case with other techniques, economic-based projections hold promise for improving projection accuracy, especially in regard to predicting net migration.

Land-use methods are particularly well suited to small-area projections such as census tracts. The major requirement is the knowledge of land use, including both the number of existing housing units and how many housing units the local area can reasonably support. Knowing that a local area has about as many housing units as it can be expected to have (maximum density) and having information on changes in the average number of persons per housing unit can help generate some relatively accurate short-run projections. However, the method relies on a great deal of qualitative analysis and is subject to errors regarding future land-use patterns. Changes in zoning ordinances or land use in small areas not completely built up can render the projections of little value.

Population Projections—Summary

Much like the procedures for estimating populations, techniques designed for population projections are varied. There are different data requirements and assumptions attached, so once again the reader is cautioned about both their use and their reliability. Projections series are important because they represent the various demographic scenerios possible given different sets of assumptions. Although one forecast must eventually be utilized for planning purposes, information on alternative demographic realities provides requisite background information on how strategies can and should be adjusted should the forecast be in error. Even for the small businessperson who does not have a great deal of time or the resources for evaluating data sources and considering alternative strategic plans, the population projections series generated by a host of federal, state, and local agencies oftentimes provide the data to be considered at little or no cost to the user. When data must be purchased, a quality evaluation of these data must take place.

BUSINESS USES OF POPULATION ESTIMATES AND PROJECTIONS: A FEW EXAMPLES

There are a host of business uses for population estimates and projections. The following paragraphs are intended to provide a few examples of some of those uses and readers should keep in mind their individual data requirements and planning needs as the uses are presented. Additional business application scenerios are presented in Chapters 11 and 12.

Many of the business needs for population estimates and projections are linked to what these data can tell the user not only about the growth of the national market but also about increases in regional and local markets. Project increases or decreases in persons of specific ages indicate potential growth or decline in a number of markets. Projections for total numbers are important as well. For example, MSA projections to the year 2000 show that of the ten metropolitan areas that will add the most population, nine are located in the South and West; six of those nine are located in California and Texas.[15] Because all markets are somehow linked to size, these areas would have to be regarded as prime prospects for almost all types of business growth, which for the reader is probably no surprise. Population projections for even smaller local areas, such as cities or counties, can also provide requisite planning information concerning overall market growth, and with the needed age, sex, and race detail, segments likely to grow the fastest can be identified.

Linking the growth in the population over age 65 to housing needs for the elderly (prevalence rates) has led some planners to forecast that in order to meet the demand for geriatric care one new 100-bed nursing home must open every day from now until the year 2000.[16] Seeing that this demand is not likely to be met, a series of "living at home projects" have been initiated which are designed to keep physically able older citizens living in relatively independent settings. The projects are targeted toward the 104 cities in the United States which have at least 10 percent of their total population age 65 and over.

In the area of health care, population estimates and projections are used to determine market penetration and to project demand for various types of services. For planning purposes, Baylor Hospital in Dallas, Texas, for example, multiplies detailed (age and sex) population projections by local-area medical incidence rates to generate "expected" cases of a variety of maladies requiring a host of treatment procedures.[17] Baptist Hospital in Memphis, Tennessee, uses detailed population projections in conjunction with other data to decide on additional hospital purchases.

Travelers Corporation has focused on the changing age structure (and projected age structure changes) to develop a job bank within its "Older American Program." While entry-level workers are expected to decline 16 percent by the end of the century, persons 65 and over should increase 28 percent. Travelers' job bank is intended to help solve the recruitment problems being experienced by some industries where there is already a shortage of workers at the lower levels. Older workers, who have different job requirements, provide a skilled labor force at less than the cost of agency temporaries.[18]

Also in regard to changes in the labor force, projected increases in female workers with young children are being linked to the growing need to provide child care services by some industries.[19] Changes in the age structure of the labor force, as stated above, are seen as presenting a serious problem in the recruiting and retention of workers as the end of this century is reached. On the other hand, the promotion squeeze being caused by the disproportionate number of workers in the 25–44 age group is, and will continue to, interrupt the upward management flow.[20] In order to counteract the negative effects of the squeeze—frustration, burnout, and low productivity—some industries are developing innovative ways of rewarding workers.

Finally, recent demographic and labor force shifts and projected population change have resulted in a new demographic segmentation of financial services.[21] Bank marketing programs are now being targeted to women, and the female market is regarded as having several distinct segments. Recent shifts and projected change in the age structure of the population have led to a targeting of middle- and older-aged individuals.

The estimates/projections use examples presented above demonstrate the variety of business uses that these data have. Once demographic data needs are determined by an organization, then the task is to determine if estimates and projections of those data are produced or can be generated. The most recent data (estimates) as well as future information (projections) are vital for the purpose of strategic planning for virtually all segments of a business.

NOTES

1. George C. Parker and Edilberto Segura. 1971. "How to Get a Better Forecast." *Harvard Business Review* (March-April): 99–109.

2. Nathan Keyfitz. 1981. "The Limits of Population Forecasting." *Population and Development Review* 7: 579–591.

3. See, for example, Michael Stoto. 1983. "The Accuracy of Population Projections." *Journal of the American Statistical Association* (March): 13–20; and

Thomas Espenshade and Jeffrey Tayman. 1982. "Confidence Intervals for Postcensal State Population Estimates." *Demography* 19: 191–210.

4. Stanley Smith. 1985. "Characteristics of Single Population Projection Techniques, with an Extension to the Construction of Confidence Intervals." Unpublished paper.

5. For example, Norfleet Rives and William Serow. 1984. *Introduction to Applied Demography*. Beverly Hills, California: Sage Publications, and seminars offered by American Demographics, Ithaca, New York.

6. See John Walker. 1980. "What Every Manager Should Know about Projections." *American Demographics* (January): 30–31, for useful comments about evaluating projections.

7. These steps are adapted from Norfleet Rives and William Serow. 1984. *Introduction to Applied Demography*, p. 43.

8. An even simpler way to arrive at an estimate would be to take the 1970–1980 growth rate (11 percent from line 2) and divide it by 2 (the interval for the estimate is only five years—one-half the 1970–1980 interval). This figure (5.5 percent) can be multiplied by 226,546,000 and that product added to the 1980 total. The resulting number (239,006,000) is the same as that seen in line 9.

9. Households and housing units are not one and the same, though they are used synonymously to simplify this example.

10. Greater detail for this procedure as well as several refinements can be found in Stanley Smith and Bart Lewis. 1980. "Some New Techniques for Applying the Housing Unit Method of Local Population Estimation." *Demography* 17: 323–339.

11. More extensive discussion regarding this method may be found in William O'Hare. 1976. "Report on a Multiple Regression Method for Making Population Estimates." *Demography* 13: 369–379; and Julia Martin and William Serow. 1978. "Estimating Demographic Characteristics Using the Ratio-Correlation Method." *Demography* 15: 223–233.

12. See, for example, Richard Irwin. 1977. *Guide for Local Area Population Projections*. Technical Paper No. 39. Washington, D.C.: U.S. Bureau of the Census; and U.S. Bureau of the Census. 1984. *Projections of the Population of the United States by Age, Sex and Race: 1983–2080*. Current Population Reports, Series P–25, No. 952. Washington, D.C.: U.S. Government Printing Office.

13. U.S. Bureau of the Census. 1984. *Projections of the Population of the United States by Age, Sex and Race: 1983–2080*, table 4.

14. Richard Irwin. 1977. *Guide for Local Area Population Projections* provides more details on these procedures.

15. Martin Holdrich. 1984. "Prospects for Metropolitan Growth." *American Demographics* (April): 33–37.

16. Brad Edmondson. 1986. "Foundations Level the Slippery Slope." *American Demographics* (January): 20–21.

17. John McWhorter. 1985. "Local Demographic Estimates: Small Is Beautiful." Paper presented at the annual meeting of the Southern Regional Demographic Group. Austin, Texas.

18. Brad Edmondson. 1986. "Travelers Hire the Un-Retired." *American Demographics* (June): 24.

19. Allyson Sherman Grossman. 1982. "More Than Half of All Children Have Working Mothers." *Monthly Labor Review* 105 (February); and Thomas-Pond Enterprises Staff. 1982. "Who's Watching the Children?" *Thomas-Pond Enterprises Human Resources Newsletter* (April).

20. Kenneth Shapiro. 1981. "Managing the Impending Promotion Squeeze." *Personnel Journal* (October): 800–804.

21. David Croisdale-Appleby. 1984. "Target Marketing of Financial Services." *The Banker* (April): 51–59.

10

Do Federal, State, and Local Population Policies Affect Business Conditions?

INTRODUCTION

Isolating and studying what has been labeled *population policy*—government actions intended to influence or control dimensions of population change—is more laborious than the reader initially might suspect. The difficulty results from the fact that almost all population policy in the United States is *not* specifically directed toward controlling or setting targets with regard to births, deaths, internal migrants, or other demographic phenomena. There are no designated national or regional goals concerning population size or growth rates, though some concern on the part of politicians, union leaders, and individuals regarding the pace of growth in some local areas has been expressed. With the exception of immigration law, numerical limits such as the urban one-child policy seen in China today have not been set. And even in the case of immigrants, the target numbers are only approximations due to year-to-year fluctuations resulting from special exemptions, changes in law, and the impact of refugees.

Nevertheless, immigration policy does determine one component of U.S. population growth as well as at least two dimensions of population composition: the racial/ethnic make-up and age structure. Without any restrictions on the number of immigrants, overall population growth would increase markedly, while a policy of completely closed borders, assuming that policy could ever be enforced, would guarantee a cessation of growth early in the next century. *Indirect policies*, those governmental actions that indirectly influence demographic factors such as fertility and mortality levels, potentially affect growth rates significantly. For example, a national policy such as the one currently being followed in the United States which places value on improved public health and establishes agencies like the National Institutes of Health and the Centers for Disease Control to improve health conditions, thus reducing mortality rates, has the indirect impact of increasing population growth rates, ceteris paribus. Other health policies that make birth control devices available at subsidized prices out of concern for the reduction of unwanted childbearing have the effect of lowering fertility levels and therefore growth rates.

Moreover, government policy in the areas of fertility and mortality and morbidity are responsible for government expenditures in the private sector for health-related goods and services. Policies that require the distribution of, for example, large numbers of contraceptives or a substantial volume of vaccine result in large private-sector purchases. Government-aided research in the areas of disease treatment frequently results in the marketing of, and therefore profit from, the introduction of new drug and surgical treatments for disease.

To the extent that direct and indirect population policies affect levels of fertility, mortality, migration, growth rates, composition, and distribution, they are at least in part responsible for conditions in the business environment. These policies affect the size, composition, and distribution of consumer segments as well as the demographic characteristics of the labor force serving consumers. They also set the stage for the future growth of customers and workers. Policy is also part of the political and social dimensions of the business environment and in some countries reflects national feelings about population growth. U.S. policy, along with proposed changes, concerning immigration (see Chapter 5) is in part an outgrowth of regional social and political forces that are demanding solutions to problems that have been associated with relatively large influxes of immigrant labor.

Population policy at the national level also determines our posture and financial assistance with regard to population growth and change in other nations. To the extent that policies are geared toward assisting less-developed nations in reducing levels of fertility and curbing high rates of population growth, monetary and advisory aid will be offered to support that policy. If that policy changes, then such aid may be withdrawn and/or concentrated in other areas of assistance.

The focus of the present chapter is on how both direct and indirect population policies are affecting demographic variables and therefore the business environment in the United States. Policies at the national, state, and local levels are examined for their commonalities and dissimilarities, and population policies from other nations are evaluated in regard to their implications for future domestic policy. That is, policies that are presently either in place or being proposed in the nations of Western and Eastern Europe, for example, may reflect the types of policies that will be discussed in the United States a short time in the future. European nations have been subject to a low-population-growth environment longer than the United States and much can be learned from their experiences. Specific policies, or lack of policy, regarding fertility, mortality and morbidity, migration, population distribution, and growth are discussed.[1] The link between demographic policy and variations in business policy are explored. Furthermore, the effects of business policy on demographic variables are considered.

FERTILITY, MORTALITY AND MORBIDITY, AND MIGRATION

Policies regarding fertility are indirect in that there are no national, regional, and local laws or legislative activities that set target fertility levels and establish the requisite infrastructures to meet those targets. However, political elements at the national and state levels are in place that indirectly affect fertility by working through the intermediate variables discussed in Chapter 3. Legislation with regard to contraception, marriage, and induced abortion can affect fertility levels even though the intent of the law is to accomplish something quite different. For example, state laws that establish a minimum age at marriage under which parental consent must be given in order to protect minors from their inexperience can reduce fertility levels by limiting to some extent exposure to intercourse.[2] However, recent data on teenage sexual activity show that these laws are no longer a major deterrent to such activity. Nevertheless, for most teens, births out of wedlock are not a desired outcome. With regard to contraception, newly passed national and state laws reducing funding for subsidized contraceptives and contraceptive counseling may have the effect of increasing fertility, though the long-term impact of such legislation is unknown. Induced abortion law provides perhaps the best illustration of the effect of law, and court rulings, on fertility potential. Complete elimination of induced abortion on demand, as discussed in Chapter 3, *could* result in more than 1 million additional births per year in the United States! Of course, this unrealistically assumes that illegal abortions would not be sought out and that contraceptive use behavior would not change. The point to be made is that legislation, court decisions, and ongoing policy with regard to the intermediate variables—factors relating to exposure to intercourse, conception, and pregnancy outcomes—affect fertility levels.

Mortality and morbidity policies are more direct than those for fertility in that the funding of health centers and the sponsoring of health-related research has the goal of reducing levels of sickness and death. The population in general benefits by the dollars spent, and population growth rates are increased due to the reduction in mortality. However, there are no government targets with regard to what life expectancy should be five or ten years from now, for example, and certainly no national goal to increase population growth at the present time. There is little general concern over tax dollars being spent on health care in general (there is great concern over the amount spent), though disagreements do arise when priorities must be established regarding on what health issues to spend money (for example, AIDS versus cancer research).

Almost all of the issues having some legal significance occur in the area of artificial life support to physically impaired children and adults, through these cases are too few in number to significantly influence mortality levels and growth rates. As the population of the United States ages, this issue is likely to be debated at even greater lengths.

Immigration and migration policies, as stated earlier, have the most visible direct impact on population size and growth. Nevertheless, even though immigration law sets total and country-specific limits on the number of persons who can legally move to the United States, public concern over population size and growth is implicit at best. While concern for growth rates, and particularly the source of growth, has been on the mind of many of the legislators who have proposed and voted for laws establishing quotas, the laws themselves do not speak to the issues of total population size and growth rates in the United States.

At the state and local levels, the intent of migration policy has been different in that some states and communities have tried to restrict movement to their localities, wishing to limit the movement of certain types of people and to control growth. States and localities have also had more at stake regarding immigration quotas, given that immigrant settlement patterns tend to be highly concentrated.

State laws that have attempted either to tax commercial carriers crossing state lines or to bring criminal penalties for transporting indigent people into a state have been ruled unconstitutional. On the other hand, local indirect restrictions on population growth have been ruled constitutional if they promote the general welfare of the resident population and do not represent an unreasonable restraint on ownership of private property. For example, immigration to a given community may be limited by reducing local building permits if it can be demonstrated that the population increase resulting from such construction would overtax services such as the ability to provide public school education.[3] While this area of the law is relatively new and additional migration-restriction legislation is certain to be written and tested in court, the effect on growth has only been realized in a relatively small number of communities. Nevertheless, the number of communities that have success-fully defended their growth-limiting legislation in the courts could well increase in the future. Businesspersons either operating in such communities or considering expansion into these places, or whose present community is or may be considering some types of restrictions, may wish to assess the potential impact of such laws on the business environment.

POPULATION POLICY IN OTHER NATIONS

While population policy in the United States is best described as nondirective, policies in other nations not only spell out goals but create the infrastructures to achieve those goals. Policy goals, and the means for attaining those goals, are quite clear in China, for example. Given the national aim of a population that numbers no more than 1.2 billion in the year 2000, policies at the province level have been instituted in order to attain this goal. Though there are interprovince policy differences, among the factors addressed in urban area policies is the advocation of a later age at marriage (24 years of age and older), and a one-child-per-couple fertility preference. Rewards for later age at marriage and reduced fertility include maternity leaves, monthly health subsidies for only children, work points or cash equivalents, and priority for housing. Disincentives or punishments for women either pregnant with second children or who have a second child include among others a substantial reduction in wages and the removal of an opportunity to obtain additional housing.[4] Though Chinese policy may be interpreted as extreme with regard to punishment, it does illustrate how a country whose population and growth rate is seen by policymakers to be too large may approach the problem. Furthermore, to the extent that the policy is successful, demographic factors such as fertility levels, growth, and population composition may be affected, thus altering the business environment. China as a market is discussed in more detail in Chapter 13, where international issues are treated.

While policies designed to reduce growth rates represent one end of the policy spectrum, policies that encourage growth are becoming more prevalent in the world today. Nations that are either in the development stages of such policies or that have actually instituted growth encouraging laws generally have two characteristics in common: (1) low growth rates that are projected to remain low and to turn negative in the relatively near future and (2) a concern over internal and international strength and thus fear of declining influence in world affairs. Since the United States has more in common with these nations than with those attempting to decrease growth rates, much may be learned from their policies.

Some European nations have expressed concern over low population growth rates since the 1960's, though the first indications of worry were voiced during the nineteenth century. For example, France's defeat by Germany in the war of 1870–1871 was seen by some of the French citizenry to be the result of low population growth and the price for practicing contraception.[5] By early in this century the French army drew from a substantially smaller pool of males than did the Germans, and defeats during World War I were blamed on this fact. During the Great Depression many European and non-European nations—the United States as well—became concerned with low rates of population growth, a stagnation in labor productivity, and a reduction in product demand.

The post–World War II baby boom and rebuilding era ended those fears for some time, though the boom lasted for a considerably shorter period of time in most countries than it did in the United States. By the mid–1960's, nations such as Romania were radically changing population policy to a strong pro-natalist stance, and laws were being passed making induced abortions illegal and contraceptives much harder to obtain. Mothers and prospective mothers were offered rewards for larger families.[6]

Other nations have initiated pro-natalist policies. Fertility inducements—increased family salaries as a reward for increased childbearing—were introduced in East Germany in the mid–1970's and continue today.[7] In Hungary, women currently receive a cash allowance for each child, paid leaves from employment lasting five months following childbirth, and food and clothing grants, among other benefits designed to increase fertility levels.[8] In recent years, French leaders have been nearly unanimous in publicly deploring continued low growth and fearful of the effects of eventual population decline.[9] They have been most adamant in calling for state intervention. Some have labeled contraception and abortion the white plague, with the declining birth rate seen as a cancer and a death wish. As a response, government intervention has resulted in cash rewards given to couples who have a third child.

Calls for an increase in fertility and growth rates are sometimes difficult to comprehend in a world whose population rhetoric in recent years has been filled with fears of a population bomb or population explosion. However, in already slow-growing nations that are experiencing total fertility rates far below replacement and whose immigration totals are relatively small, the prospects for population decline are quite real. And given the continued feeling that slow growth or loss carries with it a less rigorous, move conservative, less powerful population implication for many leaders, it is not surprising that government efforts to increase fertility and growth rates would emerge. Recent data show that of the 171 nations in the world that the Population Reference Bureau Inc. maintains and publishes data on, 22 (about 13 percent) regard their population growth as too small. In Europe, nine of twenty-seven nations (33 percent) report population growth as being too low.[10]

Questions needing answers include Do government efforts work in increasing population growth rates? and Is zero or slightly negative population growth really that bad? These questions are asked because the United States is moving toward the European scenerio—zero population growth is on the horizon—and it may not be long before political leaders begin to call for efforts to increase fertility rates. If the proposed policies are implemented and are successful in increasing fertility levels, then there are obvious implications for the business environment. That is, the business climate will be one of an increasing number of consumers overall along with a younger age structure of those buyers. If proposed policies are not initiated or they do not work, then a different business milieu will evolve. Growth will cease and the consumer population will age. Both scenarios are worthy of consideration.

ARE POLICIES INTENDED TO SPUR POPULATION GROWTH LIKELY TO BE SUCCESSFUL?

While the policy of ending immigration restrictions would certainly result in a substantial increase in the flow of people into the United States, this policy is not likely to soon be enacted. However, the volume may be increased over time, though calls for greater control of who immigrates to the United States would certainly be heard.

The policies designed to increase fertility levels that are most likely to be adopted would be like those already in place in some European nations. Have these policies worked? The answer is unclear, though the evidence points toward less success than desired. Romania has one of the longer histories of a basic pro-natalist policy complete with birth premiums, the reduction of income taxes for those families having more children, and the banning of abortions. For the first few years after the institution of what some would regard as rather draconian measures, fertility levels rose—and alarmingly from the standpoint that the demand for public services for these births exceeded the supply. For example, the total fertility rate increased from 1.8 to 3.7 between 1966 and 1967, a more than 100 percent rise. As these children became older, classroom space and other services were also inadequate. However, over the long run—twenty years and beyond—fertility rates are slowly returning to their pre–1966 levels, though they are still higher (a TFR of 2.2 in 1984) than they were earlier. Once fertility rates are low, it may be exceedingly difficult to convince women to have more children, simply because a new value system concerning the utility of children may emerge. More recent evidence with regard to birth premiums in East Germany suggests that though a small rise in the total fertility rate might be expected, the increase may not be nearly large enough to boost the TFR to replacement level. While there are additional data to be gathered and other fertility inducements are certain to be set into place, at this time it appears that such attempts will not succeed in maintaining sufficiently high birth rates over the long run. Perhaps a combination of fertility inducements and increases in immigration would be able to sustain small rates of growth.

If fertility and population growth are likely to remain low, then a discussion of the impact of low growth on the economy and the remainder of the business environment is certainly in order. As was discussed earlier, low growth has been seen as problematic in a number of nations at various points in history. During the Great Depression, Keynes discussed the low fertility/low growth of the day in terms of a stagnation thesis, arguing in general that population growth was requisite to a healthy economy.[11] Other economists and politicians feel that way today in spite of a great deal of evidence to the contrary.

THE EFFECTS OF SUSTAINED LOW GROWTH ON THE
BUSINESS ENVIRONMENT

Beyond a leveling off of the size of the population, the clearest effect that sustained low growth has on the business environment concerns the changing age structure and a concomitant shift in the demand structure for goods and services. Given the present trend toward an older age structure of the United States, the demand of products specific to younger persons will decrease while that for older persons will increase, all other factors being equal. However, several exceedingly important factors do not remain equal in this kind of shift, with the most important being the rapid increase in the number and proportion of total persons who are in their most economically productive years. The baby boom cohort, approximately 22–40 years of age in 1986, is just entering its most productive years in terms of highest income and lowest unemployment, though the youngest members of the cohort are still some time from maximum economic output. Given that the cohorts older than the baby boomers are much smaller, the ranks of the relatively well-off should increase markedly over the next several years, though increases in female labor force participation could reduce the drop in unemployed persons. Households and families should also have greater discretionary income due in part to a smaller number of child dependents. Overall, expenditures in a host of goods and services categories should increase substantially simply due to the increasing proportion of the total population that is at these productive ages. In the long run, the benefit of having large cohorts entering low-unemployment, high-income ages is lost as age cohorts become similar in size.

Another dimension of the changing age structure concerns the relative increase in older and decrease in younger members of society. While the total dependency ratio—the number of persons under age 18 and age 65 and over divided by the remaining population—should remain basically unchanged over the next several decades, the aged dependency ratio will increase as the youth dependency ratio decreases. There are potentially positive and negative aspects to these changes. Initially, a decreasing youth dependency ratio carries with it a decrease in demand for youth-related services (for example, education) and perhaps a relative decrease in public and private expenditures in these areas. On the other hand, the increase in the aged dependency ratio means a relative increase in expenditures on older persons, and to the extent that the aged are more expensive than the young, perhaps an overall increase in spending will result. Furthermore, as the smaller cohorts age and begin to enter the labor force, shortages in the labor supply for certain occupations could occur as a result of the shrinking labor pool, though further increases in female labor force participation and selecting labor force participants from older ages could easily offset the loss. Overall, younger persons are likely to experience less unemployment and higher wages due to their relative scarcity. Without question, all of these scenarios would change in the event of a long-term marked acceleration or deceleration in the economy, situations that are impossible for anyone to predict.

There are two additional factors accompanying slow or zero population growth that should be considered. The first concerns aggregate investment demand, which many studies have shown is likely to be smaller in an older population.[12] Reduced investment demand has overall implications for economic growth and job generation, though it does not necessarily imply a reduction in per capita incomes. Second, a low-growth scenario may have severe repercussions for small communities, due to the substantial loss in population and economic opportunities that might occur.[13] However, the negative impact of differential growth rates for different communities nationwide has been felt during periods of greater growth.

Overall, slowing growth and the transition to zero population growth brings changes in the economic environment, though few, if any, of the changes are completely negative. New business opportunities are being created, and at the same time the demand for some products and services is declining. The combined efforts of state and federal governments, along with activities in the private sector, are required to make the transition to low growth easier. Even if birth incentive legislation is enacted and yearly immigration quotas increased, it is unlikely that growth would return to anywhere near pre–1980's levels. Therefore, it is more of a question of how adjustments will be made than if changes are needed.

Given the data from other nations that indicate that birth incentive measures can bring about small but measurable increases in fertility rates, the issues regarding the role of business in formulating population policy require some discussion. The best example of the impact that the business community can have on demographic policy concerns immigration. Though there continues to be debate with regard to the impact and the enforcement of the immigration reform measures of 1986, there is no doubt that many members of the business community lobbied quite hard on this matter. At a later point in time, segments of the business community may become involved in legislative efforts targeted toward the increase of fertility rates, though other groups may oppose such measures.

Equally important, however, is the potential impact of business policy on demographic elements. There are private-sector business policies that are inherently pro-natalist or anti-natalist. Any policy that makes it easier for women and men to combine childbearing and child raising with work is going to be pro-natalist to some extent. Examples of such polices include relatively liberal leaves of absence with no penalty and work site day care for children. These are an integral part of governmental and private efforts in European countries.

In general, population policy can and does affect the business environment, though the degree of impact is sometimes difficult to measure. Business planners would be wise to consider both the short- and long-run business environment implications of any proposed legislation, understanding at the same time the limits to the potential effect of such laws. Businesses in smaller communities are likely to be most affected by policies or lack of policies in that it is these places where business climates are most sensitive to short-run shifts in population variables, particularly migration patterns. Over the long run, the entire nation is certain to be affected by population policy.

NOTES

1. An excellent presentation with regard to the law and population can be found in Larry D. Barnett and Emily F. Reed. 1985. *Law, Society, and Population: Issues in a New Field*. Houston, Texas: Cap and Gown Press.

2. Larry D. Barnett and Emily F. Reed. 1985. *Law, Society, and Population: Issues in a New Field*, pp. 21–27.

3. Larry D. Barnett and Emily F. Reed. 1985. *Law, Society, and Population: Issues in a New Field*, pp. 100–110.

4. Population and Development Review Staff. 1983. "On Province-Level Fertility Policy in China." *Population and Development Review* 9 (September): 553–561.

5. Michael S. Teitelbaum and Jay M. Winter. 1985. *The Fear of Population Decline*. New York: Academic Press, p. 19.

6. The Population Council Staff. 1971. *Abortion Legislation: The Romanian Experience*. Studies in Family Planning Volume 2, Number 10 (October). New York: The Population Council; and Margaret Roberts (trans.). 1984. "Romanian Population Policy." *Population and Development Review* 10 (September): 570–573.

7. Daniel Vining, Jr. 1984. "Family Salaries and the East German Birth Rate." *Population and Development Review* 19 (December): 693–696.

8. Michael S. Teitelbaum and Jay M. Winter. 1985. *The Fear of Population Decline*, p. 148.

9. Michael S. Teitelbaum and Jay S. Winter. 1985. *The Fear of Population Decline*, p. 120.

10. Mary Mederios Kent and Carl Haub. 1984. *World Population Data Sheet*. Washington, D.C.: Population Reference Bureau.

11. John M. Keynes. 1937. "The Economic Consequences of a Declining Population." *Eugenics Review* 29: 13–17.

12. Larry Neal. 1978. "Is Secular Stagnation Just around the Corner? A Survey of the Influences of Slowing Population Growth upon Investment Demand." Pp. 101–125 in Thomas J. Espenshade and William J. Serow (eds), *The Economic Consequences of Slowing Population Growth*. New York: Academic Press.

13. Peter A. Morrison. 1978. "Emerging Public Concerns over U.S. Population Movement in an Era of Slowing Growth." Pp. 225–246 in Thomas J. Espenshade and William J. Serow (eds.), *The Economic Consequences of Slowing Population Growth*.

11

How Demographic Information and the Demographic Perspective Are Used: Large Businesses and Other Organizations

As was demonstrated earlier, the U.S. population has changed considerably over the past 200 years. From a loosely organized nation of thirteen states with fewer than 4 million people in 1790 to a fifty-state superpower of more than 240 million persons in 1987, continued population growth has been the rule. However, recent years have been marked by slowing population growth, and the not-too-distant future seems to contain a point at which growth will end altogether. At the same time, demographic thinking has begun to enter organizational planning as population trends, particularly slowing growth and an aging demographic structure, have been linked to the well-being of businesses. In an organizational environment where constant and substantial population-driven market growth can no longer be assumed, planning, which includes among other things an understanding of how and why population change is occurring as well as the effects on the business environment, is essential if an organization is to survive.

The demographic–business environment connection has been shown in a variety of contexts. Demographic estimates and projections, for example, have been linked to merchandise sales, market projections in metropolitan areas, newspaper markets, television markets, and zip code markets through buying power indices constructed annually by *Sales and Marketing Management* magazine.[1] These indices reflect the purchasing potential of a variety of market segments (for example, geographic and compositional) and in turn the data are used for planning by a number of large and small businesses.

Preceding a discussion on how businesses use demographic data and analysis, a few additional indicators of population change are discussed in order to provide a context for the examples that follow.

CHANGES IN POPULATION SIZE AND HOUSEHOLD/FAMILY COMPOSITION

More detailed data on the slowing of population growth and, more importantly, on how the age structure of the United States is changing, is offered in Table 11.1. Using the middle series population projections discussed in Chapter 9, the table shows the expected size and age structure of the U.S. population at five-year intervals from now until the end of the century. While the overall population may well increase to nearly 268 million by the year 2000, the 14 percent projected population increase over a seventeen-year period is less than that experienced in the entire 1970's. Furthermore, substantial age structure shifts are likely to occur. For example, all of the age groups from 35 to 54 are projected to grow by at least one-third as the large baby boom cohorts become older. Significant growth is also projected for ages 75 and over, who in the year 2000 will number more than 17 million persons. On the other hand, growth for individual age groups under 35 will be either slow or negative. Aggregated, the age groups under age 35 will shrink from 133 to 128 million over the seventeen-year period—a decrease of 4 percent. Without question, businesses sensitive to slow growth and marked shifts in the age structure (which businesses are not sensitive?) are being affected by these trends.

Shifts in size and age structure are but a part of the changing demographic environment. Modifications in the way people live, with whom they live, and in family structure are equally important to organizations concerned with success. While the total population is expected to grow 14 percent between 1983 and 2000, the number of households could well grow nearly 17 percent just between 1985 and 1995.[2] The greater increase in households is the result of continued population growth along with decreases in average household and family size. As discussed in Chapter 7, trends in population composition indicate there has been a large decrease in household and family size over the last thirty-five years. As a point of reference, the overall population increased 53 percent over the same time period.[3] From 1950 to 1985, the average household size declined over .7 persons, or 20 percent. Family size shrank over .3 persons, or about 9 percent. Further average size reductions are likely, and by as early as 1990 households may well average only about 2.5 persons.[4]

A closer look at specific types of households as seen in Table 11.2 shows the remarkable growth in single-person households over the last thirty years. From fewer than 4 million households in 1950—less than 10 percent of all households—single-person households have increased to nearly 21 million,

Table 11.1

Projections of the Population by Age for the United States: 1983–2000

Series 14—Middle Series

Age	1983	1985	1990	1995	2000	% Change (1983-2000)
< 5	17,846[a]	18,453	19,198	18,615	17,626	- 1.2%
5-9	15,960	16,611	18,591	19,337	18,758	17.5
10-14	17,766	16,797	16,793	18,772	19,519	9.9
15-19	19,180	18,416	16,968	16,968	18,943	- 1.2
20-24	21,871	21,301	18,580	17,142	17,145	-21.6
25-29	21,170	21,838	21,522	18,822	17,396	-17.8
30-34	19,070	19,950	22,007	21,698	19,019	- 0.3
35-39	16,278	17,894	20,001	22,052	21,753	33.6
40-44	13,171	14,110	17,846	19,945	21,990	67.0
45-49	11,175	11,647	13,980	17,678	19,763	76.9
50-54	11,144	10,817	11,422	13,719	17,356	55.7
55-59	11,463	11,245	10,433	11,040	13,280	15.9
60-64	10,734	10,943	10,618	9,883	10,483	- 2.4
65-69	9,005	9,214	9,996	9,736	9,096	1.0
70-74	7,352	7,641	8,039	8,767	8,581	16.7
75-79	5,263	5,556	6,260	6,640	7,295	38.6
80-84	3,264	3,501	4,089	4,671	5,023	53.9
85+	2,512	2,697	3,313	4,074	4,906	96.1
Total	234,223	238,631	249,657	259,559	267,955	14.4

[a]Numbers in 1,000s.

Source: U.S. Bureau of the Census. 1984. Projections of the Population of
the United States by Age, Sex, and Race: 1983-2080. Current
Population Reports, Series P-25, No. 952. Washington, D.C.:
U.S. Government Printing Office, table 6.

a rise of over 400 percent. At the same time, the total number of households increased by less than 200 percent. By 1985, more than one-fifth of all U.S. households were single-person households.

Table 11.3 presents data on the number of households, what percentage were family households, and the composition of family households from

Table 11.2
Percent Single-Person Households: 1950–1986

	Single-Person Households	Percent of Total Households
1985	20,602[a]	23.7
1980	18,296	22.7
1975	13,939	19.6
1970	10,851	17.1
1960	6,896	13.1
1950	3,954	9.1

[a]Numbers in 1,000s.

Source: U.S. Bureau of the Census. 1986. Statistical Abstract of the United States, 1986. Washington, D.C.: U.S. Government Printing Office, table 54.

Table 11.3
Percent Distribution of Family Households by Type: 1950–1984

	1950	1955	1960	1965	1970	1975	1980	1984
Households	43,554[a]	47,874	52,799	57,436	63,401	71,120	80,776	85,407
% Families	90.2	87.6	85.4	83.5	81.4	78.3	73.7	72.6
% Married Couples	87.6	86.7	87.2	87.1	86.8	84.3	82.5	80.8
% Male Households[b]	3.0	3.2	2.8	2.5	2.8	2.7	2.9	3.3
% Female Households[b]	9.4	10.1	10.0	10.5	10.8	13.0	14.6	15.9

[a]Numbers in 1,000s.

[b]No spouse present.

Source: U.S. Bureau of the Census. 1986. Statistical Abstract of the United States, 1986, table 54; U.S. Bureau of the Census. 1980. Statistical Abstract of the United States, 1980, table 62.

1950 to 1984. A significant decline in the percentage of all households that were made up of families (17 percent) occurred over the nearly thirty-five year period. The last three rows of the table—percent married couples, percent male households, and percent female households—are subcategories of families. In other words, the figure for married couples in 1984 means that 80.3 percent of all families were married-couple families. Male-headed (female absent) made up 3.6 percent of all families and female-headed (male absent) made up 16.1 percent of the total families. As can be observed, a decrease from 88 to 80 in the percentage of all families who were married-couple families occurred between 1950 and 1984. The largest increase (about 7 percent) in family type was among female-headed, spouse-absent families, and in 1984 over 16 percent of all families were categorized this way.

In sum, demographic change that has occurred over the last thirty years affecting business environments include significant shifts in the age structure, decreases in average household and family size, a remarkable increase in single-person households, a decrease in married-family households, and an increase in female-headed, spouse-absent families. As the next section on business uses of demographic data and the demographic perspective unfolds, the reader should keep in mind not only these trends but also the discussions in Chapters 1 and 3 on decreasing fertility, increasing female labor force participation, and increasing numbers of persons remaining unmarried. Together these factors help form the demographic environment of the 1980's.

INDIVIDUAL BUSINESS APPLICATIONS

Levi Strauss

Levi Strauss has identified the demographic trends discussed above, particulary those involving changes in the age structure and a move toward smaller households and families.[5] As a result, Levi Strauss had adjusted its product line as well as marketing strategies in order to better compete in a changing demographic environment. One example, briefly discussed in Chapter 1, of a product adjustment (significantly altered product) made famous in their advertisements is traditional Levi's bluejeans with a "skosh" more room created for the aging baby boomer who has put on a few pounds. Levi Strauss has also responded to the increase in female labor force participants, particularly women who are in professional occupations, by offering a line of clothing called "career apparel" by Levi and Koret. At the same time, however, Levi Strauss realizes that many women are employed in blue collar occupations and so they continue to emphasize the quality and durability of traditional Levi products.

Levi Strauss is also planning for its marketing of the late 1980's and

1990's. While a decline in the population under 35 is projected between now and the year 2000, at the younger ages, those less than 14, the trend will be toward an increase in numbers (see Table 11.1). And as Levi Strauss executives have noted, there will be more 14-to-24-year-olds in 1990 than there were in 1970, and 1970 was a very good year for blue jeans sales. In sum, Levi Strauss uses demographic data to identify existing and projected markets, and with this information has adjusted product lines and marketing strategies in order to remain competitive in the apparel industry.

Dow Jones

Dow Jones, publisher of the *Wall Street Journal*, utilizes demographic information as well.[6] The *Journal*, as most businesspersons know, has experienced tremendous growth in circulation and advertising revenue in recent times. From the end of World War II to 1983, circulation increased from 76,000 to around 2 million newspapers per day. Between 1979 and 1983 alone, circulation and advertising revenue increased 34 and 170 percent, respectively. However, in 1979 the *Wall Street Journal* turned to demographic research to address such questions as Could they expect to continue to grow as fast as they were? and Who were their readers?

In general, the *Journal* has identified eight markets based on demographic and lifestyle characteristics. The nondemographic characteristics most useful in defining *Journal* markets are individual employment income, size of company employed by, job title, ownership of securities, and attitudes with regard to buying power. Demographic concerns for these markets are in regard to the present and projected sizes of the markets. Utilizing internal data gathered on current and past readers, customer profiles have been generated. Using these profiles, a circulation campaign strategy has been developed focusing on paid print, direct mail, and per inquiry television. Furthermore, the *Journal* is making circulation projections by linking the demographic characteristics of its current readers with independent projections of population income and households. The circulation projections are optimistic because at least throughout the remainder of this decade there will be a rising proportion of persons in the *Journal*'s prime markets. Finally, the *Journal* is presently conducting reader surveys every two years. With the demographic, psychographic, and other data gathered from the surveys, advertisers can identify in great detail markets they wish to target through the *Journal*.

Time Incorporated

Time Incorprated, publishers of the magazines *Time, Fortune, Sports Ilustrated, Money,* and *People,* has linked demographic characteristics to media consumption in order to better understand circulation growth/decline.

Moreover, Time has used these data to improve strategic planning.[7] Time has found that in general aggregate circulation growth closely parallels fluctuations in the adult population. However, an analysis of the performance of individual magazines suggests that a much more complex relationship between circulation and population growth exists. Media trends also reflect changes in household and family demography. For example, as the proportion of all households that were "traditional" husband-wife-children families began to decline in the 1960's, some magazines such as *Fortune* began to do better (special-interest publications) while others such as *Life, Look,* and *Saturday Evening Post* (the more general-interest magazines) folded altogether. Linked specifically to demographic change, several children's magazines failed during the 1970's as the number of 5-to-13-year-olds declined.

In addition, Time has identified the readership characteristics of its own individual magazine consumers, and examining demographic projections has developed a general outlook for each publication. For example, *Fortune* magazine has a customer age profile that peaks in the 35-to-44-year-old range and is therefore positioned to take advantage of changes in age structure presently occurring (see Table 11.1 again). *Time* has a very broad age appeal, with some concentration in the 35–44 interval, and it too should fare well. On the other hand, *Sports Illustrated*'s readership is skewed toward the young and the approaching declines in those ages could pose a threat to the magazine.

Time also uses geographic/demographic analysis to improve responses to direct mail solicitations. Mailing lists are screened for addresses with a low probability of response, and the refined lists result in a substantial savings to the company. Finally, Time has been developing an on-line data base of international demographic information with an eye toward the development of international markets. While the use of the data has been limited so far, long-term plans call for the development of what has been labeled an "early alert system" to identify international markets of future promise.

Associated Dry Goods

Associated Dry Goods (ADG), which includes stores such as Lord and Taylors, Loehmann's, J. W. Robinson, and L. S. Ayres—173 stores in all with sales of 3.2 billion in 1982—uses demographic data to support corporate and divisional-level decision making.[8] For example, ADG uses demographic information in the selection of new retail sites. Most site selection for ADG involves the purchase of an existing retail location given the ready availability of such stores. Before a site decision is reached, however, an analysis regarding a number of factors must be undertaken. First, the store's trading or market area must be identified. That is, the geographic location of present and potential customers is determined. Second, the number of people

This older age structure has serious implications for health care costs fifteen years in the future when the work force begins to enter its highest health care utilization ages, though it should be noted that GM is certainly not alone in this regard. New and creative ways of thinking about and planning for health care will be required if costs are to be held down.

GENERIC BUSINESS APPLICATIONS

Life Insurance Industry

Life insurance companies have also started to make use of demographic data for planning purposes, though many potential applications have yet to be fully realized. Almost one-third of all life insurance is purchased by persons 25 to 34 years of age, and given the data presented in Table 11.1, growth in life insurance sales can be expected to continue through 1990. However, beyond 1990 the business outlook is less certain, though an expanded view of just what services insurers can proide is opening new markets.[12]

In part, an increase in life expectancy as well as a better educated consumer market is fueling this much more expanded view. Salespersons are becoming "financial consultants" as deferred annuities, Keogh retirement plans, and other types of financial strategies are becoming an integral part of life insurance discussions. Policies are being made more readable for a clientele that wants to know more about what it is buying. In addition, more creative methods of premium payment are emerging.

One of the key changes in the life insurance sales mix has been the increase in sales to women resulting, in part, from the increase in female labor force participation. In 1970 there were nearly 2.7 male policies for every female policy. By 1980, the ratio had declined to 1.7. Measured in dollar amounts, the ratio of male to female dollars spent on insurance was about $7.00 to $1.00 in 1970, though by 1980 the ratio declined to $3.40 to $1.00. The average-sized ordinary policy for women increased 235 percent during the 1970's while the rise for men was only 150 percent.[13]

Overall, four new female insurance markets are developing. The first is labeled Career Women. In the early 1980's there were over 16 million women living on their own with no husband and no children under age 18. Their work expectancy—the number of years they would expect to work —was more than twenty three years. These women are particularly interested in disability insurance to replace their income should they become unable to work and whole life insurance, though there is certainly a question about whether this is the best way to accumulate cash for retirement.

Homemakers make up the second category. While these women hold no jobs outside the household, their economic value as providers of homemaker services is starting to be recognized. Protection against a loss of these services is seen as necessary in many families.

Two-income families, which make up the third category, have increased markedly in the past ten years. Betwen 1970 and 1985, the percentage of all families that have more than one income increased from 53.1 to 70.0 percent.[14] These types of families, many of whom are dependent on both sources of income to maintain their standard of living, are being targeted by certain insurance companies. One example is the television advertisement that shows the recent widower in his empty living room. He is selling his house (formerly theirs) because without his former wife's income he cannot pay the monthly mortgage. As the message goes, if they only had life insurance on his wife, the house would not have to be sold.

The last category is that of single parents—nearly 20 percent of all families as was seen in Table 11.3. Between 1970 and 1985 the number of female-headed, husband-absent families increased from 5.6 to 10.1 million.[15] These large numbers, coupled with historically low incomes, represent a potentially large market, albeit one that insurance companies have been slow in approaching. However, there are two products that are of particular value to single parents. The first is mortgage cancellation insurance which would provide a paid-for house in the event that the single parent died. In addition, income replacement insurance can assure the requisite funds for the proper care of the children left by a deceased parent.

Personnel Planning

Another arena where demographic change is having an effect on strategic planning is in the area of personnel planning. Table 11.4presents middle series labor force projections to the year 1995. These are the persons personnel planners will have to draw from to fill positions from now until nearly the end of the century. As a point of reference, the labor force was 69.6, 74.5, 82.8, 93.8, and 106.9 million in 1960, 1965, 1970, 1975, and 1980, respectively. Labor force growth from 1960 to 1980 was about 54 percent.[16]

Though the size of the labor force is projected to increase from 110 to 131 million workers between 1982 and 1995—an increase of 19 percent overall—the average 1.5 percent per year increase is far less than the average 2.9 percent for the 1970's. And as can be seen, the age structure of the labor force is changing in such a way as to create potential worker shortages at the younger ages while ensuring an overabundance of workers in the middle ages (again baby boomers). The pool of young workers aged 16–24 will decrease 14 percent over the interval, and workers aged 25–54 will increase 35 percent.

Among more narrowly defined age bands, the fluctuation is even greater. For 20-to-24-year-olds, the thirteen-year decline is 17 percnt. On the other

Table 11.4
Labor Force Projections for the United States to 1995: Middle Growth Pattern

Age	1982	1987	1992	1995	1982-1995 % Change
16-24	24,607	23,326	21,651	21,130	-14.1
16-19	8,526	8,251	7,500	7,804	- 8.4
20-24	16,081	15,075	14,151	13,326	-17.1
25-54	70,506	82,422	91,960	95,397	35.3
25-34	31,186	35,555	35,815	34,405	10.3
35-44	22,432	28,983	34,398	36,873	64.4
45-54	16,949	17,904	21,747	24,932	49.8
55 and over	15,092	14,653	13,976	14,047	- 6.9
55-64	12,062	11,521	10,844	10,982	- 8.9
65 and over	3,030	3,132	3,132	3,065	1.1
Total	110,204	120,421	127,587	131,387	19.2

Source: U.S. Bureau of Labor Statistics. 1984. Employment Projections for 1995. Washington, D.C.: U.S. Government Printing Office, tables 1 and A.

hand, labor force participants 35–44 years of age increase 64 percent. Furthermore, a decline, though a somewhat small one, is projected for ages 55 and over. These trends, coupled with the number of jobs projected to be eliminated by automation, the decreasing proportion of older persons remaining in the labor force, and changes in lifestyle and attitudes toward work, represent significant adjustments that personnel planners must make in order to ensure that there are enough workers in the right place at the right time to perform the tasks requisite to organizational survival.

Focusing first at the younger labor force ages, a shrinking supply of 16-to-24-year-olds in general means a smaller supply of entry-level workers, and for organizations that rely quite heavily on younger workers for their supply of labor, a change in recruitment strategy must result. That is, greater reliance on workers above age 24 need occur. A change in recruitment strategy has already been evidenced by McDonald's, Inc., which in some areas of the country has attempted to attract older workers through a series of radio advertisements emphasizing the value of the older employee and the wish that they apply for job openings at McDonald's. However, a change in recruitment emphasis is only a part of the solution because it is unrealistic to assume that younger and older workers have the same values and lifestyles and therefore can be managed in the same fashion. It is important that rewards structures, training, and management styles be adjusted to assure that older persons stay on the job.

At the middle ages, the problems are quite different. A near glut of labor force participants has created a host of problems ranging from an oversupply of executives to an increasing number of workers disgruntled because of an already existing, and likely to get worse, promotion squeeze.[17] These problems are the direct result of the tremendous amount of intra-age cohort competition that has emerged as much larger cohorts of workers (that is, baby boomers) follow the small depression cohorts through the age structure.[18] Perhaps exacerbating the problem of executive glut at the present time is the renewed emphasis on reducing the number of executives and middle managers in large corporations.[19] However, even without efforts at streamlining large corporations, the problem of too many highly trained workers with high job expectations and too few jobs for these persons is an issue that must be faced by personnel planners.

The reduction in older workers is an interesting anomaly because it comes at a time when the number of persons over 55 is increasing. However, labor force participation rates for older persons have dropped radically since 1960. As can be seen in Table 11.5, labor force participation rates have declined over 17 percent for males 55–64 and nearly 17 percent—almost one-half —for men 65 and over. For females, the pattern has been different. Women 55–64 have exhibited almost constant labor force participation rates over the twenty-two year period, though women 65 and over have shown a 3 percent decline. This pattern may not hold because organizations feeling the impact of the declining number of entry-level workers would elect to try to encourage older workers to stay on.[20] Phased retirement programs, such as those found in some European countries, could be adopted.

Housing

Population shifts, particularly those affecting age and household structure, are reshaping the housing market. Recent housing projections show two important changes worthy of attention—a shrinking overall demand for housing and the emergence of a different kind of housing consumer.[21] While household growth averaged 1.2 million households per year during the 1970's, projections for the 1980's and 1990's show a decline in growth to 1.3 and 1.0 million per year, respectively. The reduction in household growth is directly related to declines in housing demand. The gain in homeowner households is projected to grow 882,000 units per year in the early 1990's, a significant reduction from the 1.2 million per year during the 1970's. Even the renter market will be affected. Though renter households grew by more than one-half million per year during the 1970's, projections for the early 1990's show a reduction to 175,000 per year.

Table 11.5
Labor Force Participation Rates for Persons 55 Years Old and Older

Age and Sex	1960	1965	1970	1975	1980	1984
Male:						
55–64 years	86.8	84.6	83.0	75.6	72.1	·68.5
65 and over	33.1	27.9	26.8	21.6	19.0	16.3
Female:						
55–64 years	37.2	41.1	43.0	40.9	41.3	41.7
65 and over	10.8	10.0	9.7	8.2	8.1	7.5

Source: U.S. Bureau of the Census. 1986. Statistical Abstract of the United States, 1986, table 660; U.S. Bureau of the Census. 1984. Statistical Abstract of the United States, 1984, table 671.

Among those buying houses, the distribution concerning the type of house bought is changing.[22] Due partly to the increase in single-person households, condominiums sales have increased, though many buyers of condominiums view their purchase as only an intermediate step before a single-family detached house is purchased. Among single males and females, nearly one-half purchased condominiums, townhouses, or two- to three-family houses in 1981. Even among married couples with no dependents, more than one-fifth bought houses of these types. For older buyers, purchasing a non-single-family detached unit is also popular—around 40 percent of all housing sold.

Home builders are responding to these trends in a variety of ways. The development of condominiums was one response. Also, home designers and architects are changing the interior designs of houses.[23] For example, guest rooms are more and more likely to be used by children who are visiting the parent they do not live with (divorce). Floor plans and furnishings in some instances are being reworked with this trend in mind. Family rooms are being replaced by entertainment centers in part as a response to the growing number of married and cohabitating couples without children. Housing designed specifical ly for the elderly is being developed. Electrical outlets, for example, are placed higher on the wall to eliminate the need for bending. Cabinets are placed lower to prevent extensive stretching.

Furthermore, home builders are attempting to take advantage of the high purchasing power of home buyers by equipping their homes with electronic extras. Ryan Homes, for example, has installed computerized control centers in 8,000 of their new homes.[24] These control centers, called Homeminders and manufactured by General Electric, can put up to 100 lights, appliances,

Table 11.6
Consumer Expenditures on Food by Household Size: 1980–1981

Household Size	Total	Food at Home	Food Away From Home	Number of Households[a]
1 Person	$1344.68	$ 743.44	$ 601.24	20.1
2 Persons	2482.36	1634.79	847.57	20.3
3 Persons	2952.52	2058.21	894.31	11.6
4 Persons	3619.19	2252.99	1066.20	10.0
5 or More Persons	4425.62	3336.40	1089.21	8.0

[a]In millions.

Source: Consumer Research Center. 1984. How Consumers Spend Their Money. New York: The Conference Board. Data based on the 1980-1981 Consumer Expenditure Survey, Bureau of Labor Statistics.

furnaces, and air conditioners on a daily schedule. That is, they can be preset to be turned on and off from one control center. As Sternlieb and Hughes note, given the demographics of housing it will be the sale of amenities such as spas, home exercise areas, and high technology that will determine the success of the housing market in the 1990's.[25]

Consumer Expenditures—Food

Consumer expenditures vary considerably when classified by a host of demographic variables, and given the types of changes presently under way (see Chapters 1 and 7 and the earlier part of this chapter), the structure of consumer spending is likely to be considerably altered in the next several years. Table 11.6 presents data for expenditures on food cross-tabulated by household size. The data come from the 1980–1981 Consumer Expenditures Survey conducted by the Bureau of Labor Statistics and are for urban households. The data show that smaller households spend more money per capita on food than larger households. The per capita expenditure range is from $1,344.68 for one-person households to $776.42 for five-or-more-person households (data not shown in the table)—or a decrease of 42 percent in the larger households. Given a trend toward smaller households, all other factors remaining the same, one could expect an overall increase in money spent on food over the next two decades. Also of interest, particularly to restauranteurs, is what proportion of this money is spent on food away from home. While four-person households spend about 29 percent of their food

Table 11.7
Per Capita Consumer Expenditures on Food for Husband-Wife Families:
1980–1981

	No Children	Children under 6	Children 6 to 17	Children 17 and over
Food, Total	$1117.53	$ 810.37	$ 918.84	$1052.54
Food at Home	762.22	571.76	660.62	728.22
Food Away from Home	355.32	238.61	258.22	324.32
Breakfast and Brunch	19.97	14.52	13.27	16.50
Lunch	125.24	88.52	103.08	123.46
Dinner	170.21	91.69	97.93	135.25
Snacks and Nonalcoholic Beverages	39.89	43.87	43.94	49.11

Source: Consumer Research Center. 1984. How Consumers Spend Their Money. New York: The Conference Board, Inc. Data based on the 1980-1981 Consumer Expenditure Survey, Bureau of Labor Statistics.

money outside the home, one-person households spend nearly 45 percent. The link to shrinking household size is obvious.

Table 11.7 presents the same data in per capita form for husband-wife families cross-classified by the age of the oldest child. Per capita expenditures are highest for families without children, and the dollar amount increases as the age of the oldest child gets larger. The same pattern is true for food-at-home and food-away categories. Concerning the proportion of all food money spent outside the home, the greatest percentage is for families without children (32 percent) and the least for families whose oldest child is 6 to 17 years (28 percent)—certainly not a very large range. As would be expected given their larger dollar amount spent on food outside the home, families without children are the leading per capita spenders in three of the four food-away-from-home categories. These data too point toward increased expenditures on food overall as the number of families without children increases. However, as the age of the oldest child increases, the per capita amount begins to approach that of families without children.

Canada Dry offers a good example of a shift in product and marketing strategy as a result of recognized compositional changes in the food and beverage market.[26] As a recent survey by the National Soft Drink Association has found, when consumers age, their drink tastes change from a preference for caffeinated, naturally sweetened soft drinks to diet and caffeine-free drinks. This places a tremendous burden on soft drink companies that wish to appeal to a clearly segmented market (older *and* young consumers). Canada Dry has chosen to target the older market with phrases like "make your move to Canada Dry; so long to sweet things." Their strategy seems to be working because their market share has increased five points since 1981, though it should be noted that the ginger ale market is a rather small one.

Other beverage marketers that have recognized the demographically induced change in beverage tastes are producers and distributors of fruit-added sparkling wines, generically known as wine coolers. Producers of these types of drinks are taking advantage of an age structure that is more favorable to wine consumption and less favorable to beer and other alcoholic beverages. Between 1983 and 1985 alone, retail sales of wine coolers increased six times to over $700 million.[27] Presently, wine coolers account for about 7 percent of all wine sales. On the other hand, beer makers, understanding that beer consumption is highly concentrated in the younger male population and also knowing that this population is expected to decline in numbers between now and the end of the century, have invested in heavy promotional campaigns to protect and extend market share.

Finally, even the places where food and beverages are sold are responding to population shifts. Demographic change has brought with it new lifestyles. These new lifestyles include changes in not only the types of food and beverages purchased but where they are purchased. Large superstores (super supermarkets) are an attempt to appeal to what is being called the most value-conscious consumer the United States has ever known.[28] These new stores feature true minimum pricing by eliminating the need for warehouses (the store itself is a warehouse) and offering fewer services—for example, customers bag their own groceries. Furthermore, these stores emphasize nonfood items, which it turns out are accounting for 25 percent of total supermarket revenue in the 1980's.

The Mature Market

As early as the mid-1960's, marketers were aware of the coming significance of the maturity market—persons roughly over the age of 55.[29] Utilizing demographic projections and limited data on the consumption and media habits of the elderly, a separate market with distinct needs was identified. Specific consumption areas considered were automobiles—older persons buy fewer autos; durable goods—the elderly buy fewer consumer goods than other age groups; food—older persons are very price conscious and tend to shop infrequently; housing—while many older consumers own their own homes, retirement communities do represent an opportunity for sales; and services—senior citizens demand more medical, dental, and nursing services. Referring again to Table 11.1, without question the population aged 55 and over is projected to grow quite rapidly between now and the end of the century. However, to treat these segments as one homogeneous group of potential buyers is to underestimate the complexity of the market. The reader has only to look at the last six rows of Table 11.1 to see that growth rates within subcategories of the 55 and over group show tremendous variation —from 1.0 percent growth for the 65-to-69-year-olds to 96.1 percent for the 85 and over category.

Furthermore, older consumers have a great deal of money to spend. As was discussed in Chapter 4, discretionary income remains quite high beyond age 55. The mature market has an annual purchasing power of betweeh $60 and $200 billion.[30] People over age 50 control about $7 trillion of wealth, or about 70 percent of the net worth of all U.S. households.[31] In addition, only 10 percent of the population age 65 and above reside with their children, and only 5 percent live in institutions such as nursing homes. Therefore, most are free to purchase as they wish.

One way to segment the market is by age, though the reader must be careful not to overlook the large amount of heterogeneity in each age group. Doris Walsh has segmented the market into four groups.[32] The groups and a summary of their characteristics are:

(1) Age 55–64 (adolescent elderly—about 22 million persons). About 70 percent of the males and 42 percent of the females are in the labor force. This group is in relatively good health and comprises a relatively high proportion of married couples.

(2) Age 65–74 (junior elderly—about 17 million persons). This group shows a significant decline in labor force participation. They are in relative good health and only 52 percent of their households contain a married couple.

(3) Age 75–84 (middle seniors—about 8.5 million persons). This segment has very low labor force participation and declining health. Only 35 percent of the households contain a married couple.

(4) Age 85 and over (senior seniors—about 2.5 million persons). This group has almost no labor force participation. They are frail, though 80 percent are still able to take care of their daily needs. They have a low proportion of married couple households. These classifications, along with more detailed consumption information when combined with population projections, can be used by product manufacturers and service providers to plan for the needs of these different elderly groups.

The question of whether or not the elderly consumers needs are being met should be asked. A survey of elderly consumers concerning their retail store needs was reported by Lambert.[33] Among the unmet needs stated by the persons 65 and older interviewed were (1) the need for more discounts, (2) an improvement in personnel-consumer interactions, that is, more courteous treatment, (3) more help in locating products within the store, (4) making pricetags and labels easier to read, (5) providing faster checkout procedures, and (6) reducing package sizes. While it is known that in general elderly consumers have different needs than younger consumers, information on their desires (concerning products and services) is less well known.

Finally, new mature markets are being identified and targeted. For example, television advertisements that sing the praises of health insurance supplements to medicare and medicaid are targeted directly at the elderly. This targeting occurs for good reasons. Co-payments and deductibles are rising and many elderly on their relatively fixed incomes cannot pay additional health care costs. Older consumers have also been found to be heavy users of long distance telephone service, mass transit, taxicabs, and laundromats, and targeting efforts can be observed, for example, for long distance telephone service in many television and print advertisements. The large circulation of magazines geared to the mature market such as *Prime Time, 50 Plus*, and *Modern Maturity* makes the task of the marketer much easier.

THE USE OF DEMOGRAPHIC DATA AND EXPERTISE IN THE PUBLIC SECTOR

Demographic data and the demographic perspective are used in almost an unlimited number of ways in national, state, and local government planning. Some uses of these data are mandated by law such as the application of decennial census data for the reapportionment of House of Representative members or the use of population counts or estimates for the distribution of revenue-sharing monies. Other uses are quite obvious, for example, the application of the myriad of data gathered by the National Institutes of Health for the general improvement of the health and welfare of the U.S. population. (Recall the discussion of data sources in Chapter 2.) The purpose of the present section of this chapter is to point to some less commonly known areas where demographic data—particularly trends—are being used for planning purposes. Many of these uses have business environment implications.

National

The National Center for Educational Statistics (NCES) has, among other roles, the task of collecting and disseminating educationally relevant data. One of its areas of focus in recent years has been in bilingual education—in particular, not only planning for bilingual programs for one or two years in the future, but ascertaining bilingual program needs five and ten years in advance. NCES also assists states in planning by providing data at the state level. Several projects have been contracted by NCES for the collection and analysis of data to make this planning possible. In 1978, for example, the Children's English Services Study was conducted by NCES for the National Institute of Education in order to determine, among other things, the proportion of minority children ages 5 to 14 with limited English proficiency.[34]

At the same time, NCES was working with Miranda Associates on the development of a surrogate measure of limited English proficiency (LEP).[35] In 1980, NCES contracted with InterAmerica Research Associates in order to produce LEP projections by language group, age, and state to the year 2000.[36] Overall, the projections showed an impressive growth in LEP children, from 2.5 to 3.4 million—or 36 percent— between 1976 and 2000. The largest growth by language group was for Spanish-language LEPs who in 2000 should make up over 15 percent of all LEPs. Given the relatively large amount of growth projected, the planning implications are clear regardless of one's political beliefs concerning the placement of bilingual education programs in public schools. That is, the relatively large amount of growth in the number of persons with limited English skills means that unless English skill levels are improved, a substantial number of persons will be less well integrated into American society than they could be.

The U.S. Army is also interested in language skils, particularly those of its recruits. The U.S. Army Research Institute has contracted to have demographic projections of LEP Hispanic accessions in the Army.[37] An accession is an Army recruit who has been accepted and has signed a contract. The purpose in having such projections made is to establish program needs requisite for ensuring that English-language deficiency does not impair military operations. The findings of the study showed a 27 percent increase from just over 1,400 to approximately 2,000 in LEP accessions between 1980 and 2000. For the most part the increase is the direct result of the rising proportion of all accessions who are Hispanic. Although the proportion of all accessions who are LEP is relatively small, the results point to the need for continued high-quality English instruction, suitable selection and classification procedures, and an awareness of cultural differences between Hispanics and non-Hispanics.

Finally, the Internal Revenue Service (IRS) is interested in the relationship between demographic trends and their own business environment. Recent studies have shown that changing household compostion, age structure, employment patterns, and population distribution are resulting in more complex income tax statement filings as well as a changing distribution of locations where tax forms are being mailed. These trends have implications for better personnel training (the filed forms are becoming more complex) and the geographic distribution of personnel (the growth in the number of forms mailed to IRS regional offices is not matched well by the redistribution of personnel).[38]

State

States also utilize demographic analysis and data in planning for a host of programs. For example, educational enrollments are know to be demographicaly driven. In many states, school enrollment projections, vital to educational planning, are seen as a product of fertility, migration, and what proportion of the relevant population is actually enrolled in school. For instance, in order to project kindergarden enrollments for State X five years from now, one needs information regarding:

1. The number of births in State X this year
2. The estimated net effect of migration on this year's birth cohort over the next five years
3. What proportion of those persons projected from (1) and (2) will actually enroll in school.

Simple demographic analysis furnishes the information to project the number of first graders.

State demographers and state data centers provide expertise for state agencies as well as for interested individuals. As was discussed in Chapter 2, the U.S. Bureau of the Census has established federal-state programs for providing local-area population estimates as well as projections. The local-area estimates are linked to revenue-sharing allocations, though that is but one use for the data produced. There is considerable state-to-state variation in the services provided; much of the difference has to do with the priorities set by persons external to the data centers.

The North Carolina state data center, for example, is housed within the North Carolina Office of Management and Budget.[39] The center works closely with the state legislature and executive agencies in strategic planning. However, data requests and general assistance are provided at a nominal fee to other interested parties. In Montana and South Carolina, state demographers worked on reapportionment in the early 1980's. In Colorado, the state data center worked on resolving differences in local-area population estimates in conjunction with the development of shale oil. Local communities would not give companies permits to develop sites until they negotiated a contribution for the facilities, for example, roads and water the additional population they attracted would require. The state demographer helped arrive at the projections of the increase in persons likely to result from such development. In Minnesota, the data center's input is sought when large capital expenditures are being planned. Certainly population projections must play a part in determining whether or not, for example, a sewage treatment plant is constructed.[40]

States are also producing published data sets on a regular basis. Montana, for example, produces county profiles that contain sixty-five types of federal and state data for each Montana county. Illinois, Nevada, South Carolina, and several other states published statistical abstracts that contain a host of demographic data and are widely distributed throughout their respective states.[41]

The need for such projections can be illustrated in thinking about how educational enrollment figures have fluctuated for the United States as a whole over the last forty years. In 1940, for example, there were about 18 million children enrolled in grades 1–8 in the public schools. The figure peaked around 1970 at 30 million—a 65 percent increase. By 1985, however, enrollment had fallen to around 24 million, or a decrease of 20 percent.[42] Many states have undergone even greater changes. While public school enrollment in grades 9–12 fell 10 percent from 14.3 to 12.9 million between 1975 and 1981, there was a 22 percent decline in Connecticut and a 2 percent increase in Texas.[43] Without planning that includes a demographic dimension (and some states do little planning), shortages or overabundances of physical plants and teachers can occur. (They have occurred in all states at one time or another.)

Local

Demographic analysis is also a part of local-area planning. Many cities and/or counties have continuous demographic input into planning because some agency (or agencies) has been given the charge of providing such information to all local agencies. In other instances, while no specific agency is given the responsibility for tracking demographic change, demographic input occurs because key persons within these agencies understand the impact that population change can have on the issues at hand. Finally, some municipalities contract with external research and data providers for generating demographic input.

Cities use demographic data and analysis in a variety of ways such as in assisting with decisions about where to spend federal community development block grant money. Memphis, Tennessee's Division of Housing and Community Development, while collecting a great deal of demographic data for planning purposes, has contracted with a local university to select, on the basis of selected demographic characteristics, a larger number of target neighborhoods where block grant monies might be spent. A political process was then responsible for the final selection. The Metropolitan Dade County (Florida) Planning Department collects and analyzes a wide variety of demographic data to help in land use, housing, and utility planning. As was mentioned earlier, the Massachusetts Energy Facilities Siting Council studies population projections to aid in determining public utility needs.

The San Diego Association of Governments produces a complex series of population estimates and projections for subareas of San Diego County for a host of planning purposes. The planning areas where these data are used include water and air quality, regional transportation needs such as highways, and location determination for schools, fire and police stations, solid waste sites, libraries, and other public facilities.[44] Demographic estimates and projections are also an integral part of aviation forecasts—passengers, operations, air cargo, and aircraft.[45]

CONCLUSIONS

While this chapter has presented a limited number of examples where demographic input is a integral part of strategic planning, it should provide a general overview of the extent and variation of how population trends and changes have affected business organization behavior. Of course, each organization is unique, but all must compete and/or provide services in an environment shared by many businesses. From this perspective all institutions share some common demographic ground. It is the responsibility of each individual business to learn as much about the environment as possible in order to maximize the efficiency of its operations.

Concerning the use of demographic data and expertise for federal, state and local planning efforts, several factors must be considered. Aside from the obvious consulting opportunities that are created when the research is contracted to the private sector, the reports and data generated have important uses. For example, aviation forecasts have significant implications for those businesses in the travel and shipping businesses. Beyond the direct and more obvious uses of these reports and data is the additional information about the business environment that they provide. Planners in the growth sector would be wise to exploit these sources of knowledge.

NOTES

1. Richard Klein. 1986. "USA 2000." *Sales and Marketing Management* (October): 8–39.

2. American Demographics Staff. 1984. "Demographic Forecasts." *American Demographics* (April): 50.

3. U.S. Bureau of the Census. 1986. *Statistical Abstract of the United States, 1986.* Washington, D.C.: U.S. Government Printing Office, table 2.

4. Bickley Townsend. 1983. "The Changing Consumer Household." Transcript of talk given at the Consumer Demographics Conference (March). Chicago, Illinois.

5. This discussion is based on a transcript of a talk by John Wyek. 1984. "The Levi Strauss Strategy." Strategic Demographics for U.S. Markets Conference (March). San Francisco, California.

6. This discussion is based on a transcript of a talk by Tom Eglinton. 1983. "How Dow Jones Uses Demographics." Consumer Demographics Conference (September). Los Angeles, California.

7. Scott McDonald. 1984. "Uses and Limitations of Demographic Analysis in a Communications Business." Paper presented at the annual meeting of the Population Association of America (May). Minneapolis, Minnesota.

8. Francesco Turchiano. 1983. "The Retailing Perspective." Transcript of a talk given at Demographic Outlook '83 Conference (June). White Plains, New York.

9. Carl Fredrickson. 1983. "The Financial Perspective." Transcript of a talk given at Demographic Outlook '83 Conference (June). White Plains, New York.

10. Doris Walsh. 1984. "Utilities Come In from the Darkness." *American Demographics* (June): 29–31.

11. Hallie J. Kinnter and Ernest B. Smith. 1985. "A Demographic Profile of the G.M. Work Force and Dependents: Implications for Health Care." *General Motors Research Laboratories*. Publication GMR–5207. Warren, Michigan.

12. Steven Skinner. 1980. "Staying Alive." *American Demographics* (May): 11–13.

13. Doris Walsh. 1982. "Why Life Insurance Companies Are Discovering Women." *American Demographics* (April): 20–23.

14. U.S. Bureau of the Census. 1986. *Statistical Abstract of the United States, 1986*, table 676.

15. U.S. Bureau of the Census. 1986. *Statistical Abstract of the United States, 1986*, table 54.

16. U.S. Bureau of the Census. 1984. *Statistical Abstract of the United States, 1984*. Washington, D.C.: U.S. Government Printing Office, table 671.

17. Donald Lunde. 1981. "Personnel Management: What's Ahead?" *Personnel Administrator* (April): 51–60; Kenneth Shapiro. 1981. "Managing the Impending Promotion Squeeze." *Personnel Journal* (October): 800–804; and Thomas Murray. 1977. "The Coming Glut in Executives." *Dun's Review* (May): 69.

18. See Richard Easterlin. 1980. *Birth and Fortune*. New York: Basis Books, for a detailed discussion of the problems faced by baby boomers because they are members of large birth cohorts.

19. Thomas Peters and Robert Waterman. 1982. *In Search of Excellence*. New York: Warner Books; Business Week Staff. 1981. "A New Target: Reducing Staff and Levels." *Business Week* (December 21): 69–70.

20. Doris Walsh and Ann Lloyd. 1984. "Personnel Planning's New Agenda." *American Demographics* (September): 35–51.

21. George Sternlieb and James Hughes. 1985. "The Good News about Housing." *American Demographics* (August): 18–21, 49.

22. George Sternlieb and James Hughes. 1982. "Who's Buying Homes?" *American Demographics* (December): 24–27.

23. Jeffrey Rosenfeld. 1984. "Demographics and Interior Design." *American Demographics* (February): 28–31.

24. Brad Edmondson. 1984. "Ryan Homes Have Brains." *American Demographics* (August): 16.

25. George Sternlieb and James Hughes. 1985. "The Good News about Housing," p. 49.

26. Forbes Staff. 1985. "Older, Not Sweeter." *Forbes* (July 15): 107.

27. Associated Press. 1984. "Wine Coolers Tagged Hottest Trendy Drinks." *Omaha World Herald* (August 4): 18-A.

28. Edward McLaughlin and Gene German. 1985. "Supermarketing Success." *American Demographics* (August): 34–37.

29. Charles Boeldner and Henry Munn. 1964. "The Significance of the Retirement Market." *Journal of Retailing* 40:43–64.

30. Charles D. Schewe. 1985. "Gray America Goes to market." *Business* (April-June): 3–9.

31. Peter Petre. 1986. "Marketers Mine for the Gold." *Fortune* (March 31): 70–78.

32. Doris Walsh. 1984. "Segmenting the Maturity Market." Transcript of a talk given at Demographic Outlook '84 (June). New York, New York.

33. Zarrel Lambert. 1979. "An Investigation of Older Consumers' Unmet Needs and Wants at the Retail Level." *Journal of Retailing* 55: 35–57.

34. David Dubois. 1980. *The Children's English and Serivces Study: A Methodological Review.* Washington, D.C.: U.S. Department of Education, National Center for Educational Statistics.

35. Resource Development Institute, Inc. 1979. *Analysis of MELP's among CESS Respondents.* Austin, Texas: L. Miranda and Associates.

36. Rebecca Oxford, Louis Pol, David Lopez, Paul Stupp, Murray Gendell, and Samuel Peng. 1984. *Demographic Projections of Non-English-Language-Background and Limited-English-Proficient Persons in the United States to the Year 2000 by State, Age, and Language Group.* Rosalyn, Virginia: National Clearinghouse for Bilingual Education.

37. Rebecca Oxford-Carpenter, Louis Pol, and Murray Gendell. 1984. *Demographic Projections to the Year 2000 of Limited English Proficient Hispanic Accessions in the U.S. Army.* Research Report 1349, Training Research Laboratory. Alexandria, Virginia: U.S. Army Research Institute for the Behavioral and Social Sciences.

38. Peter Morrison and Paola Scommegna. 1986. *Demographic Trends Tax the IRS.* Population Trends and Public Policy Occasional paper No. 11. Washington, D.C.: Population Reference Bureau.

39. Martha Farnsworth Riche. 1981. "State Data Centers." *American Demographics* (January): 32.

40. Martha Farnsworth Riche. 1981. "State Demographics." *American Demographics* (October): 42–44.

41. For a list of the states and their publications see Martha Farnsworth Riche. 1981. "State Statistical Abstracts." *American Demographics* (August): 38–40.

42. U.S. Bureau of the Census. 1984. *Statistical Abstract of the United States, 1984,* table 217.

43. U.S. Bureau of the Census. 1984. *Statistical Abstract of the United States, 1984,* table 217.

44. San Diego Association of Governments. 1984 *Overview of the Regional Growth Forecasting System* (October): San Diego, California.

45. San Diego Association of Governments. 1984. *Aviation Demand Forecasts* (July): San Diego, California.

12

Demographic Data and Expertise in the Small-Business Context

INTRODUCTION

A likely reaction on the part of some readers to a separate chapter on the demographic perspective and small businesses concerns whether or not the distinction between large and small enterprises is a useful one. Responses to utilizing the small/large business dichotomy include the following types of questions: Don't all businesses regardless of size have the same basic concerns, that is, show a profit and operate efficiently? And, therefore, aren't demographic applications basically the same? Certainly these are legitimate queries that call for a discussion of factors that differentiate large from small businesses before a special treatment of small-business users of demographic data and the demographic perspective can be presented.

The distinction between large and small enterprises is somewhat artificial given that all businesses can best be described as possessing a continuum of characteristics. That is, whether it be the number of employees or the dollar amount of retail sales, size is a continuous variable, and any designated categories are subjective in nature and potentially misleading. Furthermore, the differential between small and large may be of substantial import or of no value at all, depending on which industry is being considered, which dimension has been chosen to distinguish small from large, and the context in which the comparisons are made.

The author wishes to thank David M. Ambrose for his helpful insights and comments concerning demography and small-business issues. Any errors of fact or interpretation are, however, my own.

Nevertheless, small businesses, as distinguished by several factors, do account for a great deal of economic activity and therefore are worthy of separate consideration. For example, businesses nationwide having fewer than 100 employees account for 56 percent of all employment and 49 percent of the total annual payroll in the 1980's. In the construction, retail, and wholesale industries, companies with fewer than 100 employees make up 74, 78, and 82 percent, respectively, of all employment.[1]

The contention here is that there are size thresholds for businesses, and once an enterprise falls below a given level, organizational and managerial characteristics change to the extent that enterprises on either side of the dividing line contain dissimilarities in organization, day-to-day operations, and planning activities. The further a business gets from the threshold on either side, the greater the dissimilarities are. These differences frequently dictate different demographic data and expertise needs.

While data on employment size categories as a measure of separating small from large businesses are discussed a few paragraphs from now, several other size measures can be found in the literature. *Forbes*, for example, has chosen its list of best small companies by selecting from a roster of more than 4,000 firms with sales between $1 million and $300 million.[2] *Business Week* distinguishes its top 1,000 companies from the rest on the basis of a company's market value, and the top 100 small corporations come from a list of companies with less than $150 million in annual sales.[3] Though this chapter is not intended to provide a lengthy discussion on the development of a definition for a small business (or what a small/large enterprise distinction should entail), it must be emphasized that there is no commonly agreed-on small-business definition, and therefore readers are advised to evaluate the discussions that follow in regard to their own business problems and opportunities.

Once it is agreed that a *general* distinction between large and small businesses can be made, some discussion of the additional factors separating both groups is warranted. That is, small- and large-business dissimilarities other than those used for definitional purposes must be considered. And, of course, these factors must be related to different demographic data and expertise needs.

One major difference between large and small businesses is that while the former are for the most part operated for profit, the latter are driven by other motivations as well. Owners of small businesses frequently are able to justify untraditional business procedures and strategies because they realize nonmonetary or psychic income as part of the reward structure. Psychic income is crucial to the survival of many small enterprises because it is often the difference between business success and failure. Psychic income is derived from various feelings: control of action, evidence of ownership, community recognition, personal challenge, and leadership. But perhaps the all-encompassing psychic income is derived from feeling that small-enterprise ownership is part of an overall way of life.[4]

As a result, many small businesses operate "irrationally" by large-business standards. And a large proportion of small businesses continue to operate even after most other organizations would have ceased functioning. For example, many small enterprises in fact lose money (or make less profit than is recognized) because they tend to redefine and underestimate the place and value of labor contributed to the business by themselves and other members of their family. The reader must be cognizant of the role of psychic income in these judgements.

Second, the seemingly irrational behavior is in part not surprising when other factors are considered, that is, all of the functions that must be performed by the small-enterprise owner. Though large organizations have specialized components to address accounting, finance, management, and marketing issues, for small businesses all of these functions frequently are performed by one or two individuals. The one or two persons making decisions simply may not have expertise in all of the areas required to keep a business operating at maximum efficiency. Therefore, owners frequently make decisions on less than precise or complete information. This lack of complex organizational and decision structures constitutes the second major difference.

The third difference concerns the sphere in which a business operates. Small businesses tend to operate regionally and/or locally and are therefore concerned with aspects of the business environment different from those that large businesses would find of concern. Small businesses need to know about regional/local economic, political, and social conditions; events, trends, and data at the national level may clearly be of limited value. As a result, small-enterprise data needs are different starting with what demographic data are available for the geographic unit in question. (Recall the discussion in Chapter 2 on the importance of the geographic units of availability for demographic data sets.) For example, data from the Consumer Expenditure Survey (national-level data only) may be of limited or no use to the retailer whose market is in northeastern Nebraska or a zip code in the Memphis MSA.

Concerning business distinctions made on the basis of variation in the number of persons employed, several small/large business differences may be observed. The first concerns growth in employment. During the 1980's, small-business-dominated industry employment (defined here as businesses with fewer than 500 workers) increased 11.4 percent while large-business-dominated industry employment grew only 5.3 percent.[5] However, very small business establishments experienced more job contraction and constant employment (versus job growth) than large businesses (500 and more workers). Between the middle 1970's and early 1980's, nearly 49 percent of businesses with fewer than twenty employees showed either no job growth or losses in employment while only 30 percent of the establishments with 500 or more employees experienced the same phenomenon.[6] With regard to closures (business failure), fewer small businesses (less than 500 employees) than large ones failed between the mid 1970's and the early 1980's; however, within the small-business category, those with fewer than 20 workers experienced the highest mortality rate of all size categories (nearly 30 percent).[7] An often-cited Illinois study of survival rates of retailers shows that large retailers, defined as retailers with more than $2.4 million in annual sales, had five-year survival rates nearly three times higher than small businesses.[8]

In sum, small businesses are different from large businesses on the basis of the rewards gained from being in business, organization and business strategy, sphere of operation, job generation, and establishment survival—though perhaps the rewards structure and the sphere of operation provide the greatest distinction. All of these factors contribute to different demographic data needs and different uses of those data from those seen in the previous chapter on large businesses.

In the following paragraphs, the general kinds of problems or opportunities that small businesses encounter where the demographic perspective can play a role are discussed in order to provide a context for the subsequent paragraphs, which include a detailed discussion of how individual small enterprises have incorporated demography into their planning and operations. The detailed individual business discussions are derived from small-business case studies performed by the author and his colleagues through the Nebraska Business Development Center. Some cases, nevertheless, were shared by colleagues at other institutions, and a few were found in the small-business literature. The cases represent businesses that vary greatly both in size and in the type of activities engaged in, though all would be classified small by most standards. The names of the businesses discussed have been changed to ensure their confidentiality.

PROBLEMS/OPPORTUNITIES

Small businesses can utilize demographic data and expertise in the context of solving problems or taking advantage of opportunities that are frequently faced. However, most small enterprises do not incorporate a demographic component because the owners of such enterprises are simply unfamiliar with the contribution that demography can make. What small-business owners are faced with is a number of day-to-day operational or planning issues that must be confronted. Put in a question format, the following issues are frequently raised by small-business owners:

1. Can demand for a product or service be estimated or forecasted?
2. Can we determine why business is declining or not growing as fast as it should?

("Should" is always difficult to define because owners or managers often do not look at historical trends in their data, nor do they engage in forecasting.)

3. What is the image of our store; that is, what do people think of us (for example, products, services, locations, and salespeople) and how does this relate to a willingness to shop with us?

4. Where should a new or existing business locate or relocate?

5. How can market boundaries be determined? What are my market boundaries?

6. Who are my customers?

7. Can new markets for products or services be identified?

8. Are there labor force supply and demand issues worthy of consideration?

Not surprisingly, these are the same types of concerns raised by larger businesses, though almost without exception small-enterprise operators must face the problems and opportunities on their own without a complex organization to seek answers. Furthermore, due to reduced size and limited financial resources, small-business proprietors tend not to engage in the types of business research that would best assist them in solving problems and capitalizing on opportunities. They feel that they have more pressing day-to-day matters to deal with such as how much inventory to have during peak sales periods and how to price products in order to be competitive with larger businesses. The lack of familiarity with business research—the ways in which research can benefit an enterprise and how research is carried out—makes the inclusion of the demographic perspective into a business plan sometimes difficult to accomplish because the data and expertise are regarded as part of a nonessential set of activities. Furthermore, as stated before, most small-business owners have only a vague idea of what demography is (they probably call it demographics) and how the demographic perspective can assist them. The key to convincing a small-business owner to incorporate demography into everyday business activities is to *demonstrate* its usefulness and importance and convince the owner that the data can be obtained relatively inexpensively (often at no cost) and can be manipulated without the assistance of a business consultant.

As is the case in any good business research, the first step in incorporating demographic data and expertise into day-to-day operations and planning is to develop a clear mental picture of just what the business problems and/or opportunities are. The next step is then methodological and involves identifying how the problems/opportunities can be studied and ultimately addressed. It is at this stage that demographic analysis becomes part of small-business operations. Demographic expertise serves as a dimension of the problem-solving/opportunity-exploiting framework. Demographic data provide information to put this dimension into operation.

One final point is worthy of note. Demographic expertise goes beyond problem solving and opportunity exploitation and can be incorporated merely to help a business operate more smoothly on a day-to-day basis by more clearly identifying business conditions and change in the marketplace. In this way, business problems can be averted and opportunities understood with greater advance notice.

USES OF DEMOGRAPHIC DATA AND EXPERTISE

This section first reclassifies the types of small-business problems/opportunities into groups with common dimensions and then presents case studies in each category that illustrate how a demographic perspective can be useful in that specific context. In several instances, potential uses of the demographic perspective are presented. The categories discussed should not be seen as mutually exclusive because frequently an individual business wishes to have answers to any number of questions that extend to several of these categories. Thus, an interest in multiple groups of information is expressed. In addition, it should be realized that as in the case of other areas of business and social research, measures of conditions and change are frequently developed that are approximations for conditions that are either unmeasurable or extremely hard to ascertain without complex and expensive methodologies. This does not lessen the value of the measure, though care must be exercised in regard to what that measure represents and how it is used.

Consumer Profiles

Business owners always seem to want to know more about their customers and potential customers. Knowing more about the people who might buy and do buy a product or service can mean anything from learning about why people do or do not purchase at their (the owners') stores to finding out about a consumer population's lifestyles, attitudes, interests, and opinions and linking those data to purchasing behavior. Among the factors of interest are what are generally known as demographics—as discussed in Chapter 1, the descriptive characteristics of those current and potential customers. It is important to note at this juncture, however, that consumer profiles should not be seen as a static, one-point-in-time undertaking. To maximize the use of consumer profiles, one should profile the populations of interest periodically or at least for more than one time period in order to ascertain the change in customers and potential customers that may be taking place.

Often, customer profiling is accomplished by surveying a sample of buyers and potential buyers and asking a host of demographic, psychographic, and behavioral questions, though this can be a costly way of obtaining information. Youth Charities, for example, wished to gather more information about the types of individuals who gave money to the organization in order to improve their targeting of potential contributors. However, their internal records contained little information about the donor base. They surveyed a sample of contributors and cross-tabulated donation behavior factors (which other charities the person gave to) with demographic factors (age, sex, and income). They found that their donors were concentrated in three general demographic-behavioral categories—low-income adult females who participated in programs, upper-income males and females who think Youth Charities programs are important to the community, and former program participants. Those data provided them with some ideas on how to expand their contributor base. They targeted noncontributors with similar demographic/behavioral characteristics through direct mail and telephone solicitations.

In another context, a survey and analysis concerning the demographic and psychographic characteristics of mall shoppers yielded the following clusters of Sunday shoppers: serious, recreational, and anti-Sunday shopper. Serious shoppers tended to be young, female, and well educated, and were most likely to be employed. Recreational shoppers were older and less well educated, and were less likely to be employed than the serious shoppers. Anti-Sunday shoppers were made up of a higher proportion of men, were older and were the most likely to be married of all three clusters. The resulting information could be used by the individual retailers in each of the malls to cater to the special interests of each cluster. For example, time and convenience were important to the serious Sunday shoppers, and advertising and in-store activities could be directed toward individuals with those attributes (for example, time- and convenience-oriented, female, and well-educated).[9]

Customer profiling can also be accompanied by taking data for existing customers from the internal records of the business (if such data do exist) and performing some simple manipulations to determine the commonalities and dissimilarities of those persons. For example, new and former customers can be profiled by looking at each group's average age, median income, residential location (block, census tract, zip code, or county), and average education. These data can be correlated with differential purchasing behavior such as size of purchase, if such data exist, and more information gathered about the good, better, and best customers.

Ace Advertisers, new to the business of specialty advertising, for example, profiled its industrial and individual customer accounts looking only at the size (dollar amount of sales) of each account. They not only identified who and where (geographically) those accounts were, but learned, as many other businesses already know, that the largest 5 percent of the accounts made up nearly 50 percent of all sales. Ace was able to single out those businesses for preferential treatment as well as identify (based on present customer profile) other businesses that could be targeted later.

Regal Auto profiled its sales force along with its customers and potential customers and found that the age structure of its current sales force was dominated by older salesmen. The present customers tended to be older too, and it was determined that if automobiles were to be sold to younger customers, younger salespersons would have to be hired.

Patient financial records have been examined with regard to the age, sex, and racial composition of admissions and discharges along with the method of payment at City Hospital. By documenting the demographic structure of the patient base for multiple points in time, the hospital is able to monitor changes in the size and composition of patients and thus to redirect marketing efforts designed to highlight hospital services. Simple counts of patients that identify seasonal variations in the number of patients, specific procedures, and length of stay allow for the better planning of personnel requirements.

It is often the case, however, that good-quality internal records have not been maintained or that the records do not contain all the information needed. In lieu of initiating an expensive survey or improving present internal data collection activities that may take some time to complete, customer profile data can be gathered through existing demographic sources, though as will be discussed at the end of this section there are some potential dangers to the use of those data.

In 1985 the Food City Grocery, an 18,000-square-foot grocery store, wished to know more about its customers, though for several reasons it was not in a position to survey its shoppers. Nevertheless, the owner was able to have the addresses of a sample of check-paying customers(addresses are on the checks) along with a sample of cash-paying customers plotted on a geographicaly detailed map. Using the map, concentrations of customers could be found in certain census tracts, blocks, and zip codes, and the demographic characteristics of those geographic units—particularly the size, age structure, and income level—were determined by gleaning the 1980 Census of Population and Housing data and post-1980 special survey demographic charcteristics in the geographic units that made up the market area.

The mapping and assigning of characteristics provided an approximate social and economic profile in that the owner learned that his customers were for the most part drawn from socially and ethnically mixed neighborhoods with moderate income, though one might argue that the owner could have obtained general impressions simply through the observation of his customers. However, a similar mapping of customers had taken place three years earlier, and though the census of population data had not changed (the latest census was in 1980), zip code–specific population updates (a special citywide survey conducted yearly) provided data on changes on the size, age structure, and income of the zip codes with the heaviest concentration of customers. Observation would have provided only general impressions and little detail about subtle changes in customer composition. Of greatest value to the owner was the knowledge that the areas in which he did most of his business had not changed much at all during the three-year interval. Furthermore, contrary to his initial impression, the population of those zip codes was growing and not declining. In sum, while the owner was unable to obtain a profile of individual customers at this store, he was able to gather, at little cost to him, information about the areas in which the customers lived.

One must be careful of what has been labeled the ecological fallacy—inferring individual characteristics from group data. Geographic-based information does provide important insight into the grouped characteristics within the market areas. There is, however, considerable variation in the individuals who make up the aggregated data for areal units. All individuals within a geographic area cannot be assumed to be the same or similar. Therefore, the profile gained from the grouped data should not be seen as a simple substitute for good-quality survey data or internal records. Mapping aggregate statistics is an intermediate step before a survey can be conducted or an internal record-keeping system developed, and in those cases where a survey is simply out of the reach of a small-business budget, the substitution of data for areal units should be evaluated with caution.

Site Selection

Many small-business owners are particularly sensitive about location because they feel that market conditions are constantly changing. For example, many owners are concerned that there are more competitors in the market area now than in the past, that the consumer market has shifted (geographically), and/or that business conditions in the present market area are less favorable than they once were. Prospective businesses simply want to know where their optimal location would be.

While there are many nondemographic considerations in location analysis (for example, availability of space and cost per square foot), a major demographic input is required to select a location that will help assure the greatest amount of success. For businesses where the clientele is particularly sensitive to the amount of time required to travel to that business, choosing a location that minimizes the aggregate distance (time) is very important. If the businessperson knows something about the demographic characteristics of those persons or organizations most likely to buy from the business in question (segmentation), and most often he or she can find out, then the demographic analysis of a small area's social and economic characteristics can aid in the selection of an optimal location. Even for a business whose customers are less time- or distance-sensitive, locating in an area favorable to business activities such as competition, physical environment, and ease of access can be the difference between success and failure. Moreover, longitudinal analysis of the changing social and economic characteristics of these small areas over time can help pinpoint locations that have substantial potential and/or those that may have already reached their business activity peak and have begun to decline. Much of this work involves a comparative analysis along a variety of dimensions for a number of potential locations.

Mid-Town Cleaners was an establishment that had been very successful in one location and wished to expand to a second. Several preliminary sites were selected on the basis of space availability and cost per square foot, and the owners wished to reduce the longer list to one or two locations worthy of in-depth consideration. Because dry cleaning customers were sensitive to the time required to secure such services—the business must either be close to home or work or be along the way between home and work—population data and traffic flow information were crucial to the selection of a site. It was determined that the site should be within or very close to an area of population growth—local-area traffic flows taken into account—and that the type of population growth most important was that resulting from an increase in the number of apartment dwellers, particularly those paying medium and above-medium rental costs since it is that type of person who is most likely to use dry cleaning services.

Using 1970 and 1980 Census of Population data for population, housing, and income for census tracts and zip codes as well as some post-1980 special survey estimates for those same variables, the geographic areas with the best business potential were identified. This was accomplished by profiling each of the locations on the initial list and making subjective judgments about each profile. Special attention was focused on the locations that seemed to have the greatest potential for future growth. Furthermore, a host of computerized models for identifying the optimal location for small retailers have been developed which can make site selection a relatively simple procedure. Most of these contain demographic components.[10]

Bernard Anthony, the potential purchaser of an existing business, had a different problem than those faced by Mid-Town Clearners. He was considering the purchase of an existing business. The business under consideration, a shoe retailing outlet, was located in an area of town he was concerned about. Though recent sales records showed strong sales volume in recent months, he was worried that changing neighborhood characteristics along with a variety of other factors would hurt business in the future. His situation was somewhat more complex than that of the dry cleaning owner discussed above because Mr. Anthony felt that customers were somewhat less time- and distance-sensitive; thus the market area was larger.

It was thought that at least 50 percent of the business would come from the near local area. Examining the same types of data looked at in the dry cleaning case—population size, age structure, income, potential for growth or decline, and traffic flow patterns for census tracts and zip codes—it was learned that the area in which the business was located, while not experiencing a population decline yet, had a relatively old age structure which made it likely that population decline would in fact occur in the near future. Furthermore, the economic development projects slated for areas adjacent to the business had been delayed and their future was in doubt. Mr. Anthony chose not to buy the business at that time and to look for other opportunities.

Demographic characteristics of the most frequent customers are used in the site selection process of fast food franchises.[11] Geographic areas containing high concentrations of such persons are selected as sites for new stores. Pizza chains, for example, have found that young males consume more of their product than do females. One such rapidly growing chain, Domino's, favors locations near college campuses and military bases in order to be near greater concentrations of customers. The use of demographic data requires a two-stage process. First, a demographic profile of existing customers is assembled. Second, geographic areas with high concentrations of similar persons are located.

Identification of Market Area(s)

Closely related to locational analysis is the identification of market areas, that is, determining over what geographic areas a business draws its customers. This activity can be relatively simple, especially when customers are time- and distance-sensitive, and as stated earlier can be accomplished by plotting all or a sample of customer addresses on a good-quality map. Distances and travel times to the business can be measured and concentrations of customers based on concentric circles of various radii can be determined. Time-specific concentration grids can also be drawn. Once the market area is determined, more can be learned about the area by studying its demographic characteristics (profiling). Small-area demographic change analysis over short or long time intervals can indicate if the market area is increasing or decreasing in size, becoming younger or older, and turning richer or poorer. Furthermore, longitudinal analysis can provide information on the expansion or contraction of a market area. If the market area is a county, for example, then yearly economic data from County Business Patterns can provide information on the number and sizes of competitors. Economic census data can provide more detailed aggregated competitor data, though only at five-year intervals.

The Center Theatre was very interested in knowing more about its market area because season's memberships and single ticket sales had dropped markedly over the last three years. A plotting of members' addresses for three different seasons showed that two areas (groups of census tracts) had experienced a significant reduction in season's members. However, the two areas had very dissimilar social and economic characteristics. One was predominately white and contained the areas of town with the highest median family and household incomes. The other area contained diverse ethnic neighborhoods and was characterized by medium- and low-income concentrations. Among many kinds of problems, several of which related to the internal organization of the theatre, was that the limited advertising budget was being spent trying to appeal to a general audience. While that may have been a good strategy for maintaining membership levels in the past, it meant that the two areas where membership had recently declined were being virtually ignored in advertising efforts. A different advertising strategy, one that targeted the types of persons characterized by the areas showing a loss of members, was developed.

A local race track was also concerned about advertising efforts in relation to the location of their clientele. By taking a sample of license plates (observation in the parking lot during the races) and linking the plate numbers to the counties of residence, track management was able to determine where people were coming from to attend the races. Furthermore, as the season went on, day-of-the-week and month-of-the-year patterns could also be identified. The information aided in determining where to concentrate current advertising dollars as well as where potential markets might be. The same pattterns monitored over several seasons could identify increasing or decreasing flows of patrons from targeted as well as nontargeted areas and assist in measuring advertising effectiveness. As these historical data are gathered and patterns identified, fine tuning the overall business strategy may occur. With the addition of a second track into the area this past season, the information became even more valuable in that the effect of the competition could be measured not only in attendance and handle but in the location of where the patrons were coming.

Demand and Sales Forecasts

While forecasting is a task most small businesses usually do not engage in or, if they do, it is the familiar "last year's sales plus 10 percent" type of activity, the inclusion of demographic data and expertise can make some types of forecasting simpler and achievable for small businesses. The implication is not that a new and better series of forecasting measures has been developed, but that some simple, little-used demographic-based techniques (in the small-business context) are better than "last year's sales plus 10 percent." Depending on the quantity and quality of data owners and managers already have (for example, sales records and information on who buys their products or services), as well as characteristics of market areas (such as size and descriptive characteristics), it is possible to link incidence or prevalence rates to consumer or industrial projections in order to produce demand or sales forecasts. If a business's sales are closely linked to a greater concentration of certain types of households in the market area, then it is possible to create an incidence rate by dividing sales by the number of households of that specific type. Given an incidence rate of 15 sales per 1,000 married-couple households, then a geographic area containing 100,000 such households could expect roughly 1,500 sales. Of course, measures of change as well as the short-run stability in this rate should be looked at. This also assumes that good-quality household projections are available.

Hand, Dunkelberg, and Sineath looked at the economic feasibility of opening a retail hardware store in a specific census tract in an MSA.[12] The census tract in mind made up what Hand and his colleagues considered to be the potential market area given the store size and competition. What they needed were profit projections to determine if the business would be viable.

They used U.S. Census of Population and Housing data as well as intercensal estimates on potential population and household growth, the proportion of households that were owner-occupied (the types of households most likely to purchase at hardware stores), and income structure to project profits.

Hand and his colleagues required a two-step procedure to project profits. First, potential hardware sales were estimated by taking hardware sales from the most recent Census of Retail Trade for the entire MSA and dividing by the number of owner-occupied houses. The resulting number was a per capita (owner-occupied households) dollar amount spent at hardware stores. This number was multiplied by the number of owner-occupied houses in the census tract, and the resulting product yielded estimated hardware sales for the tract. Future sales were forecast by projecting area owner-occupied households and adjusting the dollar amounts for changes in the consumer price index. Second, the sales estimate in dollars calculated above was allocated to various cost categories—labor, building lease, owner's salary, and cost of goods, for example—and subtracted to yield profits.

Looking at the forecasting issue in a somewhat different context, The Pines Nursing Home wished to expand its facility to include an additional fifty beds. However, before proceeding The Pines had to demonstrate that a need existed for these beds so that the local planning board would give permission to build. The owners of The Pines needed to forecast demand (sales) in the context of the changing age structure and the competitors in its market area. By linking population projections for the market area—focusing most heavily on the population age 65 and over—to incidence rates (numbers of persons 65 years old and over per 1,000 persons 65 years old and over in a nursing home including other factors such as length of stay), forecasts of the need for nursing home services were produced. This involved a simple multiplication of an age-specific incidence rate times the projected age-specific population total and summing across all age categories of interest. These forecasts were then linked to the total number of beds currently available (The Pines and competitors) to show that additional beds would be needed in the near future.

A second example comes from Midwest Livestock Feed Mill. The company had been in business for over sixty years but was experiencing difficulty in making sales forecasts because its demand forecasts were poor. It was learned that while the number of farms within the market area was being incorporated into demand estimates (Census of Agriculture and County Business Patterns data), the number of cattle on feed was not. The solution to the problem called for a development of a means for monitoring changes in the cattle population in the market area. Data to develop such a monitoring system were available from state agricultural reports.

Valley Health Spa provides a third example. Mary Robinson was interested in opening a health spa in a smaller community but was unsure about the level of demand for such a service. She had learned from national-level data that persons who join health spas are generally concentrated in the younger ages (20–40) and have middle-and-above income levels. She also knew that in general a certain critical mass of persons in those social and economic categories was needed. On examining the 1980 Census of Population and Housing data for the community of interest, along with population and income projections, Ms. Robinson concluded that the requisite critical mass did not presently exist and was not likely to be present in the future.

Market Share Estimation

Though market share is one of the most difficult issues for business researchers to address, demographic data and manipulations of those data can provide a small business with a way of approximating market share. Infrequently, market share can be calculated utilizing public records such as real estate sales for establishing a real estate company's market share within a particular area. The share is simply calculated by dividing either the number of homes sold or the dollar amount of homes sold for the company in question by the total number of households or the dollar amount of those homes in the market area. However, in most instances business researchers must rely on other sources of information for determining the denominators for market share. Frequently, economic censuses and County Business Patterns provide the baseline (denominator) data for calculating market share, though other data sources can work as well. When calculating a percentage of market share, the numerator for the proportion comes from the internal records of the business in question while the denominator is found in the data sources mentioned above.

In 1985 Shoe City Inc., a four-store local shoe retailer, was interested in learning about its market share of the shoe business. It was felt that market share, and therefore sales, was not what it should be and had in fact declined in recent years. Radical new strategies were being considered to boost sales. Taking data on Shoe City sales receipts for 1977 and 1982 and calculating market share on the basis of total sales receipts for 1977 and 1982 for SIC code 566 (shoe stores) from the Census of Retail Trade in the county that included Shoe City's market area, it was learned that market share had in fact increased between 1977 and 1982. The question that remained concerned whether or not market share had changed since 1982, the latest year that Census of Retail Trade data were available. Though no direct measures were available to estimate 1985 market share, 1985 County Business Patterns provided Shoe City with the number of shoe establishments in the county (again SIC code 566), and by comparing the 1985 data with the numbers for the late 1970's and early 1980's, it was found that the number of shoe stores in the market area had not increased. The assumption was then made that market share had not slipped, and the radical new strategies were abandoned for more moderate approaches toward increasing sales. Of course, Shoe City will want to monitor market share and when the 1987 Census of Retail Trade data are made available, they should perform new calculations.

A similar example to Shoe City is provided by Streamliner Motel, whose owners wished to know their market share and if that share had changed from the late 1970's. Using Census of Service Industries data for 1977 and 1982 for SIC annual code 7011 pt (motels, motor hotels, and tourist courts) for the MSA making up its market area, Streamliner was able to determine market share as well as the number of establishments the total share was among. Streamliner Motel internal records provided the numerators and motel service industry data for the MSA provided the denominator for calculating market share.

SUMMARY AND CONCLUSIONS

There are many uses of demographic data and the demographic perspective in the small-business context, and these applications are not merely scaled-down versions of large-business activity. This chapter contains a detailed discussion of the dissimilarities between large and small businesses and an argument that the two categories are substantially different. Applying a demographic perspective to small-enterprise analysis requires a general knowledge of the data sets that exist—which ones contain specific information—as well as the geographic units for which the data are available. Some expertise in manipulating the data is helpful, though the experience necessary to gain the expertise can be gained by reading the examples presented in this chapter while keeping one's own business problems/opportunities in mind. Furthermore, use of the data may require some creativity and imagination because using demographic data in a small-business context sometimes involves applying figures for small areas to problems and opportunities for which the data have not been used before. That is, there may be no case examples in the literature where the specific application in mind was in fact used. More importantly, however, the optimal use of demographic data in the small-enterprise context requires that the business owner have a perspective that clearly connects population phenomena to business conditions and change.

This chapter has provided the reader with several uses for demographic data in small enterprises and has presented a number of examples where the demographic perspective has been successfully applied. The major tasks that the small-business owner must accomplish in optimally using the data are (1) to frame the problem/opportunity as clearly as possible, including a general list of the data sources needed in the specific context, and (2) to apply the data in combination with internal records and/or survey information in an imaginative fashion that answers the questions at hand.

NOTES

1. U.S. Bureau of the Census. 1986. *Statistical Abstract of the United States, 1986.* Washington, D.C.: U.S. Government Printing Office, tables 880 and 881

2. Gary Slutsker. 1985. "The Cream of the Crop." *Forbes* (November 4): 126–156.

3. Judith Soveynaki. 1986. "The Business Week 1000." *Business Week* (April 18): 46–69; Pete Engardio. 1986. "Hot Growth Companies." *Business Week* (May 26): 94–108.

4. David M. Ambrose and John Hafer. 1986. "Psychic Income in the Small Business." *NBDC Report*, No. 62 (January). Nebraska Business Development Center: University of Nebraska at Omaha.

5. Small Business Administration Staff. 1985. *The State of Small Business*. A Report of the President by the U.S. Small Business Administration. Washington, D.C.: U.S. Government Printing Office, table 1.7.

6. Small Business Administration Staff. 1985. *The State of Small Business*, table 1.13.

7. Small Business Administration Staff. 1985. *The State of Small Business*, table A1.21.

8. Alvin Star and Michael Z. Massel. 1981. "Survival Rates for Retailers." *Journal of Retailing* 57 (Summer): 87–99.

9. Nora G. Barnes. 1984. "New Shopper Profiles: Implications of Sunday Sales." *Journal of Small Business Management* 22 (July): 32–39.

10. See, for example, Howard Rudd, James Vigen, and Richard Davis. 1983. "The LMMD Model: Choosing the Optimal Location for a Small Retail Business." *Journal of Small Business Management* 21 (April): 44–53; and Michael Goodchild. 1984. "ILACS: A Location-Allocation Model for Retail Site Selection." *Journal of Retailing* 60 (Spring): 84–100.

11. Dan Moreno. 1979. "Successful Sites." *American Demographics* (October): 19–23.

12. Herbert Hand, John Dunkelburg, and W. Palmer Sineath. 1979. "Economic Feasibility Analysis for Retail Locations." *Journal of Small Business Management* (July): 19–27.

13

The Demography of
International Business

INTRODUCTION

The last ten years have been marked by a significant increase in interest with regard to virtually all dimensions of international business. From monitoring the strength of the U.S. dollar to the opening of new markets throughout the world, concern for knowing more about the nations that U.S. companies are and may in the future be trading with is being expressed. Many U.S. businesses are now highly dependent on sales to other nations and are well integrated into a system of truly internationally operated organizations. Exxon, for example, obtains nearly 70 percent of its total revenue in the international market. Coca Cola derives well more than one-half of its profits from international business. Multinational corporations such as IBM, Ford, Goodyear, 3M, and Gillette all garner in excess of one-third of their sales or profits abroad.[1] For a variety of reasons, many other companies are finding that the source of business growth for the future lies beyond the boundaries of the United States.

From the perspective of the businessperson in the United States who wishes to export goods and services, information on the historical, cultural, political, economic, and demographic characteristics of those destination nations is imperative if success is to be attained and opportunities maximized. On the cultural side, a great deal of diversity in belief systems dictates to a great extent what can be sold and the manner in which selling can take place. While recent studies have demonstrated some cultural commonalities between European nations and the United States, (for example, a commit-

called the world food crisis. A typical example appeared in a recent Associated Press story carried in the *Omaha World Herald*. The article stated that nineteen countries, in particular, face severe food shortages in part because of their inability to import (purchase) enough food simply to feed their increasing numbers.[11] While this author does not wish in any way to minimize world food problems which are leading to malnutrition and death in many parts of the world, food is but one of many areas that are affected by demographic factors. Just as U.S., regional, state, and local differences in population growth rates and composition affect the ability of business to be successful in those areas, cross-national comparisons reveal that some countries contain "more favorable" demographic conditions (industry- and business-specific) than others.

Table 13.1 presents several selected demographic characteristics for nineteen nations and the world for 1986. The population of the world was estimated to be nearly 5 billion in 1986. As can be seen, there is a tremendous amount of variation in each of the demographic variables presented. Size of both the 1986 population estimate and the projection for 2000 varies from well over 1 billion persons in China to about 21 million for Kenya. Crude birth rates range from as low as ten in West Germany to fifty-four in Kenya. The highest crude death rate is eighteen in Nigeria, while the lowest is six in Mexico and Japan. Doubling time, which is a measure of how long (years) it would take a population to double in size given that its present growth rate does not change, shows a low of 17 years in Kenya and a high of 693 in Italy. That is, the population of Kenya will double from 21 to 42 million by the year 2003 if its growth rate remains constant! West Germany has no doubling time due to its negative population growth. Infant mortality rates also demonstrate a great deal of variation with the minimum figure (6.2), in Japan and the maximum (127) in Nigeria. In other words, while less than 1 percent of the births in Japan die in their first year of life, nearly 13 percent of the Nigerian births suffer that fate.

The total fertility rate (the average number of children a woman would have if current age-specific birth rates held constant), ranges from 8.0 in Kenya to 1.3 in West Germany—a difference of more than 6 children! Life expectancy at birth also has a wide differential, (26 years), with the highest (74 years) in three nations and the lowest (47 years) in Zaire. There is a 69 percentage point spread in the population living in urban areas—85 percent in West Germany, 16 percent in Kenya. Finally, per capita gross national product (GNP) ranges from $170 in Zaire to over $14,000 in the United States.

While these data to a certain extent mask the intracountry differences in composition, growth rates, and demographic factors, they do demonstrate the wide range of demographic realities in the world today. Overall, nations with the highest growth rates are also the poorest in economic (per capita GNP) terms. Furthermore, those same countries have the highest infant

Table 13.1

Demographic Characteristics for Selected Nations of the World: 1986

Country	1986 Population[a]	Population Projection 2000	Crude Birth Rate	Crude Death Rate	Population Doubling Time	Infant Mortality Rate	Total Fertility Rate	Life Expectancy at Birth	Percent Urban Population	Per Capita GNP, 1983 (US$)
World	4,942.0	6,157.0	27	11	41	82	3.7	62	43	$2,750
Egypt	50.5	71.2	37	11	27	100	5.3	58	44	690
Nigeria	105.4	150.1	48	18	23	127	6.5	49	28	770
Kenya	21.0	35.8	54	12	17	72	8.0	53	16	340
Zaire	31.3	46.9	42	14	25	106	6.1	47	34	190
South Africa	33.2	44.8	33	10	30	86	5.0	54	53	2,240
Turkey	52.3	69.7	35	10	28	92	5.1	62	46	1,250
India	785.0	1,017.0	35	13	31	110	4.5	53	23	260
Indonesia	168.4	219.9	34	13	34	84	4.4	55	22	560
China	1,050.0	1,190.0	18	8	72	50	2.1	64	32	300
Japan	121.5	128.1	13	6	107	6.2	1.8	77	76	10,100
U.S.	241.0	268.0	16	9	99	10.5	1.8	75	74	14,080
Mexico	81.7	112.8	32	6	27	53	4.4	66	70	2,180
Brazil	143.3	194.7	31	8	30	71	4.1	63	69	1,870
Argentina	31.2	37.5	24	8	44	35.3	3.4	70	83	2,510
United Kingdom	56.6	57.4	13	11	462	9.6	1.8	74	90	9,180
West Germany	60.7	58.6	10	11	--	9.6	1.3	74	85	11,400
Romania	22.8	24.5	14	10	178	23.9	2.0	71	49	2,560
Italy	57.2	58.1	10	9	693	116	1.5	74	72	6,390
U.S.S.R.	280.0	311.0	20	11	79	31	2.4	69	65	6,760

[a]numbers in millions.

Source: Population Reference Bureau Staff. 1986. World Population Data Sheet. Washington, D.C.: Population Reference Bureau.

mortality rates and the lowest life expectancies at birth. Countries with the highest growth rates also contain young age structures which are conducive to continued population growth.

Though the reader is urged to seek additional data if more information is desired about a specific country (see the next section of this chapter), other area and regional similarities and dissimilarities are worthy of note. First, the part of the world now called more developed, which includes Europe, North American, Australia, Japan, New Zealand, and the USSR, is growing much slower than the less developed world (the balance of countries). While regions like Northern and Western Europe have doubling times of 393 and 555 years, respectively, the doubling time for all of Africa is 24 years. Coupled with slow growth rates in the more developed world has come a general aging of the population. For example, while only 22 percent of the European population is under age 15, 45 percent of the African population falls in that category. On the other hand, while only 3 percent of the African population is over age 64, in Europe the percentage is 13. Furthermore, three European nations (out of twenty-seven) are now experiencing population loss, and three others have attained zero population growth (ZPG). An additional two countries have but a .1 percent annual growth rate and soon will achieve ZPG. Ten of the twenty-seven nations of Europe are projected to have a population either the same size or smaller than that exhibited today by the year 2000.

With their high rates of population growth, less developed countries exhibit the greatest potential for market growth simply because of the tremendous increase in the number of consumers. However, when growth rate data are coupled with income data (per capita GNP, which to some extent reflects the ability to buy goods and services), a very different picture emerges. Per capita GNP is only $700 annually in the less developed world, and in many countries it is less than $500, leaving most of the population unable to purchase even the least expensive goods and services. The more developed world, on the other hand, has a per capita GNP of $9,510. In other words, while the less developed world contains nearly 3.8 billion persons, its GNP totals about $2.7 trillion. The nearly 1.2 billion individuals living in more developed nations have a GNP of over $11.4 trillion. Even a relatively small country like Denmark (5.1 million population) has a $58.8 billion GNP. Pakistan, with a population of nearly 102 million (nearly twenty times larger than Denmark) has a GNP of only $40 billion.

Furthermore, the developed/less developed, low-growth/high-growth dichotomies have ramifications for other aspects of the international business environment. While developed nations have had high and stable percentages of their population living in urban areas in recent years, less developed nations have been marked by rapid urbanization over a relatively short time span. In Central and South America (for example, Brazil, Chile, Columbia, Ecuador, Peru, Venezuela, Mexico, and Nicaragua all nations have experienced a rise of 20 percent or greater in the total population classified urban since 1950.[12] Labor force shifts have also been substantial in these countries over the same time period. The percentage of the labor force classified agricultural has declined by at least 20 percent in Brazil, Columbia, Ecuador, Venezuela, Costa Rica, Mexico, Nicaragua, and Panama since 1950.[13] Certainly, these kinds of ongoing changes contribute to a restructuring of the individual consumer and industrial markets, as well as the way in which business is conducted.

Furthermore, not all of the less developed nations are poor. Brazil, for example, is presently experiencing significant economic growth and the 1986 balance of trade estimates show a $13 billion surplus.[14] South Korea and Taiwan have both been successful in international markets and represent potentially strong markets for exporters. Oil-rich nations, such as Qatar, Saudi Arabia, and The United Arab Emirates, though negatively affected by falling oil prices, all have per capita GNPs larger than that of the United States. Conversely, several more developed nations, while having the requisite income to purchase imports, have not been good markets due to a variety of trade restrictions and cultural differences. In sum, it is a combination of economic, cultural, political, and demographic factors that determines the viability of a market.

INTERNATIONAL DATA SOURCES

While the data seen in Table 13.1 are good for illustrating general demographic differences among nations of the world, the detail required for planning and strategy purposes must be obtained from other sources. The data sources discussed below do not represent an exhaustive list of all sources available, though they are illustrative of the extent of information detail in existence. Aside from these data compendia, individual-nation data can be obtained from the government statistical offices of each country. Though some desired detail may be lacking in the sources about to be discussed, the major advantage of using centralized sources for many nations is that the demographic factors presented for each country have to some extent been standardized. That is, each nation has the same information included which facilitates country-by-country comparisons.

Before presenting the data sources, one caution must be expressed. The quality of international demographic statistics is sometimes poor. Collection and tabulation methodologies, while reasonably dependable in most developed nations, are questionable in some less developed countries. The time period between data collections is also sometimes longer than what would be ideal, and therefore some data are quite old. The recommendation here is for the user to evaluate, if possible, each piece of information with regard to its timeliness, source, and methodology of collection. In the case of population estimates and projections, once again the assumptions are crucial, and therefore an examination of historical data should take place.

One of the most widely used data sources is the United Nations' *Demographic Yearbook.*[15] The *Yearbook* contains data on population size, distribution, compositional characteristics, fertility, mortality, marriage, and divorce, as well as a host of social and economic factors for the world and countries of the world. Birth and death rates are included along with life expectancies and population growth rates. Detailed data are available. For example, from the 1984 *Yearbook* tables it can be learned that there were 363,715 persons under age 1 in Canada in 1981 (latest census). These same figures are also broken down into gender and urban/rural residence components.

Part of the United Nations' publications series contains what is called *Demographic Indicators of Countries,* which includes population estimates and projections for countries of the world.[16] Alternative age, sex, and rural/urban residence projections are presented based on low-, medium-, and high-growth variants. Furthermore, the crude birth and death rates, total fertility rate, gross and net reproduction rates, net immigration, and life expectancies that are the basis for the projections are included. So, for example, the medium variant population projection for Argentina for the year 2000 is 33,222,000. This is based on an assumed total fertility rate of 2.46, a life expectancy of 71.2 years, and zero net immigration. That population would contain 8,455,000 persons under age 15, have a median age of 30.6 years, and be 87.9 percent urban. The high-growth variant shows a 33.9 million person total while the low variant generates a 31.8 million total. The range 2.9 million is less than 1 percent of any total. Also providing data on population estimates and projections is the United Nations' publication *World Population Prospects.*[17]

A wider range of social statistics is available in the United Nations' *Compendium of Social Statistics.* This publication provides data on population, health, food consumption and nutrition, education and literacy, culture and communication, land use, social security, refugees, and labor for the world, regions, countries or areas, and cities or urban agglomerations. Detailed data include, among many other factors, newspaper circulation, the number of book titles published, public expenditures on education, and pupil-teacher ratios for countries. At the city or urban agglomeration level, data on the average number of persons per household, housing conditions, population density, and environmental pollution can be found. The UNESCO *Statistical Yearbook* contains detailed economic, social, cultural, and demographic data for the world, major areas, groups of countries, and individual countries.[18] The detail provides country-specific information on characteristics such as educational enrollment by level, the number of research and development scientists, scientific and technical manpower potential, total expenditures on research and experimental development, annual cinema attendance, the number of television transmitters, the number and circulation of magazines, and the number of radio receivers.

Aside from the United Nations' publications series are two additional statistical yearbooks. The International Labour Organization's *Yearbook of Labour Statistics* contains detailed data for the world, countries, and smaller areas on employment, hours of work, labor costs, consumer prices, occupational injuries, and industrial disputes. Furthermore, time series data are included so that change can be monitored.[19] For example, wages in manufacturing for International Standard Industrial Code (ISIC) 311 rose from 8.89 to 17.19 guilders per hour between 1974 and 1983 in the Netherlands. Manufacturing labor costs increased from 12.83 to 18.88 rupees per hour in India between 1974 and 1979 for ISIC codes 311 and 312.

Second, the *Economic Handbook of the World* presents economic data for countries of the world.[20] The information contained includes gross national product per capita, international reserves, external public debt, exports (fob), imports (cif [cost includes freight]), government revenue and expenditure, and indexed consumer prices. Furthermore, a brief narrative explaining historical, political, geographic, and cultural highlights is presented along with a more detailed discussion of the structure of the economy.

The U.S. Bureau of the Census' *World Population* contains demographic estimates for the world, world regions, and individual countries.[21] Information appearing includes population size at last enumeration, a recent population estimate, birth, death, infant mortality and growth rates, and life expectancy. The references cited at the end of each country profile are particularly useful to the reader desiring additional information. Extensive country-specific unpublished data are available on request thought the U.S. Census Bureau's Center for International Research. These data include, among other factors, detailed population characteristics from the most recent and several prior censuses, along with current data on labor force activities, literacy, and health factors.

A relatively new publication, *International Demographics*, is produced monthly by American Demographics, Inc. Each issue contains a country profile—there are about fifty profiles thus far—as well as other demographic/business factors related to the international market. For example, the August 1986 issue profiles the Republic of Panama including its 1985 age and sex structure along with information on ethnicity and religion, labor and unemployment, and housing.[22] Also included is information on population growth in the region as a whole and where (other data sources) consumer information for the region can be obtained.

The Statistical Abstract of the United States contains an entire section called comparative international statistics. Aside from the country-specific demographic data much like those presented in Table 13.1, the section contains information on, for example, gross national and gross domestic product, per capita expenditures on major food commodities, ownership (percent owning) of major appliances, and consumer prices.

In sum, individually or collectively, the above demographic publications provide a great deal of information about foreign markets. So, for example, if a reader is trying to decide which country among two or three to target for the introduction of a certain good or service, comparative analysis could tell him or her how large the market was, how fast it was growing, if it had the financial capability to buy the product or service, if the political and cultural environments were conducive to the success of the business, and in what context (economic, social, and environmental) the business would exist.

On the other hand, if the question was more general and asked initially for a list of five or six countries where a given business might be successful, then the use of the information from above would be somewhat different. First, the country characteristics seen as most important to the success of that business in a foreign market would have to be identified and perhaps differentially weighted depending on the importance of each factor. Then an algorithm could be produced to identify all nations with the given set of characteristics. This could be computerized to run against a data set containing all relevant factors, and countries might be ranked from top to bottom based on their business-suitability aggregate score. The countries emerging as most likely to foster success could then be evaluated further by looking at other types of business considerations such as the costs of setting up new offices and the price of creating another level of infrastructure.

In either case, the data available provide a background from which to make better business decisions, which is the same argument made earlier with regard to the interjection of demographic data in the domestic business-planning environment. These data are not to be regarded as the only information required for good decision making, though their inclusion as a supplement to other factors should substantially improve business decisions.

This section of the chapter should not end before there is some recognition of the demographic data included in various international business reports. While these data most often come directly from the official statistics of the country in Question, or the information sources just discussed, they are generally integrated with other useful business information. For example, *Export Europe*, which is a series of country reports aimed at the exporting of various consumer products, contains useful information or population size by age and sex, population change, population concentration (in cities and towns) and income cross-classified by occupation.[23] When combined with information on domestic consumption, advertising expenditures, consumer goods ownership, and trend data on retail trade, the outcome is a very useful document for anyone wishing to enter that market. *Market Share* reports disclose trends in market size, measure changes in import demand for specific products, compare the competitive position of U.S. and foreign importers, select distribution centers for U.S. products abroad, and identify existing and potential markets for U.S. business in over eighty-eight countries.

THE IMPACT OF DEMOGRAPHIC FACTORS ON INTERNATIONAL BUSINESS DECISIONS

Demographic conditions affect international business from the earliest stages of selecting a potential market to the day-to-day operations of an existing enterprise. Each of the demographic "facts" presented in Table 13.1 represents at least one business opportunity. These opportunities range from the market for contraceptives where fertility rates are high to health care services where mortality rates are high. In moving from the stages of estimating and projecting market potential to calculating a forecasted return on investment, demographic factors (along with geographic, economic, technical, sociocultural, and national goal and plan considerations) should be viewed as indicators of market potential.[24] An assessment of the size and composition of certain consumer segments, along with a few other factors, can tell a prospective business if there is enough demand for a product or service in a given nation, and country comparisons on those factors help determine what location(s) is best for investment. The level of urbanization can greatly affect product planning.[25]

An excellent framework for utilizing demographic information for the selection of countries with appropriate business environments has been developed by Liander.[26] Using a cluster analysis approach, the demographic factors total population, population density, population growth rate, labor force participation, literacy, percentage of labor force employed in agriculture, level of urbanization, and degree of population concentration (primary) were used in conjunction with other factors in order to group countries on the basis of similar characteristics. These nations can be viewed as having similar business environments and therefore as providing similar business opportunities. A similar system for selecting the "best" countries for the purpose of foreign investment has been developed by Ehrman and Hamburg.[27] The factors of import include those related to (1) political, legal, and social concerns, (2) commercial factors, and (3) monetary/finance issues. Among the commercial factors, market size—a population-driven factor—is seen as a key to successful investment.

Among his entry strategies for international markets, Root includes a stage where market size is estimated.[28] Key components in this estimate include the size and structure of the population including its population growth rate and density. A major part of the business environment profile for Harris and Moran contains population variables such as ethnic composition, urbanization, infant mortality, literacy, per capita income, and population size.[29]

Companies engaged in international business have made use of demographic information in their formulation of strategic plans. For example,

Great Waters of France, in its marketing of Perrier in the United States, took into account not only cultural factors, but market size (population) and composition (older age structure) characteristics in its decision to target American consumers. Their success is evidenced in the fact that between 1977 and 1980 sales increased from 21 to 200 million bottles per year.[30] Eastman Kodak's international photographic operations first develops a list of various nations with sales potential and then segments the list by region and develops targets within those countries based on the demographic indicators income and family size when international expansion is considered.[31] CANAL Distribution Ltd. Sea Wing Service of Canada, which is an intermodal transportation service linking Europe and North America, took into account population, population growth, and per capita income as well as information on imports by method of transportation and transportation time in order to determine where to expand its package delivery service.[32] Minneapolis Foods ascertained the internal population distribution of Guatemala before deciding on locations through which to sell Danish pastries, cinnamon rolls, and pizza.[33] In each instance, demographic data were merged with other information in order to improve decision making.

Comparisons of less and more developed nations, with their high-growth/low-growth dichotomy, demonstrate differential marketing opportunities. Even with their low per capita GNP, the market for infant and maternity goods and school equipment is good in rapidly growing countries. The same potentially large markets exist within the population of persons between the ages of 5 and 25. On the other hand, businesses that specialize in these same product areas in developed nations have been forced to diversify in order to survive as a result of the fall in fertility rates. Maternity wards have closed and there is markedly less demand for baby products. At the other end of the age spectrum, the large increase in persons 55 years old and over is rapidly increasing demand for health and leisure products and services in more developed nations, though there is no analogous occurrence in less developed countries.

In a brief example, China illustrates how an individual country can be profiled to determine many of the important dimensions of the business climate. In Table 13.1 it is documented that China has a more than 1 billion population, a doubling time of 72 years, and a per capita income of $300 yearly. However, much more can be learned about China by combining data from other sources (Chinese census, population estimates and projections, and survey data).[34] While only about one-third of the population lives in urban areas, the percentage has nearly doubled since 1970 and shows signs of even greater increase. The highest concentration of persons is in the easternmost provinces. The age structure of the population is getting older, and by the year 2000 population projections show that there will be more than 520 million persons ages 30–64! Labor force participation is quite high—90 percent for males and 72 percent for females compared with 77 and 53 percent for males and females, respectively, in the United States. While incomes are relatively low, they are showing signs of substantial percentage increase—11.5 and 17.6 percent per year for urban workers, respectively, between 1978 and 1984. The increase in the Consumer Price Index (CPI) has been small (CPI = 160 in 1984; standard = 100 for 1950), and therefore increased spending strength is not being eroded by increases in the cost of living.

On the consumer product side, several interesting observations should be made. With regard to product ownership in 1983, for every 100 urban households there were 159 bicycles, 268 wristwatches, 83 television sets, and 27 tape recorders. For every 100 peasant households there were 63 bicycles, 132 wristwatches, 4 television sets, and 2 tape recorders. With regard to retail sales, in 1983 there was $121 billion in sales of all consumer goods out of which $66 billion was spent on food, $25 billion on clothing, and $14 billion on medicine and medical products. Overall, China is a large and diverse market with increasing business opportunities in a variety of areas.

The data above would be incomplete without an evaluation of the cultural and political environments and a more-detailed analysis of markets, distribution systems, composition, and other factors. The example, however, illustrates the value of demographic data and analysis in determining a major dimension of the business environment.

The major conclusion to be drawn from this presentation is that the demographic perspective, along with population data and analysis, is just as valuable in the international context as it is in understanding the domestic business environment. Given the trend toward international markets, the business community cannot exclude demographic input and expect to operate in an effective manner.

NOTES

1. Theodore Levitt. 1983. "The Globalization of Markets." *Harvard Business Review* 61 (May-June): 92–102.

2. International Management Staff. 1985. "New Study Finds High Level of Cynicism among U.S. and European Workforces." *International Management* (October): 76–77; International Management Staff. 1986. "Looking beyond Profitability: Where U.S. and European Cultures Meet." *International Management* (July): 54–56.

3. See, for example, George McNally. 1986. "It's Not Just Possible—It's Imperative." *Business Marketing* (April): 64–70.

4. John Quelch and Edward Hoff. 1986. "Customizing Global Marketing." *Harvard Business Review* 64 (May-June): 59–68.

5. Marvin Cetron. 1986. "Looking at the Future of American Business." *The Futurist* (March-April): 25–27.

6. E. S. Browning. 1986. "Out of Touch: Lobbying in Japan Daunts Most American Concerns." *Wall Street Journal* (May 1): 1.

7. Stephen Yoder. 1986. "Computer Chip Makers Head for Japan." *Wall Street Journal* (August 1): 6.

8. Patricia M. Schershel. 1986. "Wall Street Goes Global." *U.S. News & World Report* (March 24): 52.

9. Forbes Staff. 1986. "The Forbes Foreign Rankings." *Forbes* (July 28): 171–216.

10. Fortune Staff. 1986. "The Fortune International 500." *Fortune* (August 4): 169–205.

11. Associated Press. 1986. "Research Institute Says Third World to Face Growing Need for Food." *Omaha World Herald* (July 28): 4.

12. Thomas Merrick. 1986. *Population Pressures in Latin America*. Population Bulletin 41 (July). Washington, D.C.: Population Reference Bureau, table 6.

13. Thomas Merrick. 1986. *Population Pressures in Latin America*, table 7.

14. Jeffrey Ryser and John Pearson. 1986. "How Brazil Is Barreling into the Bigtime." *Business Week* (August 11): 38–40.

15. United Nations. 1985. *Demographic Yearbook 1984*. New York: United Nations.

16. United Nations. 1982. *Demographic Indicators of Countries*, New York: United Nations.

17. United Nations. 1985. *World Population Prospects*. Population Studies, No. 86. New York: United Nations.

18. United Nations Educational, Scientific, and Cultural Organization. 1985. *Statistical Yearbook*. Lovain (Belgium): UNESCO.

19. International Labour Office Staff. 1984. *Yearbook of Labour Statistics*. Geneva: International Labour Office.

20. Vivian Carlip, William Overstreet, and Dwight Linder (eds.). 1982. *Economic Handbook of the World: 1982*. New York: McGraw-Hill Book Company.

21. U.S. Bureau of the Census. 1986. *World Population 1985*. Washington, D.C.: U.S. Government Printing Office.

22. International Demographics Staff. 1986. "The Republic of Panama." *International Demographics 5* (August).

23. British Overseas Trade Board. 1983. *Export Europe* (reports for European nations). London: Department of Trade and Industry.

24. Douglas Sorsan, C. Samuel Craig, and Warren Keegan. 1982. "Approaches to Assessing International Marketing Opportunities for Small and Medium-Sized Business." *Columbia Journal of World Business* (Fall): 26–32.

25. John S. Hill and Richard R. Still. 1984. "Effects of Urbanization on Multinational Product Planning: Markets in Lesser Developed Countries." *Columbia Journal of Wolrd Business* (Summer): 62–67.

26. Bertil Liander. 1967. *Comparative Analysis for International Marketing*. Boston: Allyn and Bacon Co., pp. 63–90.

27. Chaim Meyer Ehrman and Morris Hamburg. 1986. "Information Search for Foreign Direct Investment Using Two-Stage Country Selection Procedures: A New Procedure." *Journal of International Business Studies* 17 (Summer): 93–116.

28. Franklin R. Root. 1987. *Entry Strategies for International Markets*. Lexington, Massachusetts: D.C. Heath and Company, pp. 36–46.

29. Philip R. Harris and Robert T. Moran. 1987. *Managing Cultural Differences* (Second editon). Houston, Texas: Gulf Publishing Company, pp. 325–370.

30. John Daniels and Lee Radebaugh. 1986. *International Business*. Reading, Massachusetts. Addison-Wesley Publishing Company, pp. 645–650.

31. Alan Rugman, Donald Lecraw, and Laurence Booth. 1985. *International Business*. New York: McGraw-Hill, pp. 342–343.

32. Philip Rosson. 1984. "CANAL Distribution Ltd.: See Wing Service." Pp. 523–535 in V. H. Kirpalani. *International Marketing*. New York: Random House..

33. Renforth, William. 1984. "Minneapolis Food Joint Venture in Guatemala." Pp. 598–603 in V. H. Kirpalani. *International Marketing*. New York: Random House.

34. The data used in the next paragraphs were gleaned from the report by Jeffrey R. Taylor and Karen A. Hardee. 1986. *Consumer Demand in China: A Statistical Factbook*. Washington, D.C.: U.S. Bureau of the Census.

14

The Demography of the Business Environment—A Summary and View toward the Future

INTRODUCTION

The preceding thirteen chapters have shown how demographic events and conditions serve as major factors in shaping the business environment. From the addition and deletion of consumers through the interaction of fertility, mortality, and migration to the changing composition and distribution of those consumers, population-related phenomena to a great extent determine the number and geographic location of buyers along with many of their buyer and economic characteristics.

As is discussed in Chapters 11–13, many businesspersons have utilized demographic information in the context of decision making to gain a competitive edge. Whether it is a large organization such as Time Inc. or the small retailer doing business in the average U.S. city, population phenomena are seen by a host of executives as important input variables in the shaping of short- and long-term strategic plans. Peter Drucker devotes an entire chapter to what he labels demographics in his book *Innovation and Entrepreneurship*.[1] In that chapter, a clear connection is made between demographic events and organizational success or failure for a number of major businesses including the House of Rothschilds, Melville, and New York's Citibank. Melville, for example, saw early on that baby boom children just a few years removed would produce a tremendous increase in the demand for footwear on the part of adolescents. They cultivated this market by redesigning products and promotional campaigns; their efforts were rewarded through a tremendous increase in sales. Melville's success was noted and copied by other shoe companies. By that time, they had geared themselves for the maturing of the baby boom cohorts and today they continue to operate successfully.

The common thread running through businesses that have used demographic data and analysis successfully is that they all have developed in one fashion or another a demographic perspective to the issues and events that affect their organizations. They have been able to view business opportunities as well as problems as being to some extent demographically driven and have learned to monitor the demographic signals that spell change for their organizations. They have not all become demographic technicians—most have not—but they have learned to identify and track the demographic factors that are a key to their success.

In summarizing and drawing useful conclusions from the preceding chapters, several issues must be addressed. These issues can be grouped under three general categories and provide the outline of the remainder of the chapter. First, a brief review of recent demographic history is provided with an eye toward the most-likely-to-occur scenerio for the remainder of this century. This should aid the reader with regard to what changes in demographic conditions to expect. Second, demographic events are once again linked to static and dynamic concerns for the business environment. These concerns include trends in the size and composition of consumer segments as well as the private and public policies that may emerge as the result of changing demographic conditions. Third, the issue of what the large- and small-business executive can do to determine the effect of demographic factors on individual business conditions is addressed. Suggestions are offered concerning how large and small businesses alike can track demographic change.

DEMOGRAPHIC HISTORY

The demographic history of the United States is one filled with changes in the levels of fertility, mortality, and migration. With the exception of the post-World War II baby boom, fertility has been declining in the United States since the nineteenth century. Declining fertility coupled with an increase in life expectancy and fluctuating but larger totals of immigrants to the United States in recent years has resulted in a slowing of growth, an aging of the population, and a demographic structure that is becoming more socially and ethnically diverse. Furthermore, population redistribution has resulted in a movement of people from the Northeast and Midwest to the South and West. More importantly, perhaps, many individual cities, communities, and smaller geographic areas have experienced marked decreases or increases in population size and changes in composition that have affected their social and economic structure including the business environment.

While the macro trends (that is, slowing growth and an aging population) at the national level are likely to continue, trends for smaller geographic areas are not likely to remain constant. So, while the South is likely to continue to grow, a great deal of division-to-division, state-to-state, and community-to-community variation will be seen. These differences already exist—some areas in the South probably will never increase in population—and changes in state and local economic conditions will continue to alter growth rates as well as other demographic factors. For example, the relationship between depressed oil prices and slowing population growth in states like Texas and Louisiana and cities like Houston is well known.

Macro-level trends are important, nevertheless, as they are responsible for the national markets as well as private and public policies that affect these markets. While the most-likely-to-occur demographic scenario for the end of the century forecasts continued population growth, the growth rate is slowing and population increase could well come to a halt by the middle of the next century. By the end of this century the population should number around 267 million, an increase of about 25 million consumers from the 1987 population. However, all of the growth will be in the South and West, with the year 2000 population totals in the Northeast and Midwest being smaller than the 1987 totals. With regard to age structure, the number of persons age 65 and above will increase from about 29 million to approximately 34 million, or nearly 15 percent. Other age groups, particularly those most affected by the post–World War II baby boom and the following baby bust, will experience even greater growth variation. For example, persons 45–64 are likely to increase from an estimated 42 million in 1987 to 59 million in 2000—a 40 percent rise! The number of persons under age 5 will actually decrease.

The reader is reminded once again that local trends will not necessarily follow those at the national level. For example, while U.S. population growth was approximately 11 percent from 1970 to 1980 and slowed to 3.5 percent in the period 1980–1984, growth in cities like Arlington, Texas; Anchorage, Alaska; Mesa, Arizona; and Tallahassee, Florida exceeded 25 percent for just the first four years of the 1980s. It is these subnational patterns that can and must be tracked.

While none of the above summary information comes as a surprise to most readers, regional and local variation can be expected and therefore must be monitored. For example, cities in the Northeast and Midwest—regions losing population—that are growing faster than the national growth rate (3.5 percent for the period 1980–1984) include Lincoln, Nebraska (4.9%); Staten Island Borough, New York (5.3%); and Omaha, Nebraska (6.4%). Metropolitan areas falling in the same category include the Nashua, New Hampshire PMSA; Grand Rapids, Michigan MSA; Minneapolis–St. Paul, Minnesota–Wisconsin MSA; Danbury, Connecticut PMSA; Poughkeepsie, New York MSA; and the Wichita, Kansas MSA.

Though it would be advantageous to be able to state unequivocally that the scenerio presented above will be fact in a few short years, all projections or forecasts are bound to contain error. Fertility and mortality assumptions, at least in the short run, are likely to be approximately "correct," though assumptions with regard to immigration and internal migration have less certainty. The impact of the recently passed immigration reform measures on the total number and characteristics of legal and illegal entrants to the United States is unknown at this time. With regard to internal migration, national, regional, and local changes in economic conditions could greatly affect the pattern of movement.

In sum, demographic scenarios are useful because they provide general information about market change, though they must be continually updated as conditions fluctuate. More important, however, is the development and continuous updating of alternative demographic scenarios for the market area of a particular business. Given that demographic data are available for a variety of geographic units, this task is not always as difficult as it might initially seem.

BUSINESS ENVIRONMENT

A great deal of attention has already been focused on the connection between population variables and the growth/decline and changing characteristics of the consuming population. While these considerations are important, there has been far too little interest in the implications of population change for labor force supply in specific industries as well as the private and public business and population policies that may result as growth approaches zero and the population becomes older.

Labor supply not only is the product of demographic forces that provide the number of potential participants but also includes educational and wage considerations. Education, in general, translates as training to perform skilled labor tasks and wages draw participants to certain occupations. As the age structure of the population changes, some industries are forced to recruit from a labor pool that is structurally different from that of the current workers. To the extent that these new workers are different—in age, lifestyle, and/or racial/ethnic composition, for example—other methods of training as well as different reward structures are required in order to guarantee a labor supply of sufficient size. As discussed earlier, the fast food industry, which traditionally has recruited teenage workers, has been forced to recruit from other age categories. Training as well as the rewards structure has been altered somewhat to accommodate these new workers. Other retail businesses are having to make similar adjustments. However, as industries that require a more-skilled labor force experience shortages in certain demographic categories, training and rewards structure adjustments will be greater than those made by retailers whose workers require less training.

With regard to changes in labor force structure, several issues are salient. First, while the total labor force is projected to grow by between 25 and 30 million members between now and 1995, all of the growth will be accounted for by increases in labor force participants 25–54 years of age. In fact, labor force participants age 16–24 and 55 and over will actually decline in number over the interval.[2] At the same time substantial growth is projected for a number of occupational groups including a number of health care categories, marketing and sales positions, several technician categories, and service worker jobs such as bartenders, waiters and waitresses, and cooks.[3] However, some occupations draw most heavily from age groups whose labor force is projected to decline in number. Over 48 percent of the waiters and waitresses in the United States today (an occupation projected to undergo substantial growth) are between 16 and 24 years of age (ages where a decline in the labor force is projected).[4] If growth in this occupational category is to materialize, then the rewards structure and/or recruiting and training strategies must undergo change. Other occupations experiencing decline include fast food counter help and related jobs (83.4% age 16–24), shoe sales (57.9% age 16–24), farmers (37.1% age 55 and above), and dressmakers (39.0% age 55 and above).[5]

From a public and private policy standpoint, there are several considerations regarding demographic change. First, there are the national demographic policies which to some extent affect both the number and structure of consumers as well as workers. These policies tend to have their greatest implications for specific areas where immigrants tend to settle, though the institution of fertility inducement laws such as those discussed in Chapter 10 could affect the entire population. Businesses and businesspersons help shape these policies through their support—votes and money—and great care must be given to these concerns. Local-area growth policies have more specific implications for businesses limited to a local or regional market, and support or opposition to such statutes can affect both customer and labor force supply.

Business policy specific to individual organizations is exceedingly important as adjustments are made to a changing demographic environment. Demographic change probably brings about as many opportunities as problems and those organizations that are flexible enough to adjust to this aspect of the changing business environment have a competitive advantage. The advantage covers both the ability to attract a sufficient amount of business activity and the requisite labor force to support those activities. Flexibility alone, however, will not suffice. Preparation for and monitoring of demographic change must occur. And even more importantly, there has to be a clear understanding of the connection between demographic change and specific characteristics of a business. Most business owners and managers know that population growth is slowing. Those that understand the connection between slowing growth and other demographic and nondemographic phenomena as well as how to adjust to change have a competitive advantage.

In addition, an understanding of the relationships among demographic factors and other dimensions of the business environment is of importance. While the direct impact of slowing growth and an aging population on the number and composition of consumers may seem important but obvious, the indirect effect of these demographic factors through other dimensions of the business environment may be less well known though just as significant. Looking at the mature market, for example, a large increase in the number of persons 65 years of age and over has presented problems for the funding of social security benefits. To the extent that the increase in the population 65 and over brings about changes in the funding of benefits—how much is paid out per person, and the age at which persons can begin to receive such payments, that is, adjustments in the political environment—consumption of goods and services as well as a host of other business-related activities in that population is likely to change. Smaller benefit increases mean fewer dollars to be spent. An older age at retirement could result in extended labor force participation and a significant change in spending behavior. Alterations in health care benefits have created a shortfall in health care insurance and a market or supplemental insurance. In sum, the indirect effects of demographic change on business conditions are substantial. The task of the businessperson is to identify what the indirect effects are.

HOW TO MONITOR CHANGE

As previously emphasized, the reader does not need to be a demographic expert to monitor and understand demographic change. And because most demographers do not have a good business perspective, the average businessperson who has some demographic exposure will be able to gain certain types of knowledge from demographic data that the demographer would overlook.

The initial task of those wanting to monitor change is first to learn how demographic phenomena are presently influencing business opportunities and problems. That is, the reader must develop a demographic perspective. Once this perspective has been developed—and no doubt it will change over time—businesspersons must find data sources that contain the requisite information and must learn how to manipulate and analyze the data. While not all data sets are available at the level of geography desired, demographic information is readily available in a variety of formats. Data in published form may be the best initial format because it is possible to directly examine the types of information available. The *Statistical Abstract of the United States*, an annual publication, provides a good start because it is a compendium of data from a large number of data sources. It is well referenced, and more detailed information than that appearing in the *Abstract* can easily be found. The data should be linked to other data sources such as those internal to the reader's own business in order to take full advantage of the information available. Such linkage can result in incidence and prevalence rates such as those discussed in Chapters 11 and 12. The rates multiplied by the population at risk derived from demographic data result in demand or business activity projections or forecasts. When more detailed data are desired, many times the published sources or data tapes make it possible to access the information needed. If the reader's interest is international in nature, the same procedures should be followed, though the initial source of information may come from a compendium such as the *United Nations Statistical Yearbook*.

Once the data have been secured for the geographic units desired, another phase of demographic information use is entered. This phase includes both the continued evaluation of the relationships among demographic and business-specific phenomena and the continued monitoring of demographic trends. Relationships among business and demographic factors are likely to change over time, and therefore continued study as well as monitoring is essential. Continued monitoring is made easy because of the updating of demographic information through frequent or continuous surveys and registration systems. These data are made available through frequent publication. Population estimates and projections allow the user to make educated guesses about unmeasured demographic phenomena as well as allow the reader to look at possible future demographic scenarios. Recurring relationship analysis is the responsibility of the data user, though the availability of good quality information internal to the organization can make the analysis relatively easy.

While locating demographic data for the desired geographic units is sometimes easy, in many cases problems arise. That is, the data are not available and/or are not accessible or reliable for the geographic units desired. Do not give up! While more demographic expertise may be required, market areas may be approximated given the limits of geography-bound data sets. Surrogate measures for the desired unavailable information may be located and/or calculated, though in some instances a market-area survey of some type may be in order. The user should exhaust all possible sources, however, before relying on surrogate measures or investing money in a survey.

In sum, given the careful reading of issues presented in the preceding pages, the reader should be on relatively sound footing for the development of a demographic perspective for a business, market, or some other type of organizational concern. The data required are readily available and the cost of such a perspective is very small. The benefits are substantial.

NOTES

1. Peter Drucker. 1985. *Innovation and Entrepreneurship*. New York: Harper and Row, pp. 88–98.

2. U.S. Bureau of Labor Statistics. 1986. *Occupational Outlook* (1986–1987 edition). Washington, D.C.: U.S. Government Printing Office, chart 5.

3. U.S. Bureau of Labor Statistics. 1986. *Occupational Projections and Training Data*. Washington, D.C.: U.S. Government Printing Office, table B–1.

4. U.S. Bureau of Labor Statistics. 1986. *Occupational Projections and Training Data*, table C–2.

5. U.S. Bureau of Labor Statistics. 1986. *Occupational Projections and Training Data*, table C–2.

Bibliography

ARTICLES

Alba, Richard, and Michael Batutis. 1985. "Migration's Toll: Lessons from New York State." *American Demographics* (June): 38–42.

Ambrose, David M., and John Hafer. 1986. "Psychic Income in the Small Business." *NBDC Report*, No. 62 (January). Nebraska Business Development Center: University of Nebraska at Omaha.

American Demographics Staff. 1984. "Demographic Forecasts." *American Demographics* (April): 50.

Associated Press. 1984. "Wine Coolers Tagged Hottest Trendy Drinks." *Omaha World Herald* (August 4): 18-A.

Associated Press. 1986. "Research Institute Says Third World to Face Growing Need for Food." *Omaha World Herald* (July 28): 4.

Bailey, Mohamed, and David F. Sly. 1985. "Metropolitan-Nonmetropolitan Migration Expectancy in the United States, 1965–1980." Paper presented at the annual meeting of the Southern Regional Demographic Group. Austin, Texas.

Barnes, Nora G. 1984. "New Shopper Profiles: Implications of Sunday Sales." *Journal of Small Business Management* 22 (July): 32–39.

Becker, Gary. 1960. "An Economic Analysis of Fertility." Pp. 209–231 in *Demographic and Economic Change in Developed Countries*. Universities-National Bureau of Economic Research Conference Series 11. Princeton, New Jersey: Princeton University Press.

Bellinger, Danny, and Humberto Valencia. 1982. "Understanding the Hispanic Market." *Business Horizons* (May-June): 49.

Boeldner, Charles, and Henry Munn. 1964. "The Significance of the Retirement Market." *Journal of Retailing* 40: 43–64.

Brown, Paul, Ellyn E. Spragins, Pete Engardino, Kirvin Ringe, and Steve Klinkerman. 1985. "Bringing Up Baby: A New Kind of Marketing Boom." *Business Week* (April 22): 58–65.

Browning, E. S. 1986. "Out of Touch: Lobbying in Japan Daunts Most American Concerns." *Wall Street Journal* (May 1): 1.

Business Week Staff. 1981. "A New Target: Reducing Staff and Levels." *Business Week* (December 21): 69–70.

Business Week Staff. 1984. "Baby Boomers Push for Power." *Business Week* (July 2): 52–62.

Butz, William, and Michael Ward. 1979. "The Emergence of Countercyclical U.S. Fertility." *American Economic Review* 69: 318–328.

Cahan, Vicky. 1985. "The Huge Pension Overflow Could Make Waves in Washington." *Business Week* (August 12): 71–75.

Cahan, Vicky. 1985. "Tremors in the Pension System Finally Wake Congress Up." *Business Week* (November 18): 45.

Cahan, Vicky, Kathleen Deveny, and Joan Hamilton. 1985. "Health Care Costs: The Fever Breaks." *Business Week* (October 21): 86–94.

Cetron, Mervin. 1986. "Looking at the Future of American Business." *The Futurist* (March-April): 25–27.

Chase, Marilyn. 1986. "AIDS Has Spread Almost Everywhere in Africa, Zaire, Doctor Tells Parley." *Wall Street Journal* (June 24): 10.

Chase, Marilyn. 1986. "Drug Firms Anticipate Big Market in Products for Immune Disorder." *Wall Street Journal* (June 26): 1, 13.

Croisdale-Appleby, David. 1984. "Target Marketing of Financial Services." *The Banker* (April): 51–59.

Davis, Kingsley, and Judith Blake. 1956. "Social Structure and Fertility: An Analytic Framework." *Economic Development and Cultural Change* 4: 211–235.

Dugas, Christine. 1985. "Smoothing Baby Boomers' Wrinkled Brows." *Business Week* (September 23): 68.

Duncan, Otis D. 1959. "Human Ecology in Population Studies." Pp. 678–716 in P. Hauser and O. D. Duncan (eds.), *The Study of Population*. Chicago: University of Chicago Press.

Dunn, William. 1985. "The Changing Face of Cosmetics." *American Demographics* (March): 40–51.

Dunn, William. 1986. "In Pursuit of the Downscale." *American Demographics* (May): 26–33.

Easterlin, Richard. 1973. "Relative Economic Status and the American Fertility Survey." Pp. 170–223 in Eleanor B. Sheldon (ed.), *Family Economic Behavior: Problems and Prospects*. Philadelphia: J. B. Lippincott Company.

Edmondson, Brad. 1984. "Ryan Homes Have Brains." *American Demographics* (August): 16.

Edmondson, Brad. 1985. "How Big Is the Baby Market?" *American Demographics* (December): 23–48.

Edmondson, Brad. 1986. "Foundations Level the Slippery Slope." *American Demographics* (January): 20–21.

Edmondson, Brad. 1986. "Travelers Hire the Un-Retired." *American Demographics* (June): 24

Eglinton, Tom. 1983. "How Dow Jones Uses Demographics." Transcripts of talk given at Consumer Demographics Conference (September). Los Angeles.

Ehrman, Chaim Meyer, and Morris Hamburg. 1986. "Information Search for Foreign Direct Investment Using Two-Stage Country Selection Procedures: A New Procedure." *Journal of International Business Studies* 17 (Summer): 93–116.

Engardio, Pete. 1986. "Hot Growth Companies." *Business Week* (May 26): 94–108.

Espenshade, Thomas J. 1984. "Demographic Forces Shaping the Future of the Family." Paper presented at the annual meeting of the Southern Regional Demographic Group. Orlando, Florida.

Espenshade, Thomas, and Jeffrey Tayman. 1982. "Confidence Intervals for Postcensal State Population Estimates." *Demography* 19: 191–210.

Forbes Staff. 1985. "Index to the Forbes Four Hundred." *Forbes* (October 28): 316–330.

Forbes Staff. 1985. "Older Not Sweeter." *Forbes* (July 15): 107.

Forbes Staff. 1986. "The Forbes Foreign Rankings." *Forbes* (July 28): 171–216.

Forstall, Richard, and Maria Elena Gonzalez. 1984. "Twenty Questions." *American Demographics* (April): 22–42.

Fortune Staff. 1986. "The Fortune International 500." *Fortune* (August 4): 169–205.

Fredrickson, Carl. 1983. "The Financial Perspective." Transcript of a talk given at Demographics Outlook '83 Conference (June). White Plains, New York.

Freedman, Deborah. 1976. "Fertility, Aspirations and Resources: A Symposium on the Easterlin Hypothesis." *Population Development Review* 2 (3–4): 411–415.

Glasser, Gerald, and Gale D. Metzger. 1975. "Radio Usage by Blacks." *Journal of Advertising Research* (October): 39–45.

Goodchild, Michael. 1984. "ILACS: A Location-Allocation Model for Retail Site Selection." *Journal of Retailing* 60 (Spring): 84–100.

Greenwood, Michael, and John McDowell. 1984. "U.S. Immigration Policy: Issues and Analysis." Unpublished manuscript.

Grossmen, Allyson Sherman. 1982. "More Than Half of All Children Have Working Mothers." *Monthly Labor Review* 105 (February).

Guseman, Patricia, and Stephen Sapp. 1986. "Fords of the Future." *American Demographics* (April): 4.

Hamford, Janet. 1986. "Hang Tough or Take the Gold Watch Early?" *Forbes* (May 5): 158–159.

Hand, Herbert, John Dunkelburg, and W. Palmer Sineath. 1979. "Economic Feasibility Analysis for Retail Locations." *Journal of Small Business Management* (July): 19–27.

Hedges, Michael. 1986. "Radio's Lifestyles." *American Demographics* (February): 32–35.

Hill, John S., and Richard R. Still. 1984. "Effect of Urbanization on Multinational Product Planning: Markets in Lesser Developed Countries." *Columbia Journal of World Business* (Summer): 62–67.

Holdrich, Martin. 1984. "Prospects for Metropolitan Growth." *American Demographics* (April): 33–37.

Hunt, Albert. 1986. "What Working Women Want." *Wall Street Journal* (June 6): 20.

International Demographics Staff. 1986. "The Republic of Panama." *International Demographics* 5 (August).

International Management Staff. 1985. "New Study Finds High Level of Cynicism among U.S. and European Workforces." *International Management* (October): 76–77.

International Management Staff. 1986. "Looking beyond Profitability: Where U.S. and European Cultures Meet." *International Management* (July): 54–56.

James, W. H. 1970. "The Incidence of Spontaneous Abortion." *Population Studies* 24: 241–245.

Kain, Edward L. 1984. "Surprising Singles." *American Demographics* (August): 16–39.

Kantrowitz, Barbara. 1986. "Three's a Crowd." *Newsweek* (September 1): 68–76.

Kaplan, Charles P., and Thomas L. Van Valey. 1980. "Geography for a Changing Society." Pp. 129–158 in Kaplan and Van Valey (eds.), *Census '80: Continuing the Factfinder Tradition*. Washington, D.C.: U.S. Government Printing Office.

Kaplan, Charles P., and Thomas L. Van Valey. 1980. "Twenty Censuses." Pp. 9–36 in Kaplan and Van Valey (eds.), *Census 80: Continuing the Factfinder Tradition*. Washington, D.C.: U.S. Government Printing Office.

Kasarda, John D., Michael D. Irwin, and Holly L. Hughes. 1986. "The South Is Still Rising." *American Demographics* (June): 33–70.

Keely, Charles. 1979. "The United States of America." Pp. 51–64 in Daniel Kubat (ed.), *The Politics of Migration*. New York: Center for Migration Studies.

Kerr, Melville G. 1971. "Perinatal Mortality and Generic Wastage in Man." *Journal of Biosocial Science* 2: 223–237.

Keyfitz, Nathan. 1981. "The Limits of Population Forecasting." *Population and Development Review* 7: 579–591.

Keynes, John M. 1937. "The Economic Consequences of a Declining Population." *Eugenics Review* 29: 13–17.

Kintner, Hallie J. and Ernest B. Smith. 1985. "A Demographic Profile of the G.M. Work Force and Dependents: Implications for Health Care." *General Motors Research Laboratories*, Publication GMR 5207. Warren, Michigan.

Klein, Richard. 1986. "USA 2000." *Sales and Marketing Management* (October): 8–39.

Kuttner, Robert. 1986. "Where the Free Market Falls Short." *Business Week* (June 30): 20.

Lambert, Zarrel. 1979. "An Investigation of Older Consumers' Unmet Needs and Wants at the Retail Level." *Journal of Retailing* 55: 35–57.

Lazer, William. 1985. "Inside the Mature Market." *American Demographics* (March): 23–49.

Levitt, Theodore. 1983. "The Globalization of Markets." *Harvard Business Review* 61 (May-June): 92–102.

Lee, Everett. 1966. "A Theory of Migration." *Demography* 3: 47–57.

Lee, Susanna. 1984. "Here Come the Baby Boomers." *U.S. News and World Report* (November 5): 68–73.

Long, Larry. 1973. "New Estimates of Migration Expectancy." *Journal of the American Statistical Association* 68: 37–45.

Lublin, Joann. 1986. "Staying Single." *Wall Street Journal* (May 28): 1, 18.

Lunde, Donald,. 1981. "Personnel Management: What's Ahead?" *Personnel Administrator* (April): 51–60.

McBee, Susanna. 1984. "Here Come the Baby Boomers." *U.S. News and World Report* (November 5): 68–73.

McDonald, Scott. 1984. "Use and Limitations of Demographic Analysis in a Communications Business." Paper presented at the annual meeting of the Population Association of America (May). Minneapolis, Minnesota.

McLaughlin, Edward, and Gene German. 1985. "Supermarketing Success." *American Demographics* (August): 34–37.

McNally, George. 1986. "It's Not Just Possible—It's Imperative." *Business Marketing* (April): 64–70.

McWorter, John. 1985. "Local Area Demographic Estimates: Small Is Beautiful." Paper presented at the annual meeting of the Southern Regional Demographic Group. Austin, Texas.

Martin, Julia, and William Serow. 1978. "Estimating Demographic Characteristics Using the Ratio-Correlation Method." *Demography* 15: 223–233.

Merwin, Mark, and Louis Pol. 1983. "Childlessness: A Panel Study of Expressed Intentions and Reported Fertility." *Social Biology* 30: 318–327.

Meyer-Ehrman, Chaim, and Morris Hamburg. 1986. "Information Search for Foreign Direct Investment Using Two-Stage Country Selection Procedures: A New Procedure." *Journal of International Business Studies* 17 (Summer): 93–116.

Morais, Richard. 1985. "Faulting the Fortune Tellers." *Forbes* (October 21): 102–104.

Moreno, Dan. 1979. "Successful Sites." *American Demographics* (October): 19–23.

Morrison, Peter A. 1978. "Emerging Public Concerns over U.S. Population Movement in an Era of Slowing Growth." Pp. 225–246 in Thomas J. Espenshade and William J. Serow (eds), *The Economic Consequences of Slowing Population Growth*. New York: Academic Press.

Murray, Thomas. 1977. "The Coming Glut in Executives." *Dun's Review* (May): 69.

Neal, Larry. 1978. "Is Secular Stagnation Just around the Corner? A Survey of the Influences of Slowing Population Growth upon Investment Demand." Pp. 101–125 in Thomas J. Espenshade and William J. Serow (eds.), *The Economic Consequences of Slowing Population Growth*. New York: Academic Press.

O'Hare, William. 1976. "Report on a Multiple Regression Method for Making Population Estimates." *Demography* 13: 369–379.

Omaha World Herald Staff. 1986. "AIDS May Kill 179,000 in U.S. in Five Years." *Omaha World Herald* (June 25): 4.

Parker, George C., and Edilberto Segura. 1971. "How to Get a Better Forecast." *Harvard Business Review* (March April): 99–109.

Petre, Peter. 1986. "Marketers Mine for the Gold." *Fortune* (March 31): 70–78.

Population and Development Review Staff. 1983. "On Province-Level Fertility Policy in China." *Population and Development Review* 9 (September): 553–561.

Population Reference Bureau Staff. 1984. "Sterilization, Breastfeeding on the Rise." *Population Today* 12 (December): 2.

Population Reference Bureau Staff. 1985. "Take a Number." *Population Today* 13 (February): 10.

Prescott, Eileen. 1983. "New Men." *American Demographics* (August): 16–45.

Quelch, John, and Edward Hoff. 1986. "Customizing Global Marketing." *Harvard Business Review* 64 (May-June): 59–68.

Renforth, William. 1984. "Minneapolis Foods Joint Venture in Guatemala." Pp. 598–603 in V. H. Kirpalani. *International Marketing*. New York: Random House.

Riche, Martha Farnsworth. 1981. "State Data Centers." *American Demographics* (January): 32.

Riche, Martha Farnsworth. 1981. "State Demographics." *American Demographics* (October): 42–44.

Riche, Martha Farnsworth. 1981. "State Statistical Abstracts." *American Demographics* (August): 38–40.

Riche, Martha Farnsworth. 1985. "The Business Guide to the Galaxy of Demographic Products and Services." *American Demographics* (June): 23–33.

Riche, Martha Farnsworth. 1985. "Directory of Demographic Products and Services." *American Demographics* (July): 34–41.

Roberts, Margaret (trans.). 1984. "Romanian Population Policy." *Population and Development Review* 10 (September): 570–573.

Robey, Bryant. 1985. "Asian Americans." *American Demographics* (May): 23–29.

Rosenfeld, Jeffrey. 1984. "Demographics and Interior Design." *American Demographics* (February): 28–31.

Rosson, Phillip. 1984. "CANAL Distribution Ltd. Sea Wing Service." Pp. 523–535 in V. H. Kirpalani. *International Marketing*. New York Random House.

Rudd, Howard, James Vigen, and Richard Davis. 1983. "The LMMD Model: Choosing the Optimal Location for a Small Retail Business." *Journal of Small Business Management* 21 (April): 44–53.

Russell, Cheryl. 1985, "The New Homemakers." *American Demographics* (October): 23–27.

Ryser, Jeffrey, and John Pearson. 1986. "How Brazil Is Barreling into the Bigtime." *Business Week* (August 11): 38–40.

Schershel, Patricia M. 1986. "Wall Street Goes Global." *U.S. News & World Report* (March 24): 52.

Schewe, Charles D. 1985. "Gray America Goes to Market." *Business* (April-June): 3–9.

Shapiro, Kenneth. 1981. "Managing the Impending Promotion Squeeze." *Personnel Journal* (October): 800–804.

Sjaastad, Larry. 1962. "The Cost and Return of Human Migration." *Journal of Political Economy* (Supplement on Investment in Human Beings) 70 (Part 2): 80–93.

Skinner, Steven. 1980. "Staying Alive." *American Demographics* (May): 11–13.

Slater, Courtenay, and Cristopher Crane. 1986. "The Net Worth of Americans." *American Demogrpahics* (July): 4–6.

Slutser, Gary. 1985. "The Cream of the Crop." *Forbes* (November 4): 126–156.

Sly, David, and Jeff Tayman. 1977. "Ecological Approach to Migration Reexamined." *American Sociological Review* 42: 783–794.

Smith, Stanley. 1985. "Characteristics of Single Population Projection Techniques, with an Extension to the Construction of Confidence Intervals." Unpublished paper.

Smith, Stanley, and Bart Lewis. 1980. "Some New Techniques for Applying the Housing Unit Method of Local Population Estimation." *Demography* 17: 323–339.

Sorsan, Doublas, C. Samual Craig, and Warren Keegan. 1982. "Approaches to Assessing International Marketing Opportunities for Small and Medium-Sized Business." *Columbia Journal of World Business* (Fall): 26–32.

Soveynaki, Judith. 1986. "The Business Week 1000." *Business Week* (April 18): 46–49.

Star, Alvin, and Michael Z. Massel. 1981. "Survival Rates for Retailers." *Journal of Retailing* 57 (Summer): 87–99.

Sternlieb, George, and James Hughes. 1982. "Who's Buying Homes?" *American Demographics* (December): 24–27.

Sternlieb, George, and James Hughes. 1985. "The Good News about Housing." *American Demographics* (August): 18–21, 49.

Stoto, Michael. 1983. "The Accuracy of Population Projections." *Journal of the American Statistical Association* (March): 13–20.

Thomas-Pond Enterprises Staff. 1982. "Who's Watching the Children?" *Thomas-Pond Enterprises Human Resources Newsletter* (April).

Thorton, Arland. 1978. "Marital Dissolution, Remarriage and Childbearing." *Demography* 15: 361–380.

Townsend, Bickley. 1983. "The Changing Consumer Household." Transcript of a talk given at the Consumer Demographics Conference (March). Chicago, Illinois.

Trafford, Abigail. 1984. "Marketplace Aims at New Breed of Burgers." *U.S. News and World Report* (November 5): 71–72.

Turchiano, Francesco. 1983. "The Retailing Perspective." Transcript of a talk given at Demographics Outlook '83 Conference (June). White Plains, New York.

Vining, Daniel, Jr. 1984. "Family Salaries and the East German Birth Rate." *Population and Development Review* 19 (December): 693–696.

Waldholz, Michael. 1986. "Drug to Block Some Ills of Aging Set for Tests in Humans This Year." *Wall Street Journal* (June 20): 17.

Walker, John. 1980. "What Every Manager Should Know about Projections." *American Demographics* (January): 30–31.

Walsh, Doris. 1982. "Why Life Insurance Companies Are Discovering Women." *American Demographics* (April): 20–23.

Walsh, Doris. 1984. "Segmenting the Maturity Market." Transcript of a talk given at Demographic Outlook '84 (June). New York, New York.

Walsh, Doris. 1984. "Utilities Come In from the Darkness." *American Demographics* (June): 29–31.

Walsh, Doris. 1985. "Targeting Teens." *American Demographics* (February): 21–41.

Walsh, Doris, and Ann Lloyd. 1984. "Personnel Planning's New Agenda." *American Demographics* (September): 35–51.

Wellington, Alphonzo. 1981. "Traditional Brand Loyalty." *Advertising Age* (May 18): 5–12.

Wolpert, Julian. 1966. "Migration As an Adjustment to Environmental Stress." *Journal of Social Issues* 22: 92–102.

Wyek, John. 1984. "The Levi Strauss Strategy." Transcript of a talk given at Strategic Demographics for U.S. Martkets Conference (March). San Francisco, California.

Yoder, Stephen. 1986. "Computer Chip Makers Head for Japan." *Wall Street Journal* (August 1): 6.

BOOKS

Barnard, William. 1950. *American Immigration Policy*. New York: Harper and Row.

Barnett, Larry D., and Emily F. Reed. 1985. *Law, Society, and Population: Issued in a New Field*. Houston, Texas: Cap and Gown Press.

Daniels, John, and Lee Radebaugh. 1986. *International Business*. Reading, Massachusetts: Addison-Wesley Publishing Company.

Drucker, Peter. 1985. *Innovations and Entrepreneurship*. New York: Harpet and Row.

Easterlin, Richard. 1980. *Birth and Fortune*. New York: Basic Books.

Goldscheider, Calvin. 1971. *Population, Modernization, and Social Structure*. Boston: Little, Brown and Company.

Harris, Philip R., and Robert T. Moran. 1987. *Managing Cultural Differences* (Second edition). Houston, Texas: Gulf Publishing Company.

Hauser, Philip, and Otis Dudley Duncan (eds.). 1959. *The Study of Population*. Chicago: University of Chicago Press.

Hawley, Amos. 1950. *Human Ecology: A Theory of Community Structure*. New York: Ronald.

Jones, Landon Y. 1980. *Great Expectations*. New York: Ballentine Books.

Keyfitz, Nathan. 1977. *Applied Mathematical Demography*. New York: Wiley-Interscience.

Lansing, John and Eva Mueller. 1967. *The Geographic Mobility of Labor*. Ann Arbor, Michigan: Institute for Social Research.

Liander, Bertil. 1967. *Comparative Analysis for International Marketing*. Boston: Allyn and Bacon Co.

Peters, Thomas, and Robert Waterman. 1982. *In Search of Excellence*. New York: Warner Books.

Potts, Malcolm, Peter Diggory, and John Peel. 1977. *Abortion*. London: Cambridge University Press.

Robey, Bryant. 1985. *The American People*. New York: Truman Talley Books.

Root, Franklin R. 1987. *Entry Strategies for Internatinal Markets*. Lexington, Massachusetts: D.C. Heath and Company.

Rugman, Alan, Donald Lecraw, and Laurence Booth. 1985. *International Business*. New York: McGraw-Hill.

Shryock, Henry S., and Jacob S. Siegel. 1973. *The Method and Materials of Demography*. Vol. 1. Washington, D.C.: U.S. Government Printing Office.

Shryock, Henry S., and Jacob S. Siegel (with Edward Stockwell). 1980. *The Methods and Materials of Demography*. Washington, D.C.: U.S. Government Printing Office.

Speare, Alden, Sidney Goldstein, and William Frey. 1975. *Residential Mobility, Migration and Metropolitan Change*. Cambridge, Massachusetts: Ballinger Publishing Co.

Spiegelman, Mortimer. 1973. *Introduction to Demography*. Cambridge, Massachusetts: Harvard University Press.

Teitelbaum, Michael S., and Jay M. Winter. 1985. *The Fear of Population Decline*. New York: Academic Press.

Tomasi, S. M., and C. B. Kelly. 1975. *Whom Have We Welcomed*. New York: Center for Migration Studies.

Weeks, John R. 1981. *Population*. Belmont, California: Wadsworth.

Weeks, John R. 1984. *Population*. (Second edition). Belmont, California: Wadsworth.

Weeks, John R. 1986. *Population: An Introduction to Concepts and Issues* (Third edition). Belmont, California: Wadsworth.

Weller, Robert, and Leon Bouvier. 1981. *Population: Demography and Policy*. New York: St. Martin's Press.

Westoff, Charles F. and Norman B. Ryder. 1977. *The Contraceptive Revolution*. Princeton, New Jersey: Princeton University Press.

Zelnick, Melvin, John Kantner, and Kathleen Ford. 1981. *Sex and Pregnancy in Adolescence*. Beverly Hills, California: Sage Publications.

MONOGRAPHS

Alan Guttmacher Institute. 1976. *11 Million Teenagers*. New York: Planned Parenthood Federation.

Bigger, Jeanne C. 1979. *The Sunning of America*. Population Bulletin Vol. 34, No. 1. Washington, D.C.: Population Reference Bureau.

Blackwell, Roger, Lee Mathews, and Carolyn Randolph. 1979. *Living in Columbus*. Columbus, Ohio: Nationwide Communications, Inc.

Bouvier, Leon. 1980. *America's Baby Boom Generation: The Fateful Bulge*. Population Bulletin Vol. 35, No. 1. Washington, D.C.: Population Reference Bureau.

Bouvier, Leon. 1981. *Immigration and Its Impact on U.S. Society*. Population and Public Policy Series No. 2. Washington, D.C.: Population Reference Bureau.

Bouvier, Leon, Cary Davis, and Robert Haupt. 1983. *Projections of the Hispanic Population in the United States 1990–2000*. Washington, D.C.: Population Reference Bureau.

Glick, Paul, and Arthur Norton. 1977. *Marrying, Divorcing and Living Together in the U.S. Today*. Population Bulletin Vol. 32, No. 5. Washington, D.C.: Population Reference Bureau.

Kalwat, Janet. 1983. *Divorce, Remarriage and Childbearing: A Study of Fertility Differences between Women in First and Second Marriages*. Unpublished Ph.D. dissertation, Princeton University.

Kubat, Daniel (ed.). 1979. *The Politics of Migration*. New York: Center for Migration Studies.

Merrick, Thomas. 1986. *Population Pressures in Latin America.* Population Bulletin 41, (July). Washington, D.C.: Population Reference Bureau.

Morrison, Peter, and Paola Scommegna. 1986. *Demographic Trends Tax the IRS.* Population Trends and Public Policy Occasional Paper No. 11. Washington, D.C.: Population Reference Bureau.

Pol, Louis. 1987. *Federal and State Government Data Sources for the Marketing Executive: Information and Uses.* New York: Audits and Surveys, Inc.

Population Reference Bureau Staff. 1982. *U.S. Population: Where We Are: Where We're Going.* Population Bulletin Vol. 37, No. 2. Washington, D.C.: Population Reference Bureau.

Pratt, W., W. Mosher, C. Bachrach, and M. Horn. 1984. *Understanding U.S. Fertility.* Population Bulletin Vol. 39, No. 5. Washington, D.C.: Population Reference Bureau.

Rives, Norfleet, and William Serow. 1984. *Introduction to Applied Demography.* Beverly Hills, California: Sage Publications.

Russell, Cheryl. 1984. *The Business of Demographics.* Population Bulletin Vol. 39, No. 3 (June). Washington, D.C.: Population Reference Bureau.

Thornton, Arland, and Deborah Freedman. 1983. *The Changing American Family.* Population Bulletin Vol. 38, No. 4. Washington, D.C.: Population Reference Bureau.

DOCUMENTS AND REPORTS

Bachrach, Christine, and William Moser. 1984. *Use of Contraception in the United States, 1982.* Advancedata from Vital and Health Statistics, No. 102. Hyattsville, Maryland: U.S. Public Health Service.

Bloom, B. 1982. *Current Estimates from the National Health Interview Survey, United States.* Vital and Health Statistics. National Center for Health Statistics. Series 10, No. 41. Washington, D.C.: U.S. Government Printing Office.

British Overseas Trade Board. 1983. *Export Europe* (reports for European nations). London: Department of Trade and Industry.

Carlip, Vivian, William Overstreet, and Dwight Linder (eds.). 1982. *Economic Handbook of the World: 1982.* New York: McGraw-Hill Company.

Dubois, David. 1980. *The Children's English and Services Study: A Methodological Review.* Washington, D.C.: U.S. Department of Education, National Center for Educational Statistics.

Graves, E. 1982. *Expected Principal Source of Payment for the Hospital Discharges: United States, 1979.* Vital and Health Statistics. National Center for Health Statistics. Advancedata, Series 2, No. 75. Washington, D.C.: U.S. Government Printing Office.

International Labour Office Staff. 1984. *Yearbook of Labour Statistics.* Geneva: International Labour Office.

Irwin, Richard. 1977. *Guide for Local Area Population Projections.* Technical Paper No. 39. Washington, D.C.: U.S. Bureau of the Census.

Kent, Mary Mederios, and Carl Haub. 1984. *World Population Data Sheet.* Washington, D.C.: Population Reference Bureau.

Kintner, Hallie J., and Ernest B. 1985. *A Demographic Profile of the G.M. Work Force and Dependents: Implications for Health Care.* General Motors Research Laboratories, Publication GMR–5207. Warren, Michigan.

Knapp, D. A., and H. Koch. 1984. *The Management of New Pain in Office-Based Ambulatory Care: National Ambulatory Medical Care Survey, 1980 and 1981*. Vital and Health Statistics. National Center for Health Statistics. Advancedata, Series 2, No. 97. Washington, D.C.: U.S. Government Printing Office.

Long, Larry, and Kristen Hansen. 1979. *Reasons for Interstate Migration*. Current Population Reports, Series P–23, No. 64. Washington, D.C.: U.S. Government Printing Office.

Oxford, Rebecca, Louis Pol, David Lopez, Paul Stupp, Murray Gendell, and Samuel Peng. 1984. *Demographic Projections of Non-English-Language-Background and Limited-English-Proficient Persons in the United States to the Year 2000 by State, Age, and Language Group*. Rosslyn, Virgina: National Clearinghouse for Bilingual Education.

Oxford-Carpenter, Rebecca, Louis Pol, and Murray Gendell,. 1984. *Demographic Projections to the Year 2000 of Limited English Proficient Hispanic Accessions in the U.S. Army*. Research Report 1349, Training Research Laboratory. Alexandria, Viriginia: U.S. Army Research Institute for the Behavioral and Social Sciences.

The Population Council Staff. 1971. *Abortion Legislation: The Romanian Experience*. Studies in Family Planning Vol. 2, No. 10 (October). New York: The Population Council.

Resource Development Institute, Inc. 1979. *Analysis of MELP's among CESS Respondents*. Austin, Texas: L. Miranda and Associates.

San Diego Association of Governments. 1984. *Aviation Demand Forecasts* (July). San Diego, California.

San Diego Association of Governments. 1984. *Overview of the Regional Growth Forecasting System* (October). San Diego, California.

Small Business Administration Staff. 1985. *The State of Small Business*. A Report of the President by the U.S. Small Business Administration. Washington, D.C.: U.S. Government Printing Office.

Taylor, Jeffrey R., and Karen A. Hardee. 1986. *Consumer Demand in China: A Statistical Factbook*. Washington, D.C.: U.S. Bureau of the Census.

United Nations. 1982. *Demographic Indicators of Countries*. New York: United Nations.

United Nations. 1984. *Demographic Yearbook 1984*. New York: United Nations.

United Nations. 1985. *World Population Prospects*. Population Studies, No. 86. New York: United Nations.

United Nations Educational, Scientific, and Cultural Organization. 1985. *Statistical Yearbook*. Lovian (Belgium): UNESCO.

U.S. Bureau of Economic Analysis. 1985. *Survey of Current Business* 65, No. 5. Washington, D.C.: U.S. Government Printing Office.

U.S. Bureau of Labor Statistics. 1984. *Employment Projections for 1995*. Bulletin 2197. Washington, D.C.: U.S. Government Printing Office.

U.S. Bureau of Labor Statistics. 1985. *Consumer Expenditure Survey: Interview Survey, 1980–81*. Bulletin 2225. Washington, D.C.: U.S. Government Printing Office.

U.S. Bureau of Labor Statistics. 1985. *Monthly Labor Review* 108 (November). Washington, D.C.: U.S. Department of Labor.

U.S. Bureau of Labor Statistics. 1986. *Consumer Expenditure Survey: Diary Survey,*

1982–1983. Bulletin 2245. Washington, D.C.: U.S. Government Printing Office.

U.S. Bureau of Labor Statistics. 1986. *Occupational Outlook* (1986–1987 edition). Washington, D.C.: U.S. Government Printing Office.

U.S. Bureau of Labor Statistics. 1986. *Occupational Projections and Training Data*. Washington, D.C.: U.S. Government Printing Office.

U.S. Bureau of the Census. 1960. *Statistical Abstract of the United States, 1960*. Washington, D.C.: U.S. Government Printing Office.

U.S. Bureau of the Census. 1975. *Historical Statistics of the United States, Colonial Times to 1970*. Bicentennial Issue, Part 1. Washington, D.C.: U.S. Government Printing Office.

U.S. Bureau of the Census. 1979. *Illustrative Projections of State Populations by Age, Race, and Sex: 1975–2000*. Current Population Reports, Series P–25, No. 796. Washington, D.C.: U.S. Government Printing Office.

U.S. Bureau of the Census. 1979. *Statistical Abstract of the United States, 1979*. Washington, D.C.: U.S. Government Printing Office.

U.S. Bureau of the Census. 1979. *Twenty Censuses*. Washington, D.C.: U.S. Government Printing Office.

U.S. Bureau of the Census. 1981. *U.S. Exports—Schedule E: Commodity by Country, February 1981*. Washington, D.C.: U.S. Government Printing Office.

U.S. Bureau of the Census. 1981. *U.S. General Imports—Schedule Commodity by Country, February 1981*. Washington, D.C.: U.S. Government Printing Office.

U.S. Bureau of the Census. 1982. 1980 Census of Population. Vol. 1, Characteristics of the Population. *General Population Characteristics*. Washington, D.C.: U.S. Government Printing Office.

U.S. Bureau of the Census. 1982. *State and Metropolitan Data Book, 1982*. Washington, D.C.: U.S. Government Printing Office.

U.S. Bureau of the Census. 1983. Factfinder for the Nation. *Agricultural Statistics*. CFF No. 3 (Rev.). Washington, D.C.: U.S. Government Printing Office.

U.S. Bureau of the Census. 1983. Factfinder for the Nation. *Construction Statistics*. CFF No. 9 (Rev.). Washington, D.C.: U.S. Government Printing Office.

U.S. Bureau of the Census. 1983. Factfinder for the Nation. *Enterprise Statistics*. CFF No. 19 (Rev.). Washington, D.C.: U.S. Government Printing Office.

U.S. Bureau of the Census. 1983. Factfinder for the Nation. *Retail Trade Statistics*. CFF No. 10 (Rev.). Washington, D.C.: U.S. Government Printing Office.

U.S. Bureau of the Census. 1983. Factfinder for the Nation. *Statistics on Governments*. CFF No. 17 (Rev.). Washington, D.C.: U.S. Government Printing Office.

U.S. Bureau of the Census. 1983. Factfinder for the Nation. *Statistics on Manufacturers*. CFF No. 15 (Rev.). Washington, D.C.: U.S. Government Printing Office.

U.S. Bureau of the Census. 1983. Factfinder for the Nation. *Statistics on Service Industries*. CFF No. 12 (Rev.). Washington, D.C.: U.S. Government Printing Office.

U.S. Bureau of the Census. 1983. Factfinder for the Nation. *Transportation Statistics*. CFF No. 13 (Rev.). Washington, D.C.: U.S. Government Printing Office.

U.S. Bureau of the Census. 1983. Factfinder for the Nation. *Wholesale Trade Sta-*

tistics. CFF No. 11 (Rev.). Washington, D.C.: U.S. Government Printing Office.

U.S. Bureau of the Census. 1983. *Geographic Mobility: March 1981 to March 1982.* Current Population Reports, Series P–20, No. 384. Washington, D.C.: U.S. Government Printing Office.

U.S. Bureau of the Census. 1983. *1982 Census of Retail Trade: Geographic Area Series—United States.* Washington, D.C.: U.S. Government Printing Office.

U.S. Bureau of the Census. 1984. *1982 Census of Governments: Government Employment, Employment of Major Local Governments.* Washington, D.C.: U.S. Government Printing Office.

U.S. Bureau of the Census. 1984. *1982 Census of Service Industries: Geographic Area Series—United States.* Washington, D.C.: U.S. Goverment Printing Office.

U.S. Bureau of the Census. 1984. *1982 Census of Wholesale Trade: Geographic Area Series—United States.* Washington, D.C.: U.S. Groverment Printing Office.

U.S. Bureau of the Census. 1984. *Projections of the Population of the United States by Age, Sex and Race: 1983–2080.* Current Population Reports, Series P–25, No,. 952. Washington, D.C.: U.S. Government Printing Office.

U.S. Bureau of the Census. 1984. *Statistical Abstract of the United States, 1984.* Washington, D.C.: U.S. Government Printing Office.

U.S. Bureau of the Census. 1985. *Annual Housing Survey: 1983.* Current Housing Reports, Series H–150–83. Washington, D.C.: U.S. Government Printing Office.

U.S. Bureau of the Census. *Consumer Expenditure Survey: 1980–81.* Bulletin 2225. Washington, D.C.: U.S. Government Printing Office.

U.S. Bureau of the Census. 1985. *County Intercensal Estimates by Age, Sex, and Race, 1970–1980.* Current Population Reports, Series P–23, No. 139. Washington, D.C.: U.S. Government Printing Office.

U.S. Bureau of the Census. 1985. *Economic Characteristics of Households in the United States: First Quarter 1984.* Current Population Reports, Series P–70, No. 3. Washington, D.C.: U.S. Government Printing Office.

U.S. Bureau of the Census. 1985. *Estimates of Households for States: 1981–1984.* Current Population Reports, Series P–25, No. 974. Washington, D.C.: U.S. Government Printing Office.

U.S. Bureau of the Census. 1985. *Estimates of the Population of the United States by Age, Sex, and Race, 1980–1984.* Current Population Reports, Series P–25, No. 965. Washington, D.C.: U.S. Government Printing Office.

U.S. Bureau of the Census. 1985. *Household and Family Characteristics: March 1984.* Current Population Reports, Series P–20, No. 398. Washington, D.C.: U.S. Government Printing Office.

U.S. Bureau of the Census. 1985. *1982 Census of Agriculture: Geographic Summary.* Washington, D.C.: U.S. Government Printing Office.

U.S. Bureau of the Census. 1985. *1982 Census of Construction Industries: Geographic Area Series—U.S. Summary.* Washington, D.C.: U.S. Government Printing Office.

U.S. Bureau of the Census. 1985. *1982 Census of Transportation: United States.* Washington, D.C.: U.S. Government Printing Office.

U.S. Bureau of the Census. 1985. *Patterns of Metropolitan Areas and County Popula-*

tion Growth: 1980–1984. Current Population Reports, Series P–25, No. 976. Washington, D.C.: U.S. Government Printing Office.

U.S. Bureau of the Census. 1985. *State Population Estimates, By Age and Components of Change: 1980 to 1984.* Current Population Reports, Series P–25, No. 970. Washington, D.C.: U.S. Government Printing Office.

U.S. Bureau of the Census. 1985. *Statistical Abstract of the United States, 1985.* Washington, D.C.: U.S. Government Printing Office.

U.S. Bureau of the Census. 1986. *County Business Patterns, 1984: United States.* Washington, D.C.: U.S. Government Printing Office.

U.S. Bureau of the Census. 1986. *Fertility of American Women: June 1985.* Current Population Reports, Series P–20, No. 406. Washington, D.C.: U.S. Government Printing Office.

U.S. Bureau of the Census. 1986. *1982 Census of Manufacturers: General Summary.* Washington, D.C.: U.S. Government Printing Office.

U.S. Bureau of the Census. 1986. *Statistical Abstract of the United States, 1986.* Washington, D.C.: U.S. Government Printing Office.

U.S. Bureau of the Census. 1986. *World Population 1985.* Washington, D.C.: U.S. Government Printing Office.

U.S. Bureau of the Census of Population. 1981. 1980 Census of Population. Vol. 1, Characteristics of the Population. *General Social and Economic Characteristics, U.S. Summary.* Washington, D.C.: U.S. Government Printing Office.

U.S. Department of Health and Human Services. National Center for Health Statistics. 1984. *Advance Report of Final Mortality Statistics, 1982.* Monthly Vital Statistics Report, Vol. 33, No. 9. Hyattsville, Maryland: U.S. Public Health Service.

U.S. Department of Health and Human Services. National Center for Health Statistics. 1984. *Vital Statistics of the United States.* Vol. 2, Section 6. Washington, D.C.: U.S. Government Printing Office.

U.S. Department of Health and Human Services. National Center for Health Statistics. 1985. Monthly Vital Statistics Report. *Advance Report of Final Marriage Statistics, 1982.* Vol. 34, No. 3, Supplement. Hyattsville, Maryland: U.S. Public Health Service.

U.S. Department of Health and Human Services. National Center for Health Statistics. 1985. *Vital Statistics of the United States, 1981.* Vol. 1—Natality. Washington, D.C.: U.S. Government Printing Office.

Index

About the Author

LOUIS G. POL, Professor of Marketing, University of Nebraska at Omaha, has consulted in both corporate and public sectors. He is the author of *Federal and State Government Data Sources for the Marketing Executive* and has written articles and contributed chapters on a variety of topics in the areas of marketing, demography, research methodology, and urban housing.